The Last Love

of

GEORGE SAND

The Last Love

of

GEORGE SAND

A LITERARY BIOGRAPHY

EVELYNE BLOCH-DANO

Translated from the French by

Allison Charette

ARCADE PUBLISHING • NEW YORK

FIRST ENGLISH-LANGUAGE EDITION

First published as *Le dernier amour de George Sand* in 2010 by Éditions Grasset et Fasquelle

Arcade Publishing books may be purchased in bulk at special discounts for sales promotion, corporate gifts, fund-raising, or educational purposes. Special editions can also be created to specifications. For details, contact the Special Sales Department, Arcade Publishing, 307 West 36th Street, 11th Floor, New York, NY 10018 or arcade@skyhorsepublishing.com.

Arcade Publishing® is a registered trademark of Skyhorse Publishing, Inc.®, a Delaware corporation.

Visit our website at www.arcadepub.com.

10 9 8 7 6 5 4 3 2 1

Library of Congress Cataloging-in-Publication Data

Bloch-Dano, Evelyne.
    [Dernier amour de George Sand. English]
    The last love of George Sand / Evelyne Bloch-Dano; translated from the French by Allison Charette. – 1st English-language ed.
        p. cm.
    Includes bibliographical references.
    ISBN 978-1-61145-716-2 (hardcover: alk. paper) 1. Sand, George, 1804-1876–Relations with men. 2. Manceau, Alexandre, 1817-1865–Relations with women. 3. Novelists, French–19th century–Biography. 4. Engravers–France–Biography. I. Title.
    PQ2414.B4813 2013
    843'.7–dc23
    [B]
                                2012036749

Printed in the United States of America

For my friends

"All of us know we must live when we have the strength of our emotions, because we must have lived when we are in the age of reflection."

Story of My Life[1]

"He is my strength and my life."

Diaries

"Let the world twitter and rail, I am still a *troubadour*: I believe in love, in art, in perfection, and I keep singing."

Armand Barbès, 1867

CONTENTS

Chapter One

"MY HEART IS A GRAVE"

At last! There's Nohant. Each homecoming offers some relief. This cold December brings a feeble hope that she might escape her inner demons. She is forty-five years old and world-weary.

Dark melancholy has enveloped these past two years. The utter failure of the revolution of '48, the mistakes, the socialists' collapse, her friends thrown in prison . . . and for what? An ultraconservative Assemblée and Louis-Napoléon Bonaparte's victory. Her political disillusions mingle with her personal sorrows, especially the rift between her and Solange, her daughter. How could she forgive her unacceptable behavior towards Chopin? The flirting, the gossip, the slander, the depraved life with her sculptor husband, Jean-Baptiste Clésinger, this unpredictably violent creature that she herself had nonetheless welcomed into the family. Solange cuts her mother to the heart, incapable to love, and, herself, badly loved. What would George Sand be without her son, her Maurice, her cherished Bouli? A hollow soulless shell.

He had been in Paris that spring, during the cholera epidemic. What if something had happened to him? She never would have survived.

So many deaths over the past few months. Her half-brother, Hippolyte, her childhood companion who finally succumbed to his alcoholism. Dearest Marie Dorval, her adorable, fragile, marvelous, and extreme Marie, her first adolescent love, Alfred de Vigny's muse, *Hernani*'s Doña Sol, *Chaterton*'s Kitty Bell, the romantic diva who told her "I want to be you"—now forgotten, fallen into quasi poverty, dead from despair when her grandson disappeared. And of course Frédéric Chopin, who died on October 17, devoured by consumption. He hadn't seen her since their brief meeting on a staircase one day in March of '48. That day he had told George Sand that Solange had given birth to a daughter, Jeanne, who passed away a few days later. George Sand never saw the child. She had barely finished her letter of congratulations when she found herself penning her condolences. The two letters reached her daughter on the same day.

Chopin had apparently wanted to see her before he died. Perhaps. But what good would it have done? During their nine years together she had been more mother than a lover, practically celibate since their return from Majorca. Life had been both chaotic and harmoniously balanced between Paris and Nohant, all at the measure of his possessive and hypersensitive genius. This incomparable musician was so troubled, so talented. He had taken Solange's side without hesitation. She felt no remorse over her break-up letter, nor for their abrupt separation. The events that followed convinced her she was right; but still, what a sad, sad failure. His death sent her spiraling into a deep depression.

She had played so many parts. From the young Aurore Dupin, running through the fields, to the rowdy and mystical pupil at the Augustinian Sisters boarding school; Baron Dudevant's restless young wife, mother of two, and living a bohemian lifestyle in Paris; author of

Indiana and *Lélia*, dressing in men's clothes, smoking men's cigars, adopting a man's name; the romantic muse of Alfred de Musset and Frédéric Chopin, her love affairs; the novelist admired by the likes of Dostoyevsky, Balzac, Delacroix, and Liszt; a liberated woman, always choosing her own lovers; the idealist faced with the harsh reality of the revolution. Such a romantic life—so brave, so taxing. What then remains? Rancor? Sorrow?

Any other woman would have accepted her fate and stayed by her husband's side. Young Aurore married Casimir Dudevant just to avoid the abhorrent suitors her mother forced upon her. A fresh-faced green girl of eighteen, horseback riding through the Berry countryside, studying philosophy passionately—oh, the hours she spent in her grandmother's library reading Aristotle, Leibniz, Rousseau, and others. She genuinely did believe she was happy with her husband. But soon, ennui settled in, eroding her courage, leaving her devoid of strength, with tears in her eyes. Casimir and Aurore had nothing in common save their republican beliefs. Everything that interested her bored or irritated him. He only found enjoyment in hunting, country living, drinking, and women—not at all a mean man, but definitely not suited for her.

"I saw how you detested music," she wrote to him in a twenty-two-page confession letter, "and how the very sound of the piano drove you away, so I put an end to it. You read only to oblige me, and no sooner had you read a few lines that your eyes closed and the book fell from your hands. As to our conversations on any subject, whether about literature, poetry, or ethics, most of the time you didn't know the authors of whom I spoke, or you dismissed my ideas as mere folly—fanatical and romantic. I simply stopped speaking."

Even the birth of their son, Maurice, who was weaned too soon, failed to shake off her depression a year later. Their marriage collapsed. She soon found a kindred spirit in the romantic Aurélien de

3

Sèze—a platonic love. A lover followed—a real lover—her child-hood friend Stéphane Ajasson de Grandsagne, "the pretty Steny." The birth of her daughter, Solange, didn't lift her depression—a banal tale of a disappointed and bored wife. But contrary to the Madame Bovary about whom her future friend Gustave Flaubert would one day write, she saw exactly what she wanted and followed her dreams to the stars.

At twenty-six, she came to an arrangement with Casimir—she would divide her time between Paris and Nohant. She settled in the capital with her new lover, Jules Sandeau, a nineteen-year-old law student with curly hair. They cowrote the novel *Pink and White* (*Rose et Blanche*) under the pseudonym J. Sand, and both worked as reporters for *The Paris Journal* (*La Revue de Paris*) and *Le Figaro*. Under the celebrated Henri Latouche's tight iron fist, Sand earned her journalistic stripes.

Everything changed in 1832 with the publication of her first novel, *Indiana*. Romantic and exotic, tempered by her bitter experience, *Indiana* shocked her readers. It spoke a modern language, breaking tradition with the popular historical novels of the day. A new romantic age awoke in the 1830s: Hugo with *Hernani*, Balzac with *The Magic Skin* (*La Peau de chagrin*), Stendhal's *The Red and the Black* (*Le Rouge et le Noir*), Théophile Gautier's *Young France* (*Jeunes-France*), Musset's *Venitian Nights* (*La Nuit vénitienne*). *Indiana* was a woman's triumph; a young woman of twenty-eight who led the charge against marriage and advocated freedom in love. Aurore Dudevant, née Dupin, became a celebrity overnight under her new chosen name, George Sand—a masculine name with an English spelling. And not without a nod towards home: "Georgeon" happens to be the word for *devil* in the Berry dialect. But however lightly she handled her name change in *Story of My Life* (*Histoire de ma vie*), it was by no means a benign choice. By abandoning both her father's and her husband's names, she created a whole new identity, that of George Sand, the author. She also broke from her female ancestry, the Aurores of her grandmother and great-grandmother, Marie-Aurore de Saxe and Aurore de Koenigsmark. She impudently feminized her male name. She made a true name for herself from a pseudonym and even passed it down to her children.

How many novels, how many plays, how many essays would follow *Indiana*? After *Valentine* came *Lélia*, proclaiming a woman's right to pleasure. Her readers thought the book to be a self-portrait, which hounded her for the rest of her life. Then came *Jacques, A Traveler's Letters* (*Lettres d'un voyageur*), *Mauprat, Spiridion, The Master Mosaic-Workers* (*Les Maîtres mosaïstes*), *The Journeyman Joiner, Or, The Companion of the Tour de France* (*Le Compagnon du Tour de France*), *Horace, Winter in Majorca* (*Un hiver à Majorque*), *Consuelo, The Countess Von Rudolstadt* (*La Comtesse de Rudolstadt*), *Jeanne, The Miller of Angibault* (*Le Meunier d'Angibault*), *The Devil's Pool* (*La Mare au diable*), *Lucrezia Floriani*, and *François the Waif* (*François le Champi*), to name but a few works of over forty novels and novellas written between 1832 and 1848.

George Sand did not fully exist except within (and because of) fiction. Imagination was the only breath of fresh air in the dull weight of Aurore's daily life. But her romantic inspiration didn't stop her from tackling issues closest to her heart: love and friendship, women and marriage, art and work, craftsmen and farmers, city folk and country folk, nature, mysticism, and secret societies. Her life was merely choices motivated by circumstances, meetings, and readings, by inspiration and conviction. George Sand, the pen flying across paper. Each book nipped at the heels of the one that came before, like each dream giving birth to the next. But writing was also how she earned her living—the iron shackles that chained her to the publishers of the journals she depended upon. They, in turn, compared her to the greatest writers. Balzac borrowed her personality for Camille Maupin in

Béatrix, and others followed suit. "What would French literature be to most European readers if not for George Sand and Balzac?" Stedhal wrote. In 1854, Nadar placed her first in his famous *Panthéon* of 250 writers, where Victor Hugo seems to bow before a pedestal crowned with the bust of George Sand at the head of a long line of artists.

She was highly sought after, admired, criticized, and ridiculed. She had a rebellious nature, this woman who declared freedom from men. Yet George Sand's freedom could not be defined by sex or gender any more than could her art. As soon as a discussion turned to literature, politics, or art, she used the masculine pronoun to refer to herself. She saw herself as an artist, not a female writer. Her contemporaries placed her in a league of her own. Flaubert would one day write to Turgenev about her, "You must know her as I have known her to see all of the femininity of this great man, to see the tremendous emotion of her genius." Her image in the 1832 lithographs became her signature look for years: a tailored frockcoat, a top hat fitted snugly over dark waves of hair, a cane or a Manila cigar resting in her hands.

Her creative activities did not limit this woman. Everything interested her; she studied natural science, medicine, and botany with passion, as well as painting, music, sewing, embroidery, gardening, and of course, her famous preserves. (She described them to her friend Jules Néraud, "the Malagasy," in 1844: "You must make them yourself, and you must not take your eyes off of them for an instant. It's just as serious as writing a novel.") And she was generous to a fault, showing great concern for others. Men like Louis Michel, the republican lawyer; Félicité Lamennais, an anticlerical Christian whose social mysticism she greatly admired and who fed her intellectual curiosity; Pierre Leroux, a socialist whom she helped to found *The Independent Journal* (*La Revue indépendante*), kept close contact with Sand. While she was accused of changing her philosophy based on who she talked to that day, she was crafting her own philosophy, like a bee gathering pollen from different flowers to make its own honey. However, the utopian within her was badly wounded by the bloody developments of June 1848 and the total failure of the Republic—one in which she could no longer recognize herself.

There wasn't a man in her life at that point, either. She, who had known such passion, so many fleeting lovers . . . What would the future hold for her?

The year 1849 is drawing to a close. Now she must take stock of her situation.

George Sand arrives by train in Châteauroux, where the coach— the *bagottoire*, as they say in Berry—comes to pick her up. This cold December strings together the browns and grays of the countryside—no cause for glad tidings. But then, it's better than Paris, which she enjoys less and less. She may have felt a certain pleasure during her visit in February '48, but this time, three weeks were too long for her. And that was despite having stayed at the Hôtel de France on the rue d'Antin, in the theater district. Her play, adapted from the pages of *François the Waif*, completely won over the audience at the Odéon (the book would not be published until the following year). What a triumph! Critical acclaim and a packed house. The love story between François, the abandoned child, and Madeleine, his adoptive mother; Marie Laurent's moving interpretation; the painstaking care that Bocage brought to his interpretation of country-living in Berry; everything had been spot on. Satisfied—she'll be able to save herself from financial ruin after the debts Solange racked up. Still, nothing brings her true happiness.

While in Paris, she had paid visits to Sainte Chapelle and the minister of public instruction. Prosper Mérmiée, her short-lived lover, had become inspector of historic monuments. She hoped he would grant historical status to the Nohant-Vic church. She had been at the center of Paris gossip when she broke off her liaisons with *Carmen*'s author. But that was such a long time ago . . . They had seen each other since, during an official dinner. She was "neither old nor young, and quite pretty, with striking dark eyes which she lowered when I looked at her. She looked better than she did twelve years ago,"[2] Mérmiée remembered. He brought her a cigar, which she gladly accepted. No words were exchanged between them. … In reality, a full fifteen years had rolled by since their affair, and the fledgling novelist had now become the most celebrated woman of the day.

Forty-five years old. Is that truly "neither old nor young"?

Alexis de Tocqueville crossed paths with George Sand for the first time at that same dinner in May '48, during the socialist enlistment. She had many friends there: Bakounine, Louis Blanc, Mazzini, Ledru-Rollin, and Barbès. The conservative from Normandy described her as "a sort of political man." Tocqueville loathed women who wrote, even more so when they spoke of revolution. He eyed her warily, but nevertheless found himself captivated by her conversation, her understanding of politics, and the accuracy of her predictions. "I did like her," he wrote. "I found her to be a rather large woman, but who held herself admirably well. Her whole being seemed to be contained within her eyes; and the rest of her face, mere matter. What surprised me most of all was recognizing the natural allure of a great mind in this woman. There was such simplicity to her thoughts and her speech that perhaps she affected a bit of the same simplemindedness in her dress."[3]

Feigned simplicity? It's far from Stendhal's opinion, who met her on the way to Italy and was inspired to write that fashion must have been George Sand's forte, she wore clothes so well! Although, he did add with some scorn that "her one flaw is her grand philosophy, her pretension." If only women would stick to talking about clothes . . .

She did admittedly enjoy beautiful fabrics and colors. Her elegant dress could not escape the feminine eye of Elizabeth Barrett Browning. The English poet was captivated by her gray serge dress and her stylish jacket, buttoned to her neck and trimmed with a collar and plain weave lawn sleeves, and thus pronounced her to be attired "with great nicety."[4] George Sand had a *look*. It was her Spartan style that contrasted with the fashion of the day and was quite shocking for such a prominent woman. Mostly, she placed comfort above everything else, wanting the freedom to move from the parlor to the garden, from the kitchen to her desk. No percale, she specified to her half-sister, Caroline, who wanted to embroider sleeves for her: Muslin was "too much clothing for how active I am."[5] Neat, yes; fashionable, no. Unless the fashion was a refusal to pay much attention to her physical appearance.

Eugène Delacroix, Alfred de Musset, Auguste Charpentier, Jean Gigoux, Luigi Calamatta, Thomas Couture, Charles Marchal, Nadar, and many others have drawn, painted, sculpted, sketched, or photographed her. Being the subject of these artists' work makes her uncomfortable. She resigns herself to the task in *Story of My Life*, the first part of which she had recently written, by making do with the physical description in her passport. "Dark hair, dark eyes, average forehead, light skin, pronounced nose, receding chin, average mouth, four feet ten inches tall, no particular distinguishing marks."[6] Does this show the epitome of modesty, a form of pride, or a validation of this woman, confident in her charms and talent?

She has not yet reached the age of accepting herself growing older. Two years earlier, she congratulated herself on her "iron constitution, affected by slight periods of painful indisposition which only cause a few hours of discomfort before lifting the next morning."[7] For the past few months, however, she has been feeling the heavy passage of time. She had gained weight and some gray hairs. She is fully aware that this year is a turning point in her life. She is finally more old than young. There. She repeats the phrase with every letter she writes—to convince herself? To exorcise the whole matter? "I'm suffering a physical breakdown in my forty-five-year-old body," she writes to her cousin René Vallet de Villeneuve. "I tire more easily than should be allowed.

I'll get over it, I'm sure, but I'm so often completely exhausted and incapable of any activity. It forces me into inaction. Hours pass by listlessly. When I recover my strength, I have so much work to do to make up for lost time that I have no more time to live." Is this what age does? Bouts of energy that come in waves, then exhaustion followed by a spurt of momentary vitality?! Despite this erratic pendulum that deprives her of the "time to live," Sand forges ahead, convinced her health will prevail. "I'll get over it."

Always sensitive to the cold, she pulls a fur coverlet she had stashed in the coach around her shoulders to warm herself. She gazes at the familiar scenery. Winter in the countryside. No one has described it better: the pale December sun, the changing jeweled hues of moss and ivy; the sparkling purple of heavily frosted nights; the primrose and Bengal roses hidden beneath leaves; the webs of crystal and ice beneath the winter sun; the thick blanket of silent snow softening the harsh scenery. But what she loves best of all, in the depths of winter, are the endless evenings by the fireplace, "those long evenings in the country, where we belong so intimately to each other, where even time seems to belong to us."[8] Contrary to Paris, where time irreversibly flies, these moments of warmth and love, the shared tales told around the fireplace leave her pensive. Nostalgia, perhaps, for those childhood evenings when she crafted *saulnée* traps for birds with a couple dozen other village kids. The fire against the bitter cold outside. People bonded together by affection, warding away the disappointments of society. A tiny universe, perhaps, but a reassuring guard against the outside world.

Today, there is joy. She is looking forward to seeing her son again and welcoming her guests to celebrate the end of year in Nohant. Two friends are expected soon from Paris: Hermann Müller-Strubing and Alexandre Manceau.

Chapter Two

"THE DREAM OF THE SIMPLE, THE GOOD, THE TRUE"

ay 1848: Resigned that the social revolution, for which she had worked so hard, was lost, George Sand withdraws to Nohant. The bloody repressions that follow in June will prove her correct. The 1848 defeat underlines clearly to her the "before," and the "after."

Throwing herself wholeheartedly into the revolution, she rushed back to Paris less than a week after Louis-Philippe's abdication, as the provisional government declared the founding of the Republic on February 24, 1848.[9] She joined in the surge of romanticism, the yearning for universal fraternity that had seized the hearts of every republican. Théophile Gautier, ablaze with excitement, was swearing that "the moment was never sweeter"[10] for artists. Universal suffrage had been declared (at least for males over the age of twenty), freedom of press and assembly reestablished, and slavery abolished, along with the death penalty for political crimes. So much to celebrate! "My lifelong dream is coming true,"[11] wrote George to her singer friend, Pauline Viardot, La Malibran's sister. Priests were blessing the freedom trees planted all over France as symbols of the sacred unity.

From the very beginning, however, two revolutionary trends grew increasingly defined and started clashing: the moderate republicans, led by the poet Alphonse de Lamartine, and the socialists, headed up by Alexandre Ledru-Rollin, lawyer and founder of *Reform* (*La Réforme*), with Louis Blanc, author of *History of the French Revolution* (*Histoire de la Révolution française*) and theorist of the state labor organization. The tricolor flag was hoisted next to the red flag of revolution thanks to Lamartine. Ambiguity and tension mounted between those for political reform and those who favored social progress and the right to work. George belonged firmly in the second camp.

After spending just enough time in Nohant to hear the declaration of the Republic and attend the mayoral inauguration of her son, Maurice (who quickly tired of his duties), returned straight to Paris, where she arrived armed with a safe-conduct pass, to serve the revolution and take an active role in the proceedings. She became both a symbolic counselor and a quasi-official propagandist, working in the highest government circles without actually using her own name—the great paradox of that century's female condition. From writing articles in the *Bulletin of the Republic* (*Bulletin de la République*), she quickly became the publisher of *Letters to the People* (*Lettres au peuple*) and other texts specifically geared towards provincial audiences. Grasping the gap between Paris and the rest of France, Sand worked to raise public awareness in rural areas.

The Théâtre de la République (formerly the Théâtre-Français) opened officially on April 6, 1848, with *Le Roi Attend*, a play she had written for the occasion. She went on to found *The People's Cause*

(*La Cause du peuple*), a weekly journal which would only print three issues, with Louis Viardot and Pierre Leroux, and collaborated with Ledru-Rollin on *Reform* and Théophile Thoré, a lawyer, on *The True Republic* (*La Vraie République*)—both journals, heavily committed to the left.

Paris was bursting with life, with new clubs, new publications, newspapers, meetings, and declarations popping up daily (parodied by Gustave Flaubert in *L'Education sentimentale*). Right in the thick of it, Sand was endowed with an inexhaustible supply of energy and passion. She lived in a small apartment in Maurice's building, at 8, rue de Condé, from where she would walk to the Ministry of the Interior, on the rue de Grenelle, to pay a visit to her friend Ledru-Rollin. The night of April 18, as fear reigned over Paris after Louis Blanc's unsuccessful demonstrations to postpone the elections, she reported: "The moonlight streams down, as beautiful as ever. Not a single cat on the streets, only patrols every twenty paces. A pedestrian will appear at the end of the street, and police will cock their rifles, turn towards him, and watch him silently as he passes."[12]

She had watched the demonstration from the workers' side, in front of the Hôtel de Ville, where she "squeezed through the mob of kids into the middle of the plaza in order to see better."[13] A few days beforehand, she had scandalized her readers with an article in the sixteenth *Bulletin of the Republic*, in which she openly championed revolution as a last resort if the legislative elections failed to promote the true social cause. "There is only one path that remains for the people who made the barricades: to demonstrate a second time and prevent decisions of a false representation of the nation."[14]

Sand lambasted the bourgeoisie who took up arms and cried, "Long live the Republic!" and "Death to the communists!"[15] The same insults were hurled at her, however, in her own Berry, where she was labeled a "communister." "Now Paris is acting like La Châtre"[16,17] she wrote. She was especially concerned about the stalled progress in social issues. The National Workshops, despite employing many workers, was barely able to combat daily unemployment. As she had feared, the legislative elections on April 23, 1848, had appointed a moderate republican majority with an outspoken conservative minority. Success for Lamartine. George Sand's socialist friends took a serious beating in the elections that had for the first time managed to bring nine million voters to the polls. Still, some of her friends were elected: Louis Blanc; Béranger, the poet, who would eventually resign; Agricol Perdiguier, a former joiner who inspired Sand's novel *The Journeyman Joiner, Or, The Companion of the Tour de France*; Armand Barbès,[18] the constant rebel, who had recently been released from prison in Carcassonne; Félicité Lamennais; Pierre Leroux; Eugène Sue; the Fourierist Victor Considerant; the communist Caber; and the anarchist Pierre-Joseph Proudhon.[19]

But George Sand realized almost immediately that the situation was deteriorating. Her last lingering illusions were shattered on May 15, 1848, when Auguste Blanqui, François Raspail, and her hero, Armand Barbès, led a battalion of between 100,000 and 200,000 unemployed laborers and revolutionaries from clubs and populist societies, overrunning the Assemblée Nationale before being arrested and thrown into prison. The workers were brutally suppressed. Fraternity had become a lost cause, a long-forgotten memory. She left for Nohant three days later, on May 18, 1848.

Tensions mounted. The social unrest swept into the National Workshops, where jobless laborers threatened to riot against the government. The provisional Assemblée diffused them by sending most of the laborers to work on far-flung provincial excavation sites, while the younger ones were drafted into the army. On June 23, the Assemblée officially dissolved the National Workshops, which immediately triggered a populist protest on the outskirts of Paris.

Over the next two days, barricades and battles in the streets plunged the capital into chaos. Laborers took up arms to fight back against the forces of Order. General Cavaignac was awarded emergency powers and turned the riot into a bloodbath: 4,000 revolutionaries were killed in combat, 1,500 executed without trial, and 11,000 others were arrested and thrown into makeshift prisons; 4,238 of them would be deported to Algeria. "I weep," wrote George Sand to her friend and publisher, Pierre-Jules Hetzel. "It is the only thing to do. The future looms so dark and black that I have an overwhelming desire, a pressing need to put a bullet through my skull."[20] These emotions can only be understood because of how committed she had been to the revolution and how much she despaired after the bloody days of June 1848.

The workday increased back to twelve hours in September. The Order and Moderate parties had won. Lamennais printed a black border around the last issue of his newspaper. This revolution, the so-called lyrical illusion, had come to an end.

George Sand took refuge at Nohant and buried herself in her new novel, *Little Fadette* (*La Petite Fadette*). It would be her fourth pastoral novel, after *Jeanne*, *The Miller of Angibault*, and *The Devil's Pool*. Her preface would later justify her escape into rural prose and idealized romance. "After the fatal days of June 1848, I find myself disturbed,[21] cut to the very depths of my soul, upset by outer turmoil. In solitude, I yearn to rediscover, if not a sense of calm, then at least my faith," she wrote, adding: "Now is a time when dark days come from man mistrusting and hating his fellow man. In such times, the artist's mission is to remember kindness, trust, and friendship. Thus, the art serves as a reminder to calloused or downtrodden men that moral purity, kind feelings, and basic equality are, or can once again be, a part of this world."[22]

The writing in *Little Fadette* was based not only on carefully measured literary motifs but also on George Sand's acute desire to revitalize herself, her provincial Berry childhood, and her love of nature. The wild Fadette lived with her grandmother and shared traits with the child that George herself had been. Far from the silly summaries given by those who hadn't read it (or had read it too early), this gorgeous novel is a highly detailed psychological analysis of two twins, or *bessons*, and the relationship between them. Sylvinet and Landry have caricaturized names, but complex emotions. A profound love links the two practically opposite brothers. Each has a different experience of both their twinning and their eventual separation, which is necessary to create two independent and autonomous people. One seeks the outside world, while the other can't handle the distance and withdraws bitterly into himself, unable to face real life. Their relationship becomes an opposition between two parts of the same whole, which a modern reader may easily interpret as the projection of an internal conflict, the artistic transposition of a deep inner dissonance.

Above all else, George Sand's idealism became her artistic wellspring. That, along with the novel's setting, her ethnographic intentions, and her ambition to craft a written version of the spoken Berrichon language, helped her escape her sorrow and despair over the political situation in Paris. "Saintliness is not my natural condition in life," she admitted, "but poetry is my reason for being, and everything that extinguishes the dream of the good, the simple, and the true— a dream which alone sustains me against the terrors of the century—is torture I avoid as much as possible."[23]

"The dream of the simple, the good, the true:" a mantra for surviving hard times, and a map to flee from the machine of history.

Mme. Dupin de Fancueil, George's grandmother, acquired the chateau in Nohant in 1793. An eighteenth century construction built for the governor of Vierzon, it sat alongside the road running from Châteauroux to La Châtre. Besides the main house, the property included a farm with stables, a barn, and a sheepfold, a courtyard lined with trees, a flower and vegetable garden, a greenhouse, a twelve-acre shaded park which melded seamlessly into a forest, and the leased lands of tenant farmers. It exuded both elegance and country charm, encased in protective greenery as well as open to the church and cemetery on the village square. The property was not just a refuge for George Sand but also the map that represented her countryside. The house and its surrounding grounds filled her mind with intimate memories, both good and bad, feeding her imagination and most likely providing the framework for her very identity. "I have always loved this countryside, its particular type of nature, its stillness," she wrote. "I not only cherish its charm but submit to its gravity and am loath to shake it off even when I perceive its dangers." Indentifying closely to her surroundings, she also feared being swallowed up by the mirror of her own weight. She had grown up in this Berry. Here she had found her first freedom as an adolescent, galloping alongside her tutor in boy's clothing. Also here she had discovered her being different very early. Not only from the peasant girls, her playmates, but she was aware that she didn't fit the child her grandmother and mother expected her to be.

She had always resisted the expectations and constraints put on a little girl of her milieu "no running, no working, avoiding sunshine and the outdoors; give up all dexterity and strength of your hands; eternal ineptitude, eternal debility; never get overtired when everything commands you not to hold back; essentially, the idea was to live under a bell jar so as to avoid being weather-beaten, chapped, or faded before your time."[24]

The adult author later decried what she, as a little girl, had rejected instinctively, not as scars of the feminine existence, but as the product of a crippling education. These connections are even more remarkable considering the romantic ideal, which would eventually win out over the ethereal woman. She had an innate refusal to conform. Rebellious? Not really. Rebels have a love of conflict, which she did not enjoy. Neither did she go looking for trouble. External pressures simply didn't take with her. Submission was foreign to her. Something was guiding her, some instinct (call it that for the moment) drove her, not necessarily to always make the right choices, but to continue down the path that had been laid out for her. She chose the less traveled road, even if it led to a dead end or triggered the ire of her mother and grandmother, as it often did.

Aurore-George lacked that option and was forced to exist in the reality of her world. She would escape within the landscape of her imagination. She undoubtedly discovered her creative powers very early. A rebel runs the risk of being suppressed; the daydreamer is a stowaway on the vehicle of life and can easily feign appeasement. She had stepped out of her daily life. "My habit of daydreaming, which began almost in the cradle and which I can hardly explain even to myself, early on gave me a 'dumb' look. Throughout my life—in childhood, convent/boarding school, the intimacy of the family—I was repeatedly told about my 'dumb' expression. It must surely have been true." She mentioned it elsewhere as well, "my usual vacant, verging on dumb, look."[25]

George Sand, dumb? The author knew that such a word would shock the readers of *Story of My Life*. But along the way, many have confirmed her absentmindedness, almost to the point of nodding off during conversations. As Berry's tranquility could seem gloomy, her meditative and quiet nature was worlds away from a lively salon. Théophile Gautier, who was once brought to Nohant by Alexandre Dumas fils, was ready to leave the day after he arrived. "But surely, you must have told him about me?" she asked Dumas. "Thick as molasses? Unable to conduct a semblance of debate in any social circumstance? Do tell our dear Théo that he was mistaken,"[26] she laughed.

Here, again, is yet another sign of a woman who gave little or no importance to appearances, focusing more on *being herself.* She had been raised in rural seclusion, with her harsh tutor, Deschartres, and her half-brother, Hippolyte Chatiron (her father's love child, her tutor, as companions), and with Ursule, a country girl who had been given to her as a playmate at the age of four and who would eventually become her dressmaker. She had not been twisted by concerns about appearance, which leeched the self of so many young girls, distorting their behavior, weakening their resolve, muddying their own desires, and ceding control back to men. She was the wild child in a good family, a child whose fundamental pillars were nature, music, and books. This refined her sensibilities, prolonged her energy, shaped her autonomy, and fed her ever-deepening well of imagination and dreams, without damaging neither will nor taste for taking action.

A noble ancestry from her father, Maurice Dupin; a populist lineage from her mother, Sophie Delaborde, the natural daughter of a bird seller on the banks of the Seine, the quai de la Mégisserie. Sophie would never be accepted by her mother-in-law, Madame Dupin de Francueil, who was herself a product of an illegitimate affair between field marshal Maurice de Saxe and the flirtatious actress Marie Rainteau. Was not the illustrious field marshal himself the bastard son of Frédéric-Auguste de Saxe and Aurore de Koenigsmark? Thus, Amantine-*Aurore*-Lucile Dupin, born on July 1, 1804, inherited a double lineage of contradictions and storybook romance, in which love ruled over destiny. Her own parents eloped a few weeks before her birth, which saved her from a life of illegitimacy, but just barely. Sophie was already mother to little Caroline, born of an unknown father. As for Maurice Dupin, he had a son, Pierre Laverdure, who took to calling himself Hippolyte Chariton after his mother, a servant at the chateau. Illegitimacy was their secret plague; it left its scarlet letter on every branch of the family tree. Aurore was in the unique position of both her parents having one "love child" each! She would always retain close ties with her half-brother, also raised in Nohant, and with her half-sister, who lived with her mother. She took care of her family—her entire family—scoffing at the contemporary social prejudices.

Two tragic events marked her arrival at Nohant at the age of four: the death of her blind younger brother, Louis, which was followed by her father's death eight days later, as he fell off of a horse on his way home from Châteauroux and was killed instantly. Her mother and grandmother hated each other and waged a bitter battle over the young girl. Eventually, Sophie granted guardianship to her mother-in-law in exchange for an allowance. Aurore would be raised at Nohant, for all intents and purposes having been bought out from her mother. Madame Dupin brought her up as the beloved son she had lost, occasionally even calling her "Maurice." While Aurore filled the empty space left by a dead son, she was being educated as a proper young lady.

What saved the little girl was taking refuge in her imaginary universe and identifying with her surrounding landscapes, Paris and Nohant. Her fierce love for her mother, that instable mother who loved her dearly and whom she longed for, was offset by her grandmother's hatred and contempt. The latter even went so far as to let slip Sophie's "loose" past, which devastated the thirteen-year-old girl. A few months later, she was sent to the convent of the Augustinian Sisters boarding school in Paris to continue her education. George Sand's personality was built on this double fracture: the premature death of a hero-father whom she was meant to replace, and the broken diamond string that held her to her mother.

On one side, there was Nohant, with its beautiful countryside; on the other, Paris, where she stayed for a few weeks every year with her grandmother. This division of her time between different places would become George Sand's pattern for the rest of her life. A strong duality marked her childhood and her very origins irreversibly, and George Sand crafted her personality and very temperament around these elements. She could easily have been trapped in some bipolar situation, but her admirable self-control and self-analysis led her to figure out how best to channel her creativity.

She was fully aware of her fluctuation between joy and sadness, her simultaneous need for solitude and company. She seemed to betray her more introverted core through her writing, which explained her need for the conviviality and exuberance of others. "A cold exterior hides a fiery soul," was her shrewd analysis of her two states of being, wholly encompassed by her life in Nohant. For only there, at her chateau in Nohant, could she balance the two inclinations. These manic-depressive cycles did not come without a cost: Her own capacity for reflection and clarity of thought often caused her depression. In the low periods, despair ripped apart her sheltering idealism to invade her very soul. But surely it was not in her nature to sit idly by. "Either my soul is obliged to succumb, or gaiety must come to my rescue."[27] Her depressed periods did not last long. Two hours of complete despondency could be followed by two or three hours of meditation and mental recuperation, where she regained her serenity. "I have to feel absolute despair in order to restore my courage," she wrote. "Only when I am at the point of telling myself 'All is lost!' can I begin to accept everything."[28]

George Sand understood her tendency towards melancholy and knew equally well that she could depend on those around her to snap her out of it. She needed them to lead her once more back into the lively whirlwind, which she called "an exchange of life." She had successfully directed the flow of her alternative needs towards Nohant, with days of physical activity within her merry band, and nights of writing, during which Aurore the dreamer gave birth to George, the artist.

Over the years, George Sand learned how to turn the contradictions and opposite poles that often afflicted her into a plus. She cleverly crafted a balance from her cycles. This binary situation formed the core of her life and her work: Fully recognizing it, she learned to master it. Experience had taught her that each dark depression had its end, which could then give birth to a creative spark, a source of energy. There were, however, periods of melancholy that could stretch out longer and weigh more. Thus, in this cold December of 1849 . . .

Chapter Three

"ALWAYS, WE ARE RULED BY WEAKER MINDS"

The two men who arrived in Nohant for the New Year's festivities couldn't have been more dissimilar. One was German, the other from Paris; one was strong and broad shouldered, the other scrawny; one was unbridled, the other more reserved; the list goes on. The two guests of George Sand, Hermann Müller-Strubing and Alexandre Manceau, were practically opposites of each other.

Hermann Müller-Strubing was a thirty-seven-year-old German revolutionary. Having been sentenced to death after the Frankfurt uprising on April 3, 1833, with his sentence commuted to life imprisonment, he was released seven years later under a general amnesty. He had used his years in prison to his advantage, studying music and Greek, becoming quite the scholar. This brawny man, who could allegedly hoist the diminutive Louise Viardot above his head with one hand, was equally strong of mind. Active in the March Revolution of 1848, he was once again arrested and sentenced to death for a second time. He managed to take refuge in Paris, where he met George Sand through their mutual friends, the Viardots. George agreed to take him in secluded Nohant and keep him away from the Paris police.

According to the singer Pauline Viardot's account, Müller-Strubing fell immediately under his hostess's charms. As for George, she found the worldly *bon vivant* quite attractive. He quickly relaxed into Nohant's lighthearted atmosphere. Less than a week after his arrival, George wrote to her publisher and confidant, Hetzel: "I'm very pleased ... with myself and *the other one*. We've made a straight and true start of things. The rest is in God's hands."[29] Then, honing in on the reason for her attraction: "For the first time in my life, I am drawn to a man of robust character and physicality. Up until now, I had some maternal instinct leading me towards weakness that I could indulge and mollycoddle as a weak, motherly dupe. Always, we are ruled by weaker minds. Perhaps I can find equality at last, in a strong spirit."[30]

Such clarity in these words! An idealized father left her an orphan, and strong-willed women raised her. She had hardly known any men in her youth who were not subservient or simply mediocre. Not to mention those closest to her, the half-brother and the husband. And then there were all the fragile men she had loved, from the apathetic Jules Sandeau to Alfred de Musset, from the lawyer Michel to Frédéric Chopin. All men of talent, some even possessed of genius, but base and unreliable in romantic affairs. Add all her short-lived lovers to the list, where each time she found the balance of power so completely skewed, and the source of her conclusion is blindingly obvious. "Always, we are ruled by weaker minds."

Her friend Maxime Du Camp professed that she always proved herself superior to every single man she had once submitted to. Therein lies the complex philosophical argument between the masculine and feminine, strength and weakness, dependence and power in love. George Sand seems to me to be one of Françoise Heritier's "with the heart of a man" from the Piegan tribe, blossoming into their power as they mature in age, bestowed with social standing and a freedom of behavior usually reserved to men. The Piegan women take responsibility for their own sexual experiences until a ripe old age and choose their own, often younger, partners. They are "strong"[31] women.

But how could George Sand reconcile her work, her independence as an autonomous and liberated woman, with her quest for love which is neither maternal nor dominating? Could she resist her own instinct to "spoil [her] children rotten"?

Her most recent lover, Victor Borie, had entered her life in August 1847, two weeks after the wrenching breakup with Frédéric Chopin. Borie, a staunch republican, had served as her secretary and accountant, and had shared her hopes and dreams for the Revolution of 1848. But this "poor *Pôtu*," (Berrichon for "clumsy oaf"), this "tub of blubber," had inspired little passion in her. And he had revealed himself to be slightly dishonest with his finances. Convicted of political crimes as publisher of the republican newspaper *The Indre Laborer* (*Le Travailleur de l'Indre*) he was sentenced to a year in prison and a fine of 2,000 francs. Borie was forced to flee in exile to Brussels. "He possesses all the necessary qualities," she wrote to Hertzel, her publisher, in February of 1850, "and he has a good soul, but he is above all else a weak creature. I'm quite lucky that fate intervened when she did."[32] Was this written with underlying cynicism or just refreshing frankness?

Another weakling, this *Pôtu*.

And so, she found herself alone. But "I can't, I shan't live without love,"[33] she wrote to her publisher. This mantra came from the experiences of a woman of forty-five, who was starting to take control of her own decisions. But her life had been so weighed down with these men-children she had cared for, who had depended upon her completely. So she turned first to herself, taking a close look at her instinct to seek out and choose, as she described in *Story of My Life*, men "to whom I could have been a mother, give or take a few years."[34] One more weak man down. For the rest of her life, she cared less about her maternal tendencies than her need to be surrounded by young folk more carefree, more optimistic, more idealistic than her own peers.

But then, what did she mean by a strong man?

She essentially wanted Müller-Strubing to be a partner worthy of her character—which is no small thing, for George Sand! This liberated woman's idea of "true love" was a strikingly modern one: "when the heart, body, and soul combine, complement, and embrace one another."[35] Her concept of "loving" someone referred to the most sensual, physical aspect of love.

It was too soon for her to make any decision about her "German friend." She didn't know him well enough yet. She liked him, admired his skill and bravery, but was waiting to see about the rest.

The chateau of Nohant is a modest edifice with a classical style. Every nook and cranny, from guestrooms to annex buildings, had been adapted for the numerous and regular guests, such as the old farmhouse of Delacroix that had also been converted to receive numerous guests. Room assignments changed often, especially during the summer and early fall, and the house was in a constant state of transformation, much like the garden. Few rooms steadfastly retained their original arrangements, except the dining room, with its wide oval table, its gray-painted woodwork panels, its Venetian chandelier in sky blue and pink glass, and its French doors opening onto the terrace and garden. In the parlor, the manor's beating heart, with its embroidered petit point armchairs, its large sofa, its Louis XV writing table, its Renaissance buffet, its family portraits, statues in Chinese bronze, and ancient porcelain, everyone gathered at the table for the evening. It was around that table that guests would gather to converse, read, draw, paint, even compose or craft marionettes or scale models of theater sets, each one rubbing elbows with everyone else. And of course, across in the court-yard, was the kitchen, with its permanent installations of brass pots and pans, along with the brick oven. The oven was depicted in Eugène Lambert's painting *Nohant's Kitchen* (*La Cuisine de Nohant*),[36] having fallen into shambles, where a few chickens and a cocker spaniel had taken up residence among old vegetable peelings. One can only hope that the artist, a longtime Nohant boarder, was indulging his fondness for wildlife scenes! At any rate, the kitchen would soon be furnished with a hot water supply, a furnace, a modern stove, and an indicator board for the servants' bells in each of the chateau's rooms, which no self-respecting manor house could be without. The bedroom on the ground floor had been Madame Dupin's bedroom, then the master suite for Aurore and Casimir when they were married, later reserved for the most important guests, such as Honoré de Balzac, Franz Liszt and Marie d'Agoult, Eugène Delacroix, and Pauline Viardot.

A large stone staircase led up to the second floor. George had moved into Frédéric Chopin's old bedroom, across the hall from hers, which became her office and library. She had a lovely view of the park, with the two cedar trees she had planted when her children were born. Down the hall was a guestroom, equipped with an anteroom and wardrobe. Maurice's domain was across the way, looking out on the courtyard, directly above the billiard room (which would become the theater). The entire second-floor hallway was paved with terracotta tiles, its terminus marked with the mailbox which Théophile Gautier had raved about during his stay at Nohant in 1863. "You write down anything that you require, noting your name and room. I needed a comb, for example. I wrote, 'M. Théophile Gautier,' such-and-such room, my request, and the next morning at 6 o'clock, I had thirty combs to choose from!"[37]

The household at Nohant marked the passage of time over gen-erations, with romance and breakups, friends and guests, and all the staff, the cooks, maids, chambermaids, butlers, servants, coachmen, and gardeners. They ate simply and decidedly provincially: fruits and vegetables from the garden, poultry from the farm, wild game and mushrooms in the fall, seasonal morels and truffles, and Berrichon desserts, such as *poirat*, a pear turnover. George favored oysters and shellfish. The household combined good education and bohemian living, in the image of its owner. There one rule observed daily was: Around 11 p.m. or midnight, the lady of the chateau would retire to her quarters to write for a few hours. She would not reappear until the next day's breakfast . . . except in special cases.

The end-of-year festivities in 1849 were drawing a boisterous crowd. Besides Maurice and the two new arrivals, the guests included Eugène "Lambrouche" Lambert, a young painter and Maurice's friend, a permanent resident for the previous five years; Laure, George's childhood friend, along with her two girls and her husband, Alphonse "Le Gaulois" Fleury, a lawyer who had become a Prefect of the Republic. (George Sand's friends certainly loved their nicknames!) That week, the program called for a "comedy and pantomime to the death!" On Christmas night, they performed *The Stranger* (*L'Inconnu*) and *Pierrot Kidnapped* (*Pierrot enlevé*); on December 26, *Herdsman Pierrot* (*Pierrot berger*) and *A Night in Ferrare* (*Une nuit à Ferrare*) were shown. Nohant's "Grand Théâtre" had originally begun with Maurice's handcrafted marionettes, his great passion. They transformed the billiard room into a stage and called on all of their friends to play the parts. Sand wrote the texts. Maurice and Lambert painted the sets. Müller obliged by stepping into Victor Borie's old role—the former lover, it made perfect sense—while the unassuming Alexandre Manceau followed the play's progress from the hall. The audience consisted of Alphonse Fleury; Félix Aulard, the mayor; and Ursule Jos, the childhood companion turned seamstress, promoted to dresser for the occasion; as well as the actors who weren't in that particular scene.

The players, in costumes, hurried through the great hall, and improvised a mime show accompanied by the piano, under the direction of Müller or George Sand. "The play in three acts finished at midnight. The pantomime, also in three acts, finished at three in the morning. We fled the hall for the parlor, where heat and warmth and supper sat waiting for us, and we laughed over tales of our adventures in theater until five or six in the morning. The next day, we did it all over again,"[38] explained George to her friend Emmanuel, the son of the astronomer François Arago. Emmanuel "Le Bignat" Arago was one of her closest confidants.

Ah, the good life!

But her letters told a different story, and deception started rearing its ugly head. In spite of Müller's qualities—"good, perfect"—she was still seeking the perfect balance in her daily life, one step at a time. Starting on January 12, she confessed that beneath her lighthearted exterior, "I'm having bouts of melancholic depression, and one of these days, I'll put a bullet through my skull."[39]

By a few weeks later, the last flame had sputtered out of existence. "I have gained an excellent friend with a heart of gold, but a *brother*, nothing more. I could never see him with different eyes, so . . ."[40] She couldn't have said it any better. Müller was learned, helpful, loyal, calm, and kind, and he held no grudges. But, well, he was thick, and a little slow. She got bored. "We are like two pals, together through thick or thin . . . two good friends, two men."[41] He would not be her strong man.

A true philosopher, Müller accepted his lot, translating Greek with her, playing music, and accompanying her on long walks. He seemed content.

"You might say that such a feeling has no worth, but I tell you that it is worth it with this man," Sand wrote in the same letter, "and I'll tell you something else, too, when we next see each other."

The mystery remains . . .

Exit Müller. He left Nohant in September for La Châtre, where he became the tutor for the Duvernet children before spending two years in England, where he would live in poverty until his death in 1893. Poor Müller.

Chapter Four

"AS PURE AS GOLD"

The need to love, yes; the desire for seduction, most certainly; the fear of being alone, definitely. But something in George Sand also longed for the spark that she had found at times in the throes of passion, like with Alfred de Musset or Michel de Bourges, and at other times in a more matronly companionship, like with Jules Sandeau or Frédéric Chopin. Love fed her creativity. It gave her a real zest for life. When she was thirty years old, she had been astonished to wake up one morning and discover that she had not felt the slightest attraction for three months! That wouldn't last long, though—she was about to meet Musset. But what is temptation, if not another word for desire? Love is just one of its manifestations.

She had naïvely mistaken Müller's physical prowess for strength of character, confusing masculinity and manliness, believing that we can choose whom we love. She just wanted a change—which she would find, but not with the athletically built revolutionary.

Alexandre Manceau and George Sand's beginnings are shrouded in uncertainty, except for the fact that he must have witnessed the debut of her adventure with Müller, followed by its abrupt end. Otherwise, there is no exact timeline, no evidence of whether they took a direct path or meandered along on their way to love. Some of her biographers place the beginning of their affair in mid-March. Others, including this biographer, say it was a bit earlier. No one has any proof.

At any rate, this thin young man was familiar to her. The thirty-two-year-old engraver was a friend of her son's, whom he may have met in a painter's studio (Delacroix's, perhaps—Maurice was a student there starting in 1840), or in the theater world, in which both were involved. Manceau's studio at 3, rue Racine was not far from Maurice's lodgings on the rue de Condé. Maurice had also spent the previous year in some of the many hotels in the Latin Quarter. They could have crossed paths in the neighborhood cafes, where artists and bohemians mingled, in those cramped spaces in constant motion where chance meetings happened easily. Alexandre and Maurice were close enough to share the services of the same maid, Elisa. This was the maid from whom George Sand had had to gather the keys to her son's apartment in March of 1848. "I found neither the keys nor Elisa at your place. I had to rush to Manceau's place; no Manceau."[42] A few days later, she gave him permission to sell a Lambert painting. "That should get him a nice chunk of change,"[43] she explained. She was already in direct contact with Manceau, without going through Maurice.

So, this was hardly love at first sight for her. This boy, thirteen years her junior, had only been a friend of her son's for two years. She hadn't been available, didn't really *see* him. She hadn't been ready. And when he came to stay at Nohant during the winter of 1849, she had only eyes for Hermann Müller.

And Manceau? How had he perceived her, the mother of his friend? So many men had succumbed to her charms. How could he, too, not have dreamt of this fascinating woman? This woman, who had lunch at Pinson's on the rue de l'Ancienne-Comédie for a few pennies, who lived just down the street, so near and yet so far away. Had he promised himself that he would be loved by such a woman someday? Or had he only imagined it in his wildest dreams? According to Sand, Manceau could be both impulsive and rationally restrained. He knew how to achieve his goals. And as for "his meager opinion of himself," it miraculously became "the secret pride of being loved by [her]."[44] You could read the same story in any novel from that time: an older woman from a higher social class who loves a poor young man, an artist. Alexandre, out of a storybook, a Julien Sorel[45] who "desired neither fortune nor fame,"[46] but who yearned for the love and respect of such a grand woman as George Sand, heroine of her century.

He was highly intuitive and intelligent. While Sand pursued her German giant, he observed her from a distance. He noticed when she teased Müller for being thickheaded. He chose to bide his time. But in the meantime, he shared his theatrical talents, helped George Sand out with little tasks here and there, showed his generosity of spirit, his energy, his character, and sometimes even his influence among his peers. Ever present, ever attentive, he would bring her a glass of water or a light for her cigarette even before she requested it. His only thoughts were of pleasing her. He was charming, and seductive, and she began seeing him in a different light.

And then, one day, he stepped out of the shadows.

According to portraits of the time, this man with narrow shoulders and a small stature had a thin, well-defined face, a hooked nose, and a solemn expression. A graphite drawing from October 8, 1849, by Auguste Lehmann, shows him in his artist's smock. His face is cast in shadow, and he appears worried, even wary, but the effect is of a deep, complex, and private person, both malleable and resolute. Fifteen years later, Nadar's photographs would confirm these representations. Another drawing from that period was from Maurice Sand's hand, of "Manceau the Actor." He is completely unrecognizable, made up as an old man, proof of his theatrical skill. In spite of his slim figure, he does not appear fragile at all, possibly due to his hands (huge) and his legs (muscular). The Goncourts described him as "a small man, average looks, just like anyone else."[47] An 1858 sketch by Eugène Grandsire, *A. Manceau, Butterfly Hunter* (*A. Manceau, chasseur de papillons*), wryly depicts the slender butterfly catcher in full big-game-hunter regalia: safari jacket, leather boots, and explorer hat, with a box strapped across his chest and a butterfly net perched on his shoulder. He was no sportsman, but his physique was on a par with George Sand's taste.

Not to remain in the wings for long, the engraver took an active role in the theatrical productions. "Manceau came, saw, and critiqued,"[48] Sand recalled to her friend Emmanuel Arago, another man who had once fallen in love with her. *Veni, vidi, vici*, yes? It was all hands on deck: He led the renovations of the rafters and backstage areas, and crafted new set pieces. He also took roles in the performances, as the love-struck Léandre or the puffed-up Fracasse or, in an ambitious adaptation of Shakespeare's *Henry IV*, the role of Prince Hal, a stirring and "distinguished" performance.

Alexandre fit in very well at Nohant. He brought everyone around to his theatrical visions, a sign not only of his experience but of the respect and even authority he was gaining in the community. His hostess, searching for a strong man, couldn't help but notice him. He did manage, however, to rub the chateau's beloved son the wrong way. Was Maurice's quiet friend starting to outshine him? He had to respond, and respond he did, with a caustic caricature from January 1850. The caption reads, "From the very beginning, Manceau fancied himself director of the Nohant troupe. Here, he lists off the rules, to loud complaint." Manceau is standing, pounding his fists on the table: "Anyone who misses rehearsal will pay the price: a hefty fine!" All the usual faces of the Grand Theater of Nohant are depicted in uproar, even those who were not present that month, such as Victor Borie. Complaints rise from all sides: "What a dictator!" "Such a reactionist." "Why don't you pay us a salary if you're going to fine us." "This isn't fun anymore, it's just work." And, from his mother's lips, this dictum: "A little overzealous." A bit jealous, Bouli?

As early as January 15, George Sand had written of Manceau to Augustine, her young cousin and ward: "You remember Manceau, Maurice and Lambert's friend. He's our lead actor now, taking on both comedic and dramatic roles. And the costumes he makes, the masks, the makeup, the scenery, he's absolutely first class!"[49]

Pure admiration.

Sand knew how dangerous confidants were, especially as a famous author. She had suffered the bitter consequences of leaked secrets about her husband, Musset, and Chopin. Now, she was keeping her secret garden hidden, asking correspondents to burn any compromising letters—she herself had burned all her letters to and from Chopin. But as a writer and someone who excelled at the dramatic, she would drop hints to arouse curiosity, saving the revelation for the final climactic scene. She would enjoy drawing out the mystery. All the while, she was making sly allusions to this man who, just maybe, was already something more than Maurice's friend.

The letter to Hetzel on February 3 had barely put her aborted affair with Müller to rest with the explanation of her mere friendship with the German lad. Yet Hetzel knew his novelist well; in that same letter, a few words must have caught her publisher's eye: "I have something else to tell you when we next see each other." Something else? The beginnings of a budding romance maybe? Her friend Rozanne

Bourgoing got the same morsel: "I have so much to tell you, hundreds of things that will shock, stun, and amaze you!"[50] That was how she piqued the curiosity of the fair Rozanne, who was herself going through a complicated romantic escapade. Three weeks later, a new hook in another letter to Hetzel: She had spoken of Lambert, Müller, Maurice, and then "there is a fourth who I won't mention, which is all I can say here."[51] She's just dying to write more!

Within a few weeks, Alexandre Manceau had made himself indispensible to the Grand Theater at Nohant. In mid-March, though, performances were suspended until further notice. Why? Because the engraver had returned to Paris.

What would they have done without him?

George fell ill. Her migraines came back, she started coughing up veritable streams of blood, which tired her tremendously. Mancea was absent. She didn't know when he would return; she waited. Pain on top of loneliness made it difficult for her to work. "All my ideas fly out of my head at the slightest distraction. My mind has started wandering just like yours,"[52] this workhorse admitted to Bocage, to whom she owed a new play.

In fact, her rhythm had been disrupted since January. The whirlwind of activity in Nohant during the first few months of the year had intensified her migraines as well as her mood swings and had made Sand unable to concentrate. She was spreading herself too thin, and she blamed herself for it. But what else could she do? The house was full to bursting, and no one went to bed until the wee hours of the morning. Even during her normally productive nighttime hours, she was unable to find peace. Torn between the need for work and the desire for play, she struggled to find a balance. "Am I not supposed to rest and lounge around at my age?" she wrote to Lise, the wife of Gricol Perdiguier, the former joiner. "I try, really I do, but I never. But my busy life is overwhelming, I can only work in fits and starts."[53]

An artist who needed to earn her own living. Work, work, work. She would never stop.

On March 23, just after Alexandre Manceau had returned from Paris, she wrote to Hetzel: "I now feel that things will improve, I will get better. I have recovered the will and strength to work and live. I'll tell you more later."[54]

On that subject, she wrote again in a letter three weeks later: "You ask if I am truly resigned at being sad and strong. Not at all! But I hesitate to write a single word to the contrary, which will of course shock you, coming from me. Any such word would seem absurd for me, wholly convinced that happiness can only be found in the total absence of sadness."[55]

She didn't yet dare put all her faith into the idea, thinking it only an illusion, an unachievable dream. "Let me stay a while in this oasis," she continued—a recurring symbol of happiness for Sand.

Then came these words, these incredibly moving words: "I am happy. I think I have finally grasped something as pure as gold."[56]

This revelation came in a long letter to her publisher at the end of April. George Sand poured out her passion onto the page, via a portrait of Alexandre Manceau, where the word "love" recurs like a leitmotif. "Yes, I love him!" "I love him! I love him with all my soul . . . I love him for everything he is. And there is a surprising tranquility in this love, despite our ages . . ."[57] She left no doubt if her love was returned. "He loves like I have never seen anyone love before."[58] Finally, this seasoned woman had found the man of her dreams in this young engraver.

Her love and the certainty of it were dazzling, but they had not blinded her. These pages contain a remarkable analysis of the man she loved, "with all his faults, all the oddities that others see, all the wrongs he has done and mistakes he has made, all of which he has shared with me . . ."[59] Sand's maturity and generosity of spirit are quite evident in this rare love, laying herself bare for the other person's gaze and scrutiny, examining the mysterious attraction between two human beings, the way they fit together that was so inconceivable to the outside world. The forty-five-year-old woman reveled in talking about a new love. The artist used the written word with her publisher to breathe life into ideas. She was interested in the passion-filled discovery of this other being, complete with his own limits, his shortcomings. His purity was, to her, gold.

This "worker who made his living from working"[60] came from a humble background. Sand's words. Born in poverty, with little education, he had gone straight into apprenticeship. His social status and lack of education proved to be a handicap for such an intelligent person. But he was upwardly mobile. Not out of simple ambition, but out of a deep self-respect, a yearning to learn, a need to find his own self-worth. "*He likes himself*," Sand wisely observed. He understood and valued his dignity. The difference in social class would not be a problem for her, the republican who had been so crushed by the events in 1848, the artist who wrote both of bucolic country life and of factory towns and workers' unions; not for the daughter of Sophie Delaborde; and certainly not for the woman who was so unconstrained by the prejudices of her day. A born teacher, it fell to her to help Manceau, to answer certain questions he had. "He is extraordinarily intelligent," she wrote, hungry to learn. Above all, "he is an incredibly intellectual artist."[61] His instinct and insight as an artist more than made up for every gap in his education. "He may not know how to spell, but he writes beautiful poetry. That one detail sums up his entire character."[62]

But these qualities didn't seem to be perceived by the outside world. Sand's entourage accused him of being proud, mistrustful, offensive, bossy, and dominating, even to the point of violence. There were those who even claimed that he was acting out of self-interest. Such criticisms came directly from George's inner circle. In rebuttal, she maintained that Manceau was "generous to the point of extravagance." The future would prove her correct.

The love-struck woman also extolled her lover's ability to be "simultaneously a cuddling cat and a loyal hound."[63] These amusing metaphors point to Manceau's double role as a sensual lover and a devoted companion. "He was once quite a libertine, but he is chaste in matters of true love, as chaste and fervent as the heart, mind, and body can possibly imagine."[64] This passionate and experienced man possessed all the qualities of a perfect lover, and we know how much she valued that. The age gap was inconsequential. There she was, shattering stereotypes once again!

She had "let herself be completely and willingly *seduced*." The sly fox saw how important it was to let this proud man take control in their liaison, or at least to let him believe that. In the meantime, she would not ignore her power as the more famous older woman. He had made the first move. Now, she took pleasure in helping him please her, this expert lover who reveled in her femininity.

A subtle balance existed between her and Manceau. He could, of course, appear naïve "as a prepubescent boy." She certainly tried to "soften his edges a bit," to make him less grating to others. She would be the Madame de Warens to the Jean-Jacques Rousseau of him.

Still, the engraver was no child. He was most certainly a man, in his chosen roles as a lover in the affair and as a "devoted admirer" in courtly love. A true knight, he adored his lady. He respected her, served her, pampered her. He was attentive, prompt, and skilled (contrary to most men, noted George). "He thinks of everything and pours all of his energy into the glass of water he offers me, or the cigarette he lights for me. ... When I fall ill, I need only see him bring my slippers or turn down my bed, and I am cured. I, who ask nothing and accept nothing from anyone, I need his attention, his pampering, as surely as if I had been born with such a trait."[65] He became the mother she had lacked as a child. Finally, she could let herself be a little girl. He cared for her, spoiled her even. But these skills he had, which were like those of a "skillful, ingenious, active woman," did nothing to diminish his masculinity. They merely provided additional proof of his devotion, of his quality as a lover. His strong-enough personality—a unique character and "extraordinary internal resources"—had earned her respect.

Alexandre Manceau was truly the man she had been waiting for. Neither the age difference, nor the social gap, nor any of her reservations, nor even the open hostility of her friends proved to be any obstacle. Something about him reassured her. She had faith and trust in her love for him. And for what may have been the first time, she had a profound sense of security with him: "I have been transformed. I feel good, calm, *happy*. I can survive anything, *even his absence*, which says it all . . . I could never survive that before."[66]

This outpouring of love, a true cri du coeur marked the beginning of a new period in Sand's life: her life with Alexandre Manceau.

Chapter Five

"ENGRAVING IS A SERIOUS ART"

Life can change almost overnight. Manceau only needed about ten days in Paris that March to put his affairs in order before packing up the tools and engraving supplies that he would bring to Nohant. He wouldn't return to Paris until the end of October, to work on Thomas Couture's portrait of George Sand, which would go on exhibition in the Salon of December 1850. The young engraver was a popular artist, who had been working for years and "earning his living from his work."

It couldn't have been easy for him to start out as an engraver, although it was probably less out of necessity than Sand had described to Hetzel. Manceau had been born in Trappes on May 3, 1817. His father, Jean-Louise Manceau, worked as a "lemonade vendor" and "billiards manager" like his father before him, an innkeeper in La Verriere.[67] His father had most likely served in Napoléon's army, like many of his contemporaries. Shortly after his son's birth, he moved with his wife to Paris, where he became a civil servant. Subsequent documents show him "employed as a senior officer in the exclusivity of Paris tax bureau," a position reserved for veterans. The Parisian municipality had reintroduced the tax on alcoholic beverages and certain foodstuffs coming into the capital. The Manceaus lived at 12, rue Jean-Jacques-Rousseau, in a working-class neighborhood near the Saint-Eustache church. Three other children were born there: Emile, on February 2, 1825; Laure, on May 16, 1837; and Henri, on December 12, 1839. In an ironic twist of fate, that very street held a cafe-turned-club at the other end of the Hôtel de Postes courtyard, where Ledru-Rollin, Louis Blanc, and other republican friends of George Sand planned the revolution of 1848.

The family lived modestly but was certainly not poor. The Manceau family was always very closely-knit, and Sand herself visited them often, as their letters show.

The young Manceau found himself in the same situation as other young men of his status: He had to compensate for the gaps in his education on his own. He had left school at age thirteen and had chosen to apprentice under an engraver because of his talent and taste in drawing. His "natural artistic talent" was quickly revealed. Engraving would have seemed a good career option, as demand increased with the booming press and publishing industries. Some lithographers, such as Achille Devéria, had already achieved widespread recognition for their illustrations of novels.

The Artist (*L'Artiste*), a review dedicated to arts and letters, had reported: "Engraving and lithography are seen in a better light [than architecture], and their popularity is just as legitimate as that of pastels and watercolors. They introduce the works of other artists, painters, and sculptors, to the masses and cheaply reproduce and disseminate a large number of rare pleasures. Only a privileged few can boast collections of canvasses, while everyone has the right to enjoy engravings and lithographs without much trouble. Such works can appear in the most magnificent of galleries just as easily as in the most modest of parlors. If we are here permitted to speak of moral and social considerations: They keep the grand historical events alive in the people's memory and spark a healthy excitement within them. ... What's more, the number of eminent artists in these domains increases by the day."[68]

After five or six years of apprenticeship, most likely under Alexandre Sixdeniers, a renowned artist of the day, Manceau started receiving his own commissions. His first works would have been letterheads or illustrations for books and periodicals, small jobs which allowed him to practice his craft while earning a bit of money.

"Engraving is at one and the same time a high art and a hard, exacting craft," George Sand would write in *Story of My Life* regarding her friend Luigi Calamatta, "whose method—enemy of inspiration— might better be renamed the genius of patience. The engraver must be an able craftsman before dreaming of being an artist."[69] Should the engraver be faithful to the model, or did he have the freedom to interpret? Much like the work of a translator, she reasoned that for an artistic work, the engraver's duty was to serve the model. His goal, what the public expected, was to make the work accessible to the masses and to preserve the work in collective memory. Thus, she concluded that engraving should be a "faithful and literal translation." If he wished to interpret, he should create his own work. This was every engraver's dilemma at the time, and she most likely had long debates on the subject with her companion, whom she had seen work for three years. This issue of the distinction between artist and artisan, art and job, perfectly describes the talent and career of Alexandre Manceau, for he was an accomplished engraver, but not an artist, contrary to the likes of Philippon, Daumier, Devéria, Johannot, Bodmer, or Gustave Doré.

Manceau had been showing his work at the Salon, the indisputable pinnacle of artistic achievement, since he was twenty-four years old. The young engraver had debuted at the Salon with an original portrait of the Marquise de Montaigu. *The Artist* praised his talent in a piece from 1841: "The portrait of the Marquise of M . . . by Monsieur Manceau may be marred by a few dull tones, but unquestionably atones for that shortcoming with the realistic and multilayered depiction of the armchair and the shawl, the fabrics, lace work, and furs."[70] The review was accompanied by a print of Manceau's engraving of *Hamlet*, a De Rudder painting which had been on exhibit the year before.[71] Hamlet's face was strong, and the overall impression dramatic. Manceau was henceforth regularly invited back to participate in future Salons.

He was a man of many talents. His work provided an insight into the fashions of the time and the flexibility demanded of an engraver to capture every facet thereof. One project Manceau worked on was Karl Bodmer's *Journey to the Center of North America with Prince Wied-Nieuwied* (*Voyage à l'intérieur de l'Amérique du Nord du prince Wied-Nieuwied*).[72] Bodmer, a Swiss painter and lithographer, had accompanied Prince Maximilien zu Wied-Nieuwied on a twenty-eight-month voyage to America. His watercolors provided a unique insight into the lives of Native Americans. Several engravers were required to reproduce all eighty-two of his paintings. The resulting book introduced real Native American life to a public which had acquired a taste for such exoticism from reading *The Last of the Mohicans*, by Fenimore Cooper.

The most striking aspect of Manceau's execution and choice of paintings is their sense of motion. The young engraver had been entrusted with fairly complex works, two of which depicted animated scenes that demanded a very precise brushstroke. The aquatint technique in particular amazed his contemporaries and allowed him to harmonize delicacy and strength in the picturesque illustrations.

He would continue to show his work in all following Salons.[73] Every piece exhibited the same fidelity to the original, with a real eye for contrast and dramatic composition. At that time, he appeared to prefer the seemingly rarer group scenes to portraits. Literature was at the forefront of his interests: *Hamlet, Don Quixote, Mysteries of Paris* (*Les Mystères de Paris*). Some of his engravings also depicted historical or even political subjects, such as the Compte-Calix painting *God and Country* (*Dieu et Patrie*). Engraved in 1848, it shows a priest reading his prayer book while standing guard, gun cradled in his arm.

A series of thirty-seven anatomical plates were commissioned by the *Newsletter of Medical-Surgical Knowledge* (*Journal des connaissances médico-chirurgicales*) in 1845, which would illustrate articles on eye surgery, by Doctor Desmarres, and genitourinary equipment, by Doctor Phillips. This precise scientific documentation demanded the highest artistic detail. Manceau jumped at the chance to attend operations for cataracts and other maladies in order to apply the necessary rigor to reproducing anatomy.[74]

Alexandre Manceau took professional initiative, pursuing success in his career. He never wanted for commissions, and his abilities afforded him a certain comfort. In 1846, he left his old studio on the place de la Sorbonne and moved into the same building as his teacher, Alexandre Sixdeniers, at 3, rue Racine. His fifth-floor apartment was lined with wood paneling, with a workshop and small bedroom facing the street, and a parlor, kitchen, and powder room across the hall. He paid 500 francs per month. Later, won over, George Sand would rave about his "lovely little den."

Alexandre Manceau was making a crucial decision by moving to Nohant. Would he dedicate himself entirely to the woman of his dreams, or would he reserve enough independence and work time to successfully further his own career? Wouldn't he be forced to sacrifice at least some of his professional ambitions? There was certainly much at stake. It was one of the balancing factors of their relationship.

Chapter Six

"I PREFER TO KEEP PRESSING FORWARD"

"The good Lady of Nohant." Condescending and patronizing words veiled the artist under the faded glory of an old patron. Yes, George Sand was generous with her money; yes, she lived in the Nohant chateau. But she refused to be labeled and trapped in such a formulaic rut. It would stifle her, bury her alive.

To some, George Sand's return to the region after 1848 was perceived as an old woman's retirement, filled only with acts of charity and a few scrawled pastoral stories to amuse other elderly Berrichon. Was the whirling devil reduced to a recluse?

Of course not! This woman of forty-six years, who moved back into her autumn quarters at Nohant, was a prolific writer, a woman overflowing with life. Her newfound love helped her take flight. Alexandre Manceau had awakened a new sentiment within her, one of trust. Yes, it was still a fragile thing, but distinct enough to show in her letters to Hetzel, her favorite confidant, in July 1850. "Oh yes, I am well, and I am very happy, incredibly happy. I truly think that I am coming to this realization for the first time in my entire life. I can give myself over to this feeling with just a bit of pride. ... I can't be bothered to wonder if this will last, or if it should. I'd rather not think about it. This thing I have found, I did not seek, although perhaps I've deserved it, after an unhappy life of patiently waiting. But I am not owed more than can be given, and when much can be given, I have no right to demand more. I can resign myself to losing everything, but never to boredom, that much I know. But, by God in Heaven, it is so good to be loved, and to love fully, and such a love! I would be a fool to predict its end."[75]

This is a mature woman possessed of happiness, with the capacity to enjoy it and an understanding of its delicacy. Also, someone with the intention of changing, of learning to be comfortable with her place on the receiving end, no longer just the constant giver. To love and be loved. No drama, no neuroses. This is what George Sand discovered thanks to a man who was neither brilliant nor mad, neither bizarre nor bad, and above all, certainly not "*weak.*"[76] (How many different ways had that word deceived her?) Finally, she could depend upon something against her own anguish. This love would last. She felt immense gratitude for such a noble young man.

But what of her own age? At thirty, she was praised by Balzac. Now, she was said to have one foot already in the grave. "I am forty-six years old, and I have a few white hairs. What of it? Older women are better loved than younger women; I see that now. It isn't the person which must last, it is love. May God look down, see that it is good, and let it endure!"[77]

Alexandre Manceau offered George Sand the privilege of enjoying her life to the fullest, even in middle age. So what if he was thirteen years her junior? She had decided to take advantage of as much of life as possible and to make her love endure.

This period marked a fertile time of great creativity. George Sand published no fewer than twenty-six novels, out of fifty total books, and about twenty plays (seventeen of which were staged in Paris) between 1850 and 1865, along with her memoirs and hundreds of letters, articles, and prefaces. But this abundance of writing, paired with her enormous capacity to work, was scorned by a few misogynist writers, including Baudelaire and Nietzsche. The former outdid himself by referring to her as a "dump;"[78] the latter used "writing pack mule." Edmond de Goncourt was equally inspired by the four-legged metaphor and called her "a brooding sphinx, the bull Apis," or even better, "an abyss of talent." Apparently, her good health and calm demeanor made others green with envy! She was an easy target for this sort of thing, whether through humility or blissful ignorance. She had, after all, once written to her good friend Bocage, "My garden is full of beautiful flowers, and I find it appallingly easy to slap down novel after novel."[79]

Up until then, for the longest time, writing was not an accepted and respectable career for women. If some of the sarcastic remarks may betray a certain lack of respect towards George Sand, it remained clear that she had actually earned the right over the years to call herself a professional writer, one who made a living with her pen and ink. Even so, she usually underplayed her talent. She shied away from taking her own creative power seriously. This set her apart from most of her male colleagues, particularly Balzac, of whom she gave a rich description in *Story of My Life*: "Everyone knows how self-satisfied he is, a satisfaction so innate in him that we excuse its gushing forth." She, on the other hand, suffered from an excess of modesty.

"My work is only *botched stuff*," she wrote to Flaubert, for whom writing was a completely engaging process.[80] Was this part of her belief that literature was just one of life's many pursuits,[81] not any more or less noble than gardening or sewing? "If I write a bad novel, the damage will not be much," she wrote to Pierre Leroux. She did not put her writing on a pedestal, which may explain why George Sand was often relegated to the role of a lover or lady of the house, even caricaturized. It is clear, however, that George Sand was not wiling away her days jarring gooseberry preserves.

For the moment, she was diving headlong into her next theatrical adventure. But why theater? Plays earned money, which she needed. The post-revolution years were hard, business was slow, and she had a large household to run. She lived day by day, barely managing to pay her debts. The previous winter, she had gone without heat in her bedroom and had walked around in slippers instead of buying new shoes. She hadn't invited her friends to Nohant nor given her usual contributions to charity."[82] She was counting on her memoirs to lift her financially, but her publisher was also suffering hard times and wasn't ready. Her *Story of My Life* wouldn't appear for a few more years. Still, she had already written the first volume and had taken up her pen once more in June 1848.

François the Waif, her play, had a promising success at the Odéon. On March 20, 1850, they celebrated its hundredth performance. The Théâtre des Variétés tried to jump on the bandwagon by producing an unauthorized adaptation of *Little Fadette*. She was beside herself. Her texts were her intellectual property, and they had been violated. This prompted her to bang out a new play, *Marielle*, which she sent to her actor/director friend Bocage in June.

Pierre Tousé, called "Bocage," had carved out a name for himself in literary roles. He had been hugely successful in Hugo's *Marion de Lorme*, Alexandre Dumas' *Nesle Tower* (*La Tour de Nesle*), and opposite the sublime Marie Dorval in *Antony*. He was also the manager of the Odéon theater. This aging seducer with eyes of fire shared George Sand's socialist convictions—and also her bed, for a brief period in 1837, from whence sprung a recurring ex-lover's jealousy. She called him a "stuffed shirt;" he called her a "nagging genius." She trusted him completely and was unfailingly loyal to him as an author, which of course gave him free reign to complicate matters. This time, he turned his nose up at the offering. He wanted another pastoral theme over this inspired play about the lives of actors.

"I don't wish to write two plays in a row about my countryside. I don't have to," she protested. "I prefer to keep pressing forward as an artist and avoid retracing my footsteps."[83]

She wouldn't budge an inch. Well, not yet, anyway.

Bocage then went and gave a free performance of *François the Waif* for the working class on the anniversary of the founding of the Republic. They sang *La Marseillaise*, the anthem of the "Reds." And, well, that didn't go over well: by July, he was dismissed from the Odéon—a national theater on the same level as the Comédie-Française. The Republic of Louis-Napoléon Bonaparte did not fool around with law and order. Sand tried in vain to withdraw her play from their repertory. A court representing commercial businesses ruled that *François the Waif* belonged to the Odéon, and prohibited Bocage from mounting a production in any other theater.

Undeterred, she wrote a new play, *Claudie*, which was performed in Nohant in August. Berrichon, of course. Extraordinarily bucolic. It told the story of a poor young woman, seduced then abandoned, whose child died of starvation. This theme—the reform of a young mother—may seem overly dramatic, but it lined up beautifully with the social issues of 1850, a vehement protest against the "low-down nouveau riche." The issue was near and dear to her heart, and it would still cause a scandal over a century later. Claudie was far from a pitiful victim. She was a proud young woman, flooded with suffering, forced to be suspicious of men. There would have been many such Claudies, abused by the village Don Juan.

Theater was just another facet of George Sand's prolific talent. Writing for theater, she was able to indulge in improvisation, multiple roles, costumes, game playing, farce, and burlesque. Plus, at Nohant, the freedom and lack of constraints from "high-society theater" was a breath of fresh air. They performed what they wished, for and among friends. That intimate stage inspired many of her scenes.

The Théâtre de Nohant quickly evolved from a simple parlor game to a serious workshop. The "salon theater" let the author see her work "in person," giving her the opportunity to polish it and, as she explained, "to above all *hear* its style, which I've had in my mind but not in my ear."[84] An interesting insight into her creative process.

Alexandre Manceau's role in the theater was becoming more apparent each day. Their common ground, a shared passion, the chance for the engraver to be actively involved in a wonderful adventure, which would grow with him. From that point forward, the rehearsals and workshops at Nohant played an integral part in Sand's theatrical writing. Maurice too had a chance to explore his own talent as an actor and artist.

Bocage would attend one of these intimate workshops and share his opinions, before his own professional troupe started rehearsing *Claudie*. The play opened in January 1851 at the Théâtre de la Porte-Saint-Martin to wild acclaim. It depicted "la Gerbaude," the harvest festival in Berry, very accurately, with expressions and manners borrowed directly from a bricklayer who worked for Sand, who sang "in the true Berrichon style."[85] But the censors defaced it unrecognizably, and it wouldn't run for more than forty performances. *Marielle* became *Molière* and opened in May that year at the Théâtre de la Gaîté on the boulevard du Temple, along the famous stretch dubbed the "Boulevard du Crime." A third play was scheduled to open on November 26, 1851, at the Théâtre du Gymnase on the boulevard Bonne-Nouvelle, whose manager was hedging his bets on the feel-good genre. Unfortunately for Sand, another drama and other crimes intervened—Louis-Napoléon Bonaparte's coup d'état would be played out at the same time, on an infinitely larger stage, bringing an end to the performances.

In spite of the offers from the Comédie-Française, George Sand swore her allegiance to street theater, where the "more open and naïve" public seemed "more malleable." She wanted to make them laugh and cry. She also had a political goal: "to provide the people with moral, moving, and comforting plays"[86] which would speak to their very souls. Theater was a platform for her, and she would continue to "preach goodness and honor in the face of censors and committees,"[87] as she explained to the revolutionary Armand Barbès, imprisoned at the Doullens fort. This political and pedagogical freedom was inseparable from Sand's idealistic nature, and she would have sacrificed anything for it. Reality was a bit, well, disappointing. But with Manceau at her side, a man of the people and a lover of theater in his own right, her convictions only grew stronger. The Boulevard du Crime had its theaters, outdoor stages, stalls, peddlers, animal trainers, mimes, acrobats, cabarets, cafes, and thousands of Parisians wandering around every night. That was her public. This "lady of Nohant" intended to be heard among these "children of the revolution."

She also agreed to participate in a collection organized by her friend, publisher Pierre-Jules Hetzel. The collection was entitled "Le Magasin des enfants." Jules Verne's future publisher proudly showed his editorial prowess by asking some of the best authors of the day to write children's stories. Alexandre Dumas, Charles Nodier, Paul de Musset, and Arsène Houssaye all made contributions, and so did as P. J. Stahl, which was of course the penname of the publisher himself (he wrote the well-known *Adventures of Tom Thumb*)!

For him, she wrote *The Mysterious Tale of Gentle Jack and Lord Bumblebee* (*Histoire du veritable Gribouille*), a fairytale with characters borrowed from a world she knew quite well: the insect world. Ants, honeybees, hornets, beetles, and spiders drew the poor Gribouille, whose naiveté bordered on stupidity, into a fantasy world. Maurice Sand provided the illustrations for the volume. This time, at least, the mother had succeeded in promoting her son's talent.

A lifelong republican, Pierre-Jules Hetzel had made a name for himself as a publisher with the 1839 *Scenes from the Public and Private Lives of Animals* (*Scènes de la vie publique et privée des animaux*), a satirical series of studies on contemporary morals. He had collaborated with Honoré de Balzac, the Musset brothers, Louis Viardot, Jules Janin, and George Sand, whom he had met for the first time through the project. She had penned the *Story of a Parisian Sparrow* (*Histoire d'un moineau de Paris*). That book's success had given Hetzel the opportunity to co-edit the first volumes of *The Human Comedy* (*La Comédie humaine*) with Dubochet and Furnes. Perceptive, accommodating, generous, Hetzel was a god among his authors. Trust had been established almost instantaneously between him and Sand, and soon she was coming to him for advice. He became her unofficial literary agent almost before being her publisher.

Hetzel had participated in the 1848 revolution and was named chief secretary for foreign affairs under Lamartine. Filling both of his roles simultaneously, he retained his governmental post until December 20, 1848, when Louis-Napoléon Bonaparte was elected. One of his final acts as chief secretary was to recommend Gerard de Nerval as France's ambassador to Germany.

The correspondence between Sand and Hetzel, over the years, became gradually more personal. She shared with him her family issues, her daily life, her duties, her loves. But she could just as easily ask him to publish one of her books, to pull some strings for one of her protégés—the mason-poet Charles Poncy or the husband of her cousin Augustine de Bertholdi, for example—or even to help her find a new cook or a furry Marquise for her own dog, Marquis. The patience of this man with his authors was without bounds. Although he had been born in Chartres, this sturdy man with his well-groomed beard, full head of hair, and meticulous dress was a true Parisian who loved the cafes and the cobblestones. Sand made sure to waft the countryside his way. But this naturally courteous publisher was not bereft of pride or a strong character. "He will never kneel before anyone, *and recognizes no man as his master* . . . Even among the most important people, he retains his free will and frank manner. He behaves as an editor in every situation and will always take the trouble to correct everyone," wrote one of his many friends, Edouard Grenier, a poet.[88]

He was always very open with his opinions, like in the case of Sand's *Molière*. Its stage adaptation had disfigured it. A critical failure, it would only run for twelve performances.

"Thank you for telling me what you think," Sand reassured him, "and please, never handle me with kid gloves. Whether or not I will yield to your advice, I always know that you care about me with all of your being."[89] Besides, she already had another play in the bag! Nothing about her literary career would ever prove discouraging for her.

From 1851 on, Pierre-Jules Hetzel would manage all of George Sand's affairs, including sitting in on the rehearsals for her plays. In that first year alone, she wrote over eighty letters to him, most of them lengthy.

But what better way did George Sand have to prove her trust in her publisher friend than to share her thoughts, her secret about Alexandre?

Chapter Seven

"WE ALL HAVE OUR SECRETS"

"Experience has taught me that I must not tell others my secrets. We all have our secrets, and we must not allow others to discuss them," wrote George Sand to Hetzel.[90] Such prudence was the result of ugly episodes in her past. Her love life and celebrity status were easy fodder for the rumor mills, and she had been victim of every kind of malicious gossip. She would not allow that to happen again. She wanted to protect Manceau, to shelter their relationship. She asked even Hetzel to burn the letter in which she revealed her love for Manceau. Fortunately for history, he did no such thing.

She remained insistent that she had not shared this secret with anyone else.

But how long would her close friends look past her relationship with the young engraver. The fact that Manceau had moved in to Nohant to stay didn't send any signal, even for Maurice—his friend

Eugène Lambert had lived there with them for years. With Manceau, however, there had been "bad storms" to weather as he settled in. The "senseless slander" continued to spread about him. Sand's friends had not been fooled, in spite of her caution. In fact, it had the opposite effect and made them protest all the more loudly.

Rumors reached Paris, where even Bocage became suspicious. When Sand came to Manceau's defense, harshly accused by Paul, the actor's nephew, Sand riposted by displaying her acerbic wrath as she took "the flightless bird under her wing."[91] She, in no uncertain terms, put Bocage firmly back in his place. "Surely, your virulent defense of Manceau betrays your love for him?" "How dare you be so indiscreet? I don't recall bringing you into my confidence and gave you neither permission to write these words nor an excuse to forget yourself."[92]

As for Manceau, he was also accused of staying with her for his own interests, turning her into "an old lady whose last resort was to purchase lovers!"

She had already had an earlier confrontation with the Bocages. While passing through Paris, she had found Elisa Barberousse, Manceau and Maurice's maid, dead drunk. This time, Sand lost her temper. After handing Elisa her final check, Sand sent her off. Manceau had never noticed her drinking. But Paul was only too happy to use this incident to vilify the young man's past life. This said, both young men did admit a certain penchant for indulging . . . in what, it wasn't made clear to Sand.

In a letter to Hetzel, George Sand once more insists that her love for Manceau goes beyond all his youthful past. All of which he had shared with her. "I love him! I love him with all my soul, with all his faults, all his oddities, *all the wrongs he has done and mistakes he has made, all of which he has shared with me . . .*"[93]

What mistakes were those?

Alexandre Manceau had fathered an illegitimate son, Auguste Guy, whom he never legally recognized. In 1871, this son, who never met his father, would write to George Sand to ask her for a recommendation for a position with the Paris-Lyon-Méditerranée (PLM) Railway Company. She did help him. All contact between them stopped until August 1875. Further correspondence has been lost.

What would Manceau's attitude have been towards the mother of this child? What could George Sand actually have known? She may have borrowed something for the plot of *Claudie*. Perhaps some links exist between Manceau's history and the drama of the Berry peasant girl, young, impregnated, and abandoned. Manceau's secrets planted the idea in the writer's head. Hopefully, he had at least acted more decently than Claudie's seducer.

Here is where a biographer's work resembles reconstructing a puzzle whose pieces have been scattered or even destroyed by the ravages of time. The remaining fragments, imagination, and logic combine to create a plot and characters. Other supplementary sources may confirm the delicate story, or else shake it apart once again.

Here a few things are known: The young Louis Auguste Guy was born in Paris's fifth arrondissement on December 29, 1842.[94] Marie-Joséphine Guy was not a young girl, but rather a thirty-two-year-old woman, seven years older than Alexandre Manceau. Clearly, he had a taste for older women! He had already gained some attention for his engravings, as his work had been exhibited in the previous year's Salon. The mother's history is less clear. Only the names of her parents are known: Jean Guy and Marie-Catherine Buzenne.

How did they meet? In 1829, Marie-Joséphine's sister, Marguerite, married Jean-Baptiste Roemhild de Romentahl, an engraver living on the rue Saint-Jacques who specialized in historical scenes.[95] His works ranged from *Scenes from the Russian Campaign: The Colonel's Departure (Episodes de la campagne de Russie: Le Départ du colonel*) and *The Colonel's Return* (*Le Retour du colonel*) in 1830 to *David Receives Wellington* (*David recevant Wellington*), an engraving of de Rudder's painting—an artist who also inspired Alexandre Manceau's works, such as *Hamlet*. Roemhild may have been one of the young apprentice's first teachers. Manceau, then living at 3, place de la Sorbonne, could have begun a love affair with Roemhild's sister-in-law.

Or another theory: Maybe the Manceaus already knew the Guy family, as Marguerite had lived on the rue des Vieux-Augustins before her marriage, just around the corner from the Manceaus on the rue Jean-Jacques-Rousseau in the current first arrondissement. As was the custom, Roemhild could have taken the boy as an apprentice on his thirteenth birthday. Then, the young Alexandre could have found his passion for the profession by watching Jean Carles, another engraver with rooms on the rue Jean-Jacques-Rousseau, who practiced both lithography and copper plate printing.

Marguerite and Jean-Baptiste Roemhild would have two children: a girl (Amélie, born in 1833) and a boy (Charles, born four years later).[96] Amélie would become a painter herself, show works each year at future Salons, and marry Eugène Dumas, a civil engineer living at 25, rue du Four.[97] She would pass away at the age of thirty-five. As for Charles, he would follow in his brother-in-law's footsteps and enter the civil engineering profession.

The Roemhild de Romenthals seemed to be well-off financially and gave the impression of being fairly successful on the whole.

Marie-Joséphine was not as lucky! The life of Alexandre's mistress would be quite different from her sister's. Thirty-two years old and still single, she was an old maid! Balzac would eventually tell her story, of a young woman with a married sister and long-dead parents. Was she hoping for a new future with the young engraver? Did he promise her that? Was it a liaison that began to bore him? Was she too old, the "mistress" who initiated the affair? To borrow a word from George Sand, could it have been a mere "libertine" amusement for him?

Her baby was born "of an unnamed father." Manceau had not legally acknowledged him. He may not have ever seen the child, abandoning Marie-Joséphine as soon as she revealed her condition, but he did at least know the child existed, as his confessions to George Sand prove. The boy would have been seven years old when his relations with the writer began. Marie-Joséphine would never marry. She remained a single mother, raising her son in destitute poverty, in spite of a small allowance, which paid for their apartment. Auguste never left his mother's side. He lived with her until the very end.

When he turned twenty, he joined the other young men of his age to register for the military and was declared fit for service.[98] He undoubtedly got a lucky draw and didn't have to enlist, so he went to work as a civil engineer. His relative, Eugène Dumas, had most likely found him the job. Mother and son lived at 7, rue de Gallois in the twelveth arrondissement, in an alley that ran into the quai de Bercy on the Right Bank, past the bridge. They lived in a single room on the ground floor of a five-story building, with a construction site just off their backyard. The rent was 180 francs per month, in the name of the Guy lady.[99] The commune of Bercy had recently been annexed to the city of Paris. Their neighborhood, the Rapée Quarter, was a large outdoor warehouse, piled high with barrels of wine, brandy, oil, and vinegar to be shipped over land or water to the entire country. The Paris-Lyon-Marseille train line passed directly behind them with the toll bridge from Bercy spanning from one bank to the other. Woodshops, factories, tiles, fabric, and slate formed a lively working landscape.

By the time he turned twenty-five, Auguste had become an industrial designer and lived on the avenue Daumesnil, still with his mother. He would never leave the working class neighborhoods east of the capital that later became the first areas to take action in the insurrections. He had met Augustine Demailly who was only seventeen years old when their first daughter, Marie-Sophie, was born on April 18, 1868.[100] Augustine came from a working class family in Pas-de-Calais; her mother was a tailor, and her father a fruit seller. This story came directly out of Zola's writings. Auguste, who had suffered from his own father's absence, legally recognized his little girl the day after her birth. Shortly thereafter, the young couple formed a household. Then, the war of 1870 came and dashed their dreams, as Auguste explained in his first letter to George Sand. Choosing his words carefully and writing with a meticulous script, he respectfully explained his situation:

Paris, September 14, 1871

Madame,

In the name of my father, the late Alexandre Manceau, I write to you to humbly ask that you honor me with your protection.

I have lost the position of civil engineer, which I had held for the past ten years, because of the war. On July 26, I sent an employment application to the Railway Company in Paris, Lyon, and the Mediterranean, but I have not yet received a reply.

I inquired to a few of my colleagues who work at that company to tell me the reason for their silence. The fact that I come without any recommendations is why they remained silent.

Thus I am asking you, Madame, to do me the honor of promoting my cause to the influential persons of this company or such similar organizations as you might know.

It would give me great pleasure, Madame, to present my case to you in person. I would also like to take advantage of such an opportunity to discuss my father with you. I never had the pleasure of knowing my father and would be delighted to hear you speak of him.

I beg you, please pardon the boldness of this request.

Respectfully yours,

Auguste Guy

39, boulevard de Reuilly[101]

What he didn't mention in the letter was that his companion was expecting a second child. Cécile would be born on December 4, 1871.[102] He especially avoided telling her about his father-in-law, a Communard, who had been deported to the Ile d'Aix in Charente-Maritime and was being held in Fort Liedot with other political prisoners from the short-lived Commune. He also neglected to mention that Auguste Joseph Demailly had recently passed away at the military hospital two days before, at the age of fifty. He had wasted away from the harsh prison conditions, along with dozens of his companions.[103]

Always ready to lend a helping hand, George Sand immediately called on her friend Edouard Rodrigues, a broker and philanthropic manager, who often took in her protégés. He, in turn, spoke with his son-in-law, Ernest Gouin, director of the Paris-Lyon line, which gave Auguste Guy a free pass into the PLM Railway Company, exactly as he had wished. He would remain with the company until his death.

Auguste and Augustine married two years later to legitimize their young daughters.[104] They had moved into a modest house not far from the Reuilly barracks before moving once again, this time to 76, boulevard Mazas (now the boulevard Diderot). A kitchen, two rooms, and a small vestibule made up their quarters on the fourth floor of a building at the end of a courtyard, just down the road from the Vincennes shelter. The two children slept with their parents, and the grandmother took the other room, which also served as their dining room.

Marie-Joséphine would take her final breaths there, at age sixty-five. Her nephew, Charles Roemhild de Roventhal was also a civil engineer, like his father. He was present at the time of her passing—the two sides of the family hadn't burned any bridges. She died on January 29, 1876, in the same year as George Sand.[105]

These two women loved the same man. One lived in total obscurity, the other with public acclaim. Both would have two granddaughters to carry on their lineage.

Auguste Guy would live for only a few years after his mother's death. Manceau's son would die on January 21, 1889, at the age of forty-six.[106] Perhaps he suffered from the same illness that took his father's life at almost the same age. But more about that later.

All of those details, not known at the time by George Sand, do shed light on Alexandre Manceau's character. They can also, in part, explain the reluctance of George Sand's friends to accept this potential nouveau riche. Maybe he simply hadn't loved that other woman, Auguste Guy's mother. Sand did notice his desire to rise from his social standing, and his dogged determination in everything he did. All moral judgments aside, it appears simply that Manceau reflexively avoided a situation which would have made it difficult for him to become the man he wished to be. It would be nice to believe that he was the one who provided the small allowance to his son's mother. His sister, Laure Manceau, a flannel vest maker, surely knew his secret, but she did not betray him throughout all her long years.[107] In any case, this story reveals the distinct boundary between two social classes: one, of the Manceaus and the Guys. Small folk versus the great George Sand, Baroness Dudevant, a famous writer.

Alexandre Manceau, the engraver artist, chose his own destiny between two women. But he would not see his child grow up, and he would never have another. As for Maurice and Solange, they never fully accepted him. His chance at paternity would come later, with the latter's daughter, Jeanne. Until then, he would devote himself completely to the woman of his dreams, although such devotion was not immune from a bit of secret guilt.

"He's in Paris on business," Sand confided to Hetzel in November 1850. "I love him, and *you alone know my secret, and he does not know that you know.* ... Be kind and gentle to him. He is not happy. He needs it; he has enemies among my friends. But I will defend him, I will see justice done. I'll tell you everything when we meet, I'm sure you will feel compassion for him. I ask you to do this thing, for him."[108]

Manceau was not unanimously loved, and Sand was barely successful at introducing her new love into the fold. Even Maurice, for whom she pled Bocage's assistance, showed little enthusiasm. The mother and son were tightly knit together. The birth of George Sand's son had been the most glorious day of her life, and their love had only grown stronger since then. Each was incapable of living without the other. She had once written, "He is my best friend, my love," to her friend Zoé Leroy, in Cauterets. Without him, she became "a hollow, soulless shell."[109] She wrote to him in June 1849, telling him to return, for "it is so lovely here and you are doing so poorly there. Your bad fortune troubles me, and I take no pleasure in anything without you."[110] For Maurice, her sadness "drives him mad, and he knows not what he does or what he wants."[111] "He and I are one,"[112] she assured Bocage.

A curious child, this Maurice, who once announced to his mother, by mail, his unexpected intention to marry a young ingénue, likely a permanent star in the Théâtre de Nohant. He earned an earful in return, a letter filled with motherly advice on marriage. Sand was clearly dismayed by her twenty-seven-year-old son's immaturity, and that he "wasn't acting his age."[113] "You are not yet a man of your years. Give yourself time to mature,"[114] she pled. Poor Bouli! He had a rough time balancing his desires with his mother's. He was a handsome lad with brown locks, and he looked very much like his mother, expect for his shy, uncertain demeanor. He had once fallen in love with George's friend Pauline Viardot, and the two had had a brief affair when he was only twenty-one. Then, he had half-heartedly wooed his protégé, Augustine, just to make her happy. And now, he jumped at marrying the first girl who came along. But George cautioned that "marriage without love is like a life-long imprisonment." She knew whereof she spoke. But no matter, Maurice wouldn't budge, not even for black-mail: She would be forced to leave Nohant if she didn't get along with her daughter-in-law. She begged him unceasingly: "I'm afraid that *you* will harm yourself. Your indecision, your criticism, your teasing, your disgust at times, your lack of commitment, especially about the seri-ous consequences of conjugal life." Above all, she concluded, "you have not yet proven yourself to me. Not as a man, not as a husband, not as a father."[115]

This beloved son probably was not pleased that his friend became his mother's lover. At the beginning, he may have hoped for a brief and fleeting affair. But by December 1850, once his mother reported on the work that was being done around the house, he realized that Manceau was there to stay, like Chopin before him.

Sand took advantage of her son's trip to Paris to rearrange Manceau's "adorable" living quarters, as the latter had returned from the capital to spend some quality time with George. She would no longer stand to live alone in Nohant.

Alexandre Manceau had occupied rooms on the second floor, over-looking the garden, since he arrived. He moved his bed into the room he had been using as a studio, and his armoire and engraving materials into his former bedroom, and left a cubbyhole for his dressing table. The exchange meant that he and George would only be separated by the writer's library-office.[116] Maurice had moved the previous Novem-ber into the large master bedroom on the ground floor, directly below his mother's. "He has such princely quarters, and as usual, his head is full to 'busting' [*sic*: bursting] with inventions and new ways to use the knickknacks that surround him."[117]

The lady of the house had also installed a water heater into her bedroom, so she would no longer freeze when she was so preoccupied by her work that she forgot to put another log in the fire.

In return, they prepared a surprise for Maurice: They knocked down the wall between the theater and the billiards room, to make one large theater hall. His mother expected him to be overjoyed.

And thus, the little community would live in peace and harmony.

Sand took her own trip to Paris at the end of December to attend rehearsals for *Claudie*. She convinced a reluctant Maurice to let her stay with Manceau on the rue Racine. Those quarters were more convenient, more comfortable, especially for "eternally constipated people" like herself. She would make her own bed. And what of the gossipmongers? Well, they wouldn't say anything if Maurice was the one sleeping in the studio and Manceau in his own apartment on the place de Furstenberg. "Oh yes, a young man loans his apartment to a provincial lady all the time, especially when she's forty-six years old." Maurice had suffered since childhood from his friends' teasing about his mother. "They say all sorts of things," he admitted at thirteen, calling her his good old George. "It's because you're a woman who writes, and you're not a prude like everybody else's mother in junior high. Well, yeah, . . . they call you, I can't tell you the word because it's too mean, a***, I can't help it, but you need to know everything in my mind, in my heart, in the heart of a good son and a true friend."[118]

But although her son carefully guarded her reputation, George took a different path.[119]

December 25, 1850: The Salon opens, which bears witness to Alexandre Manceau's artistic talents. He exhibits a portrait of George

Sand, based on a drawing by Thomas Couture, which Eugène Delacroix says is the most lifelike portrait anyone had done of her. "We saw a true masterpiece in Paris," Emmanuel Arago would write to her, "the engraving of your portrait by Couture, really a superb engraving by one of these young kins Manceau artists of Nohant [what witty wordplay!]." George Sand hastens to pass this glowing review on to her son. How could she not be proud of her companion? His success provides the best reply to the accusations against him.

December 31, 1850: Alexandre and George celebrate the anniversary of the engraver's arrival in Nohant. Alone.

Only this secret from their friends could guarantee a few months of peace at the beginning of their life together. The peace—officially, at any rate—ended up lasting longer than anyone could have guessed. For a long time, Sand's pen included Manceau in the list of her troupe of "children," along with Maurice; the "little Lambert," a teasing jokester; and Palognon, their name for the blond Léon Villevielle, a post office worker and amateur painter.

A new couple needs some time to settle into their rhythm, to parse out their new role distribution. George Sand and Alexandre Manceau achieved balance straightaway, and a very uncommon balance, too! She was the man, the head of the household. He served her lovingly, completely devoted, without putting his dignity at risk. Little by little, he rendered himself indispensible, making her life easier without demeaning himself in return. She was his lady. He addressed her as "Madame," or, in the *Diaries* (*Agendas*) which he kept for her starting in 1852, "my lady." He was always formal in his address, while she spoke to him like an old friend. As for his more intimate pet names for her, no traces remain. All of their correspondence has been destroyed, either by George Sand herself or by Maurice, who would even cut out all allusion to Manceau in the first published edition of his mother's letters.

One letter, though, has managed to survive intact and gives an idea of their relationship. Manceau wrote this letter from Nohant when George Sand was in Paris for the premiere of her play *Molière*.

May 9, 1851

Dear Madame,

If you could have any doubts, even for a moment, of my continuing interest in *Molière* and the joy it would bring me to see you a few days earlier, I would leave tomorrow. But I know this is not the truth of the matter. Thus I pray you to understand the long hours I must toil on each engraving; that I will begin my second in four or five days at the latest; that if I came to Paris, I would be forced—it would be impossible to put off—to see so-and-so and pay a visit to Rambouillet; and that it would probably serve me better to save those few pennies to buy my plates. It seems to me that I can better express my gratitude for all your goodness while I work here rather than flit about Paris.

Still, Madame, if Maurice intends to stay there, if I can come to fetch you, if I may be of the slightest service to you, make your life the tiniest bit easier, simply say the word, and I will be at your side with more speed than any letter can reach you.

I would love to leave. I should really stay. What must I do?

I send you all of my love, from the bottom of my heart, and wish you a pleasant evening, Madame.

A. Manceau

Since I will not receive your reply to this letter before *Molière*'s premiere, tomorrow or the next day, just send me word—say "Maurice stays. Come," or simply, "*Come.*" I will come as soon as I can, no matter what the reason.[120]

Torn between desire and duty, between his mistress's invitation (or summons) and his own desire, between devotion and work, this is how Manceau expresses his love and his availability without renouncing his own will. How could anyone resist a man who wrote, "If you send me the word—*Come*—I will come as soon as I can"?

To all outward appearances, he held a lower, subservient, unequal position. She made the decisions, she organized the outings, she gave the orders, and he carried them out. But each found more than adequate value in their own role, including in the bedroom. He only waited on her hand and foot because he truly wanted to. He loved her. He was financially stable on his own, "he is a skillful worker, he has more work than he knows what to do with."[121] She respects him for that, and she needs him. He was as hardworking as she, without competing with each other. Their age gap protected their egos. Each fulfilled what the other lacked: a perfectly complementary couple. Their relationship was less narcissistic, less storybook than an affair with a Musset or a Chopin, but they were by no means mere companions. Her knight in shining armor honored her in every sense of the word. From her letter to Hetzel onward, it is fairly obvious that their relationship included a deep physical understanding. It is probably one of the main reasons their relationship had such stability and longevity. It is right there, in black and white: "I send you all of my love, from the bottom of my heart."

He made it his ongoing mission to spare her from the frustrations of daily life as much as possible. He used his unremitting energy to intervene on her behalf in tedious obligations, like a protective shield. "When you love someone with all your heart, you must, as much as it is possible, masticate happiness for them, as a mother bird, so that they only have to swallow it."[122]

Besides his theater activities, which were shared by all the guests of Nohant, he happily performed all the tasks which would eventually make him necessary to Sand's life. He copied her manuscripts—she herself admitted to be a terrible copyist, unable to remain loyal to the original version, always modifying the text as she went along. Thus, Manceau took over this daily chore, which, because of the writer's rate of production, could take several hours to complete each day. He also filed her documents and mail, and wrote some personal letters. By the end of the month, he had become her secretary, her handyman, and her trusted confidant. She never hesitated to show her gratitude, as she explained to her son: "He takes care of a thousand little things—making copies, organizing everything—and lifts the weight from my shoulders. It sits well with me, his unfailing helpfulness, how agreeable he is to completing all of the chores. ... He spares me trouble and saves me time."[123] A few days later, she continued, "I really see him as a friend, my voluntary servant who renders me countless services: copying manuscripts, writing letters, keeping my accounts in order, taking care of all the little details that I couldn't, not without losing precious work time."[124]

This constant devotion would not escape the watchful eye of Théophile Gautier, who would write to the Goncourt brothers about Manceau's attention for his lady. "For example, Manceau has redesigned Nohant specifically for writing! She barely settles into a chair before he has conjured up pens, blue ink, lined notepaper, cigarette paper, and Turkish tobacco."[125]

Alexandre Manceau shadowed George Sand and fulfilled the role of so many companions of creative minds. The magic of this relationship was that he was not emasculated by his role, that his gestures were proof of his love and never of inferiority. He surely would have had to prove himself manly enough for Sand, this "woman among women," who would never have loved him otherwise. This writer had chosen a male penname and often spoke of herself with masculine pronouns, found in Alexandre the ideal companion, a modest conqueror, both man and woman at the same time, just like her.

Chapter Eight

"THIS WILD AND UNPREDICTABLE NATURE"

"I am speechless. My daughter arrived last Friday," George Sand wrote to Hetzel in early February 1851. Solange had arrived without warning with her daughter, Jeanne whom they called "Nini." The two women made an attempt at explaining themselves. George accepted Solange's presence at Nohant warily but would not open the door to her husband, the sculptor Jean-Baptiste "Auguste" Clésinger. Their reconciliation only scratched the surface, though, for, according to her mother, Solange had not accepted responsibility for any of her mistakes and tended to weasel her way out of any difficult situation. "I am not happy about this at all," she decided.

But had she ever been truly happy? The relationship between George Sand and her daughter was a long tale of misunderstandings. Just a month prior, she had once again deterred Maurice from going to his sister's place for dinner, fearing that the devilish couple would cast an evil spell on him. "Don't eat there, don't drink there," she urged.

In the same letter, as she explained their failed relations as a string of disappointments, she showed a rare violent outburst. "I don't love her anymore, at least I don't think I do. To me, she's a cold jail cell, an unknown being, completely foreign to the ideas and emotions on my plane of existence."[126]

Jean-Baptiste Clésinger who had married George Sand's daughter, Solange, was the son of a Franche-Comté sculptor, who taught him the trade and took him to Italy to learn about Michelangelo. From a very young age, he showed both talent and mental instability. He continued his sculptures while serving in a regiment of cuirassiers in the army. He joined David d'Angers' studio for a brief time but proved himself unable to conform to the required discipline, fleeing instead to Switzerland and Italy, strewing trouble and piling debts in his wake. Back in Paris, he opened his own studio and finally bowed to a self-imposed regular work schedule. He was ambitious, calculating, charming, extravagant, imposing, and violent, but very talented and aiming to please. The sturdy, black-bearded, rugged man would finally achieve fame at the age of thirty-three.

In fact, he was the talk of the season at the Salon of 1847. There was one statue in the Louvre's sculpture room on the ground floor which caught everyone's eye, called *Woman Bitten by a Snake* (*LaFemme piquée par un serpent*). It showed a woman's body on a bed of roses, writhing not in agony, but in pleasure. As for the little bronze reptile around her leg, "this is the immortal and invincible serpent of Sensuality," exclaimed an enthusiastic Théophile Thoré in his review for *Le Constitutionnel*. The model had been none other than the beautiful Apollonie Sabatier, called "La Présidente," who would later be Baudelaire's muse. She had posed for the statue at the request of her rich protector, the industrialist Alfred Mosselman, who longed to see his mistress's . . . statuesque form immortalized in marble. Close by in the Salon, another admirer, Théophile Gautier, saw her protrusion in another stately bust with round breasts: "The bust of Madame *** is quite similar. Lucky woman!"

Clésinger had used a new method to express the flushed face lasciviousness with such realism: Instead of sculpting, he had made a cast of Madame Sabatier's body. "M. Clésinger's procedure is to statuary as the daguerreotype is to painting," pronounced the critic Gustave Planche. In other words, it was not art. Opinions may have been divided, but everyone was talking about it, and Clésinger's career took off.

A few weeks earlier, on February 18, 1847, George and Solange had visited Clésinger's studio at the recommendation of the jovial Captain Stanislas d'Arpentigny. Clésinger had already tried to attract George Sand's attention to his work a year earlier. This time, though, mother and daughter fell under his charms and even allowed him to sculpt their busts. He also gave them a bronze fawn he had sculpted. They had come to Paris to complete the final touches for Solange's marriage to Fernand de Preaulx, a slightly clumsy but completly devoted country gentleman. The artist started to woo the young woman of eighteen, and he fascinated her. Delacroix met him at George Sand's place on March 12 and left with "an unfavorable impression," which supported Stanislas d'Arpentigny's opinions. The retired captain, a card trick magician, immediately regretted having introduced the sculptor to these women. This king of hearts could very well reveal himself to be black as the ace of spades. Clésinger, however, intervened and saw to it that such a wedding wouldn't take place. Fernand, the kind little suitor, was dismissed. Clésinger, the former cuirassier piled visits on top of invitations. He even followed George and Solange to Nohant in April 1847 to wrap everything up. He "arrived here like Caesar; his will and resolution and stubbornness would suffer neither indecision nor delay. He required a yes or no answer within twenty-four hours," wrote George Sand. Emmanuel Arago, Eugène Delacroix, Frédéric

Chopin, and all their other friends knew of this brute's horrible reputation: a drunken man, drowning in debt, who beat his mistress, got her pregnant, and abandoned her, telling her to try finding a husband. They tried to warn George but broached the issue too carefully, it seemed. She remained convinced that this authoritarian man would figure out how to subdue Solange's difficult personality and that her daughter would be happy with him. On May 19, 1847, Solange married Jean-Baptiste Clésinger in Nohant.

Frédéric Chopin was appalled. To spare him while sick, Sand hadn't discussed the situation with him, backing him into a corner. He feared the worst for Solange. She had only been nine years old when the musician moved in with George in 1838. The little girl hadn't trusted him at first, but gradually had developed a sincere affection for her "Chip Chip" over the years. He had seen her grow up and had been her protector, partway stepfather and a big brother. He knew her very well. Although Chopin admitted that Clésinger didn't lack for talent and that there was no immodesty in art, he gave the couple less than a year of living together. "I guarantee you that at the next exhibition, the public will be contemplating new statues, of the breasts and stomach of his wife. ... This man will sculpt Sol's little bottom in white marble," he predicted furiously.[127] He would not attend the wedding.

It wouldn't take long for George Sand to realize her mistake, but by then, it was too late. The couple lived in the lap of luxury, and their debts piled up. She reprimanded the sculptor in a long letter, accusing him in particular of hiding the catastrophic state of his fortune from her, encouraging Solange's expensive tastes, and abusing rum, which made him vile and violent to everyone.

July 1847: Things take a turn for the worse when she invites the couple to Nohant. Clésinger proposes that Sand mortgage Nohant to pay off his debts. George Sand refuses. Before leaving the house, the sculptor and his young wife try to make off with anything they can get their hands on, cramming candlesticks, silk quilts, vases, and even Clésinger's bronze fawn into their trunks. An argument breaks out, and a furious Clésinger swings the hammer he was using to nail down the trunks, at Maurice's head. George steps between them, grabs her son-in-law's hair, and receives a punch in the chest. Blind with rage, Maurice dashes off in search of his pistols. The priest and a servant rush in and manage to subdue Clésinger. George throws out "the couple" from hell—her own expression.

But the trouble didn't stop there. Frédéric Chopin, who hadn't witnessed the argument, took Solange's side. After a brief period of reflection, he decided never to set foot in Nohant again. George Sand was sickened. Their friends tried to reconcile them, without success. Granted, their relationship had already fallen prey to certain weariness, and George Sand had admitted she was tired of Chopin's possessive and demanding nature. Maurice's jealousy and incessant nagging had added to the situation. Yet George accused her daughter of having coyly beguiled and seduced the musician to fall under her charms. She would never forgive her. The private townhouse that she had given to Solange as a dowry, and restored at great cost, was sold. The Clésingers were ruined, or very nearly. Their relationship morphed from fighting to compromising. A wonderful portrait of Solange by Clésinger shows her in a low-cut, gauzy dress, hair swept up on the nape of her neck in the romantic style, seductive and mysterious. This creature is both inviting and aggressive, both sensual and haughty, much like the sculptor saw his wife.

Frédéric Chopin and George Sand split brutally and definitively.

"Adieu, my friend. May you find swift healing from your illnesses, I hope for this now (I have my reasons), and I thank God for this strange conclusion to nine years of exclusive friendship. Send me your news sometimes. There's no point in ever dwelling on the rest."[128]

Those were the last words George ever wrote to Frédéric, in the only letter of their entire correspondence that she would never burn.

As for Solange, she remained close to Frédéric until the end. When two years later, on October 17, 1849, Chopin died, it is Solange who closed his eyes. Jean-Baptiste Clésinger would sculpt his death mask.

It is easy to understand the mix of resentment and guilt felt by the two women, each for her own reasons.

Nothing had ever been easy between the two. Aurore Dupin (young George Sand) and Casimir Dudevant's marriage was already disintegrating when the young woman became pregnant with her daughter. Many suggest that the real father was Stéphane d'Ajasson de Gransagne, Sand's childhood friend. Aurore had become his mistress the previous autumn and had met up with him in Paris nine months before giving birth. Casimir Dudevant, himself born of adultery but legally recognized, would mention this fact during the separation hearings.[129] It was a confusing time. In addition to everything else, Aurore's platonic love, Aurelien de Seze, happened to be present at Nohant for the delivery on September 13, 1828.

She wanted a little girl, and yet when Solange arrived, she didn't feel "the same joy as when Maurice was born." Bad omen?[130] From the very beginning, Sand's concern about the baby's health, her anxiety, doubt, and anger mingled with her love for Solange.

Two years later, in July 1830, Aurore met Jules Sandeau. The two left for Paris within a few months, leaving the children behind in Nohant. She returned every three months to see them. It was April 1832 when Sand finally decided to bring Solange with her to Paris. The little girl was three and a half years old. She shared in the bohemian life of her mother and her love, and became the mascot for the artists and Berrichon friends who spent time at the apartment on the quai Saint-Michel where Aurore lived with Jules.

It is at that time that Aurore Dudevant became George Sand upon the publication of *Indiana*. Meanwhile, she took excellent care of her daughter, in spite of the scandalously freethinking way (for the era) she lived her life. "This is a superb family. I pamper my daughter, spoil her, clean her, beat her, dress her up, rock her, and stuff her full of food. Silly, and simple, and ridiculous, as though I were a *good mother* and an *honest wife*," she wrote her childhood friend Charles Duvernet.[131]

Early on, Sand was concerned about her "little girl's whims, sometimes so ludicrous, so deeply rooted, one could mistake her for an adult."[132] In another letter, she shared her fear that all those tantrums of hers, her "wild and unpredictable nature," already so pronounced at four years of age, might influence her future behavior.

This characteristic would become more pronounced over the years. The young girl was happy with her mother close, lavishing attention on her, but she suffered when they were separated, and felt neglected. As for Maurice, he was fairing no better: He couldn't stand the militaristic discipline of his boarding school. The catastrophic beginning to his studies at the Henri IV secondary school showed all the symptoms of psychosomatic issues.

That same year, in 1833, George Sand fell in love with Alfred de Musset. Passion trumped all. They decided to leave for Venice in December. George and her husband, Casimir Dudevant, having rediscovered their own freedoms, maintained a very good relationship. Casimir agreed to care for Solange, while Maurice stayed in boarding school. Their doctor friend, Gustave Papet, took the boy in on his school leave.

Eleven-year-old Maurice's "traveler of a mother" could write him loving and attentive letters, while five-year-old Solange was left in the caring and sometimes abusive hands of the servants. She felt horribly abandoned.

"What is this thing they call a mother's love?" the young mother wrote to Musset, who had returned to Paris before her. "It continues to be a mystery to me. These concerns and worries, a hundred times more poignant than a lover's love, and yet less joy and passion of possession. Separation hardly matters in the first few days, but becomes feverishly ardent and cruel as the days wear on."[133]

She had remained in Venice with the seductive doctor, Pietro Pagello, who had cared for Musset. He would return to Paris with her in July 1834, but she would, however, resume seeing the poet again. Their passion came in fits and starts before a final break. In despair, George Sand cut her hair and sent it to her lover. Her friend Eugène Delacroix would paint her as such—pale, almost ghostlike—in a portrait that would become famous. At the end of that mad year, she fled Paris for Nohant. As always, her work and the tranquility of the countryside saved her.

But what about Solange? Where did she fit into this whirlwind romance?

Both her childhood and adolescence were defined by a fluctuation between presence and separation and absence, attention and distance of her mother. George Sand never stopped loving her children. Both were present in her mind at all times. But from time to time, she had a burning need to live her life intensely. Nothing else seemed to matter in those moments, compared to this urge. By the time she was thirty, she had already tasted dazzling fame, passion, and independence. Far from consuming her, that fire fed her work. Her creative power seemed limitless, much like that of Balzac, who was also just starting out. This said, her children suffered for it, especially Solange.

George Sand wanted it all. She didn't want to sacrifice anything. Not work, not love, nor her children. She tried to be a good mother. Her commitment to being maternal, the "instinct" as she called it, superseded all other feelings. Including love and friendship. The fact is, with children, motherhood also includes the practical concerns of organization, time management, education, and decision making. Following a violent incident in which a drunken Casimir Dudevant struck her, she decided to report him and ask for a legal separation.[134] On February 16, 1836, thanks to her skillful new lover, the lawyer François Michel (whom they called Michel de Bourges), she won the separation in her favor with full custody of the children. She raised them by herself, assuming both roles of "father and mother of the family."

George Sand decided to take her children's education into her own hands and even tried homeschooling them. She had pulled Maurice out of junior high for good! But she soon became frustrated with his lack of interest in academic work, and in her daughter's stubborn refusal to work, in spite of her ability. Confident that the latter could succeed academically, she sent her to boarding school. This was an utter failure. Solange was a difficult child. Sand recognized that she was gifted and intelligent, but rebellious, aggressive, unfulfilled, jealous, complaining constantly, impish, shallow, and a bully, and systematically did the opposite of everything her mother wished. Her mother was forced to admit that, at eight years old, though "highly superior to her brother, Solange was less likable."

The sketch by the Swiss portraitist Nancy Mérienne shows a striking contrast between the two children aged eight and eleven. Maurice stands in profile, with a faraway look in his eyes, as if daydreaming or peering into the horizon. Solange is very pretty in a white dress with puffy sleeves, with long curls, arms crossed, holding a few flowers, tilting her head slightly, and fixing the viewer with a defiant look.

Balzac criticized George Sand for dressing her daughter in boy's clothing; Clara Gazul's portrait of Maurice dressed as a girl illustrates the mélange of gender norms that George Sand so enjoyed.

The conflicted young girl wanted desperately to please her mother, to be admired or even just noticed, but her every action was the incarnation of all that George Sand hated. Their letters to each other show the sad misunderstandings between mother and daughter. Solange begged George to let her leave boarding school or to come visit her, imploring page after page: "Come here, come, come here, Mommy." But in vain: Her trips home to Nohant hinged on her academic results. The more Sand preached to her daughter a love of work, the need to show an effort, to read, the less inclined Solange was to satisfy her. Mostly, she was bored—a deeply foreign feeling to her mother. Despite all her efforts, George Sand failed to impart a moral backbone to her daughter, which she herself had received from her grandmother.

Still, Solange had character and was the only person to hold out against George Sand. She couldn't do it tactfully, though, and it was usually for the wrong reasons. She felt an insatiable need to be found worthy in her eyes. Even though Sand loved her son with absolute, unconditional love, her daughter had to prove herself all her life. And she would never quite manage. George Sand felt exasperated and disappointed.

Her daughter reminded her of Sophie, her own mother, whose wild, unstable, explosive, unfair, combative, hypercritical nature she had feared. Maybe she realized that she forced the same suffering from her own childhood onto Solange by her absences and the distance between them: the old pattern of an adored but absent mother.

In a sad letter to Maurice in January 1851, she writes, "I love the memory of this little girl, so pretty and smart, whom we both spoiled, who fought us and made us unhappy, but whom we believed we could change, who should have become the perfect girl of our sweetest dreams."

The desire to create her version of a perfect girl might have been her downfall.

Solange had let her down, so George chose some "new" daughters, but they only reminded her of her disappointment with her own child. There was her young cousin Augustine Brault, whom she considered her adopted daughter and whom she wanted to marry off to Maurice, and the singer Pauline Viardot, her "little girl," who was very talented.[135] Ambivalent feelings for George Sand.

From a very young age, Pauline had started comparing herself to the heroines of her "mother's novels, the women of pen and ink. "Edmonde is the most beautiful of all your girls. I am the worst looking," she confided to Sand.[136]

Marie d'Agoult's *Mémoires* includes a detailed portrait of Solange as a child, whom she knew during her friendship with George Sand. "A personality as strong as her body; an intelligence that seems to be made for hard sciences; a loving heart, a passionate mind, and uncontrollable. Solange is destined to reach the extreme of either good or evil. Her life will be full of obstacles and battles. She will not bow to normal rules. Her faults will be great mistakes, her virtues will be sublime perfection."

She had also turned her prophetic eye onto Maurice and singled out the differences in character between the brother and sister who were so attached to each other. "Maurice seems to be the living antithesis of his sister. He will be a man of common sense, of discipline, of the usual virtues. His life will be dominated by morality. His studies will continue until he finds affection, of which there will be a small amount. His tastes will tend towards simple pleasures and a landlord's life, if his sizeable talent doesn't launch him into an artistic career, which is highly likely."[137]

Solange's negative tendencies were becoming increasingly more pronounced, as the following anecdote from Pauline Viardot shows. Invited to the singer's country home in Brie, the Sand family was walking through the garden on a winding path bordered by lilies, irises, gladiolus, and narcissus; adults in front, children behind them. "While chatting with Madame Sand," Pauline recalled, "I heard the constant swish of a whip behind me. Turning around, I saw that, walking along, Solange was whacking the flowers with a riding crop, breaking their stems instantly, while the flowers hung down, crushed." Horrified by this unwarranted action, the singer determined that "This was how it had always been: Solange can't help but do bad things the way artists make art for art's sake."[138]

While continuing to watch over Pauline and meet up with her in Paris from time to time, George Sand kept her distance, especially since the events of 1847.

As for her daughter's arrival, she knew full well that it would disturb Nohant's very precious peace, and she dreaded it. "Roses do well to brace themselves and stiffen their beautiful, frail necks," warned a menacing Solange, echoing Pauline Viardot's story, "for I am Robespierre to flowers."

Maybe George Sand was also apprehensive about Solange's meeting Manceau. It's not impossible. But for now, Solange only passed through in her search for a summer home. The brief visit did serve, however, as an occasion for George Sand and Alexandre Manceau to become better acquainted with a tiny person who would play a significant role in their lives: Nini, Solange's adorable little three-year-old daughter.

Their next visit, in June 1851, required weeks of logistical preparation. For George Sand and Manceau. The young woman was planning to bring from Paris her horse, and a stable had to be found as well as housing for her English groom and a nanny for her daughter. Solange loved horseback riding, enough to jump back in the saddle the day after she gave birth, which drew a harsh reprimand from her mother. Outlets for her endless energy. For Solange, riding was part and parcel of a rising young Parisian education. George Sand, on the other hand, who spent hours at her writing table, barely making ends meet, was shocked by her daughter's extravagance. She had had to do without a new cloak and a summer dress from her skilled seamstress and half-sister, Caroline, for lack of funds. "I don't follow fashion too closely, and I'm wearing my rags down to the bone," she wrote as an excuse.[139] She couldn't understand this "fine young lady," her daughter, with her need for luxury. Still, their relationship seemed to improve. They exchanged letters and saw each other the following May in Paris, when Sand arrived to attend the first rehearsals of her play *Molière* at the Théâtre de la Gaîté. Solange welcomed Manceau into her home—George and Alexandre's relationship seemed to be official now, as he was also invited to Bocage's for dinner.

As always, Solange seemed suspicious at first. Sand related a story to her about Manceau, the Parisian discovering the countryside's bucolic charms, who had been scared to death by the sight of a snake. Solange sniggered. Always concerned with staying in her good graces, Sand also wrote, "Manceau is very taken with your daughter."[140] "Nini no longer remembers Mademoiselle Manceau, who is scared of snakes,"[141] came the curt reply. However, man and child ("very cute and very difficult,"[142] according to her grandmother) had been smitten with each other at first sight.

As planned, Solange arrived at the end of June with a child and luggage in tow. Their options in Nohant were endless: theater, George's brood of fledglings, butterfly chasing (Maurice and Manceau's new passion), some swimming in the river in spite of the cold, and long strolls. Solange was making a real effort. "Right now, I think she's very nice," George beamed. "Everyone is very happy. Everything is good."[143]

Too good, perhaps?

As she woke one morning, Sand was surprised to discover a note scribbled in pencil: "I'm really leaving. It's better. The style here does nothing for me. And anyway, I want to know if it's just a tantrum or if he actually needs me for something or if [*sic*] is unhappy without me.

Adieu deary, or rather farewell. I leave Nini in your care. Manceau should take her around for a walk every morning. She woke up in the night to say 'wonderful grandmommy.' Solange Clésinger."[144]

Was that a couple's spat, a hint of flirtation, a husband's jealousy? Never mind the real reason she left—the note gives an idea of Solange's impulsiveness. Leaving her daughter with her mother and her companion, however, solidified their roles as far as Nini was concerned.

Unwilling to start another conflict with her daughter nor to receive Clésinger in Nohant, George Sand subtly found a way out by sending Nini home by train with her nurse. Her scratched cheek from falling into a rosebush was washed by Sand with arnica. Like all grandmothers, she couldn't refrain from commenting on how "Nini's food is poorly regulated, she eats all the time!"[145]

After that, Solange and her mother maintained regular epistolary contact for several months. Their everlasting debate continued: one's idleness and ennui, the other's passion in working. Neither leeches nor homeopathic treatments nor "male-style horseback riding" seemed to lift Solange out of her asthenia. Meanwhile, overcoming fever, coughs, rheumatism, and migraines, George Sand put the finishing touches on a new play. *The Vanderke Family* (*La Famille Vanderke*), a comedy in three acts, would play that November as *Victorine's Marriage* (*Le Mariage de Victorine*), "to follow Sedaine's *Philosophy without Knowing It* (*Philosophe sans le savoir*)." She worked six hours each day and six hours each night. She had also written *Berry Customs and Morals* (*Mœurs et coutumes du Berry*), another play (*Nello*), and the first draft of *Master Favilla* (*Maître Favilla*); edited several notes for Hetzel's illustrated edition of her works, including *The Devil's Pool* and *Mauprat*; finished *The Devil in the Fields* (*Le Diable aux champs*), a "mammoth comedy, or a novel in dialogue;" not to mention some features in different journals—all since June. *The Devil in the Fields*, a fantasy with two overlapping plots, told of the preparations for a play with marionettes. The characters were Maurice, Eugène, Emile, and Damien—obviously her son, Eugène Lambert, Emile Aucante (a young law clerk), and Manceau, whose middle name was Damien. The text would be dedicated to him in 1855. She left him the task of explaining the idea behind the play: "So I would say that theater should correct morals with moral portraits but should not change opinions by appealing to any opinions. ... Don't be afraid of the riveted audience member who will laugh or shed tears over himself without thinking of himself. The next day, he will already be a better or wiser person, without knowing how it came about."[146]

How could Solange be bored? George wondered. She had everything: a husband, an adorable child, books, music, a piano (Chopin had taught her to play—few people can say that!), an early disposition towards music and literature, intelligence, and a good memory. Why didn't she write? "I can tell that you, you are talented, you will write, and you will write well,"[147] she declared to her daughter. She even attempted giving a few writing lessons by mail, which, in George Sand's hand, never ceases to amaze. Try keeping a journal, she advised, and jotting down impressions or a particularly interesting conversation. Train yourself to write, read, start out by finding the shape of a piece. And for that, no better exercise than reading Bossuet![148]

Alas, it would take more effort, more will power, more perseverance to succeed than Solange was willing to put forth. Poor George Sand, who had worked so hard to instill in her children a bit of her own energy! "My life hadn't truly begun until the day I started working for my living,"[149] she wrote, a full century before Simone de Beauvoir, in a time when working women were limited to the working class. "Working is an artist's greatest joy."[150] She felt a connection with all who, like her, had "the fire of work at their backs."[151] The older she got, the more she believed in work, even fatigued as she was from six months of finishing three separate plays. But neither of her children would follow in her footsteps: not Maurice, who she doubted would ever have the ability to earn his own living, nor Solange, who lived her life with "arms crossed."

George was obsessed with that idea. "I'm not sure there is anything more essential in this world than work to calm the soul and the mind,"[152] she confided to Pierre-Jules Hetzel. Work represented another link between her and Manceau, her right-hand man, who offered his assistance in her work while still keeping up with his own commissions.

In spite of her mother's best efforts, Solange still complained about being bored, and miscarried once again. George Sand blamed "male-style horseback riding" and yet marveled: "You're pregnant without realizing it? How does that work? You had your monthly time while you were here, yet you still say you were already pregnant. This is impossible. You know nothing of yourself, you take no more interest in your body than if it didn't exist, and this makes me very concerned for the future."[153] Very few women in the mid-nineteenth century were able to give that advice to their daughters: listen to your body.

The never-ending fights between Solange and her husband were yet another cause for concern.

Solange would return to Nohant for a few days in November, however, looking for a mother's comfort. At least she made one person happy: Manceau, Nini's not-so-secret admirer. Sand joked that he feared the little cutie's whims would intrude into their relationship. "I pointed out that he will have regressed to childhood by the time she is old enough to marry, and that she'd be even more difficult to control than she is now."[154]

What a nice, tacit arrangement, both humorous and caring, for the couple who would never have a child of their own. George Sand, in yet another homage of her love for him, gave the engraver exclusive use of her likeness and refused to have her portrait done by anyone else.

November 14, 1851: Together with Solange and Nini, they all left for Paris to attend rehearsals for *Victorine's Marriage* at the Théâtre du Gymnase. Everything was going so well . . .

Chapter Nine

"I AM NO MADAME
DE STAËL"

After a harried arrival—the train pulled up to the station an hour early, and a slightly crazed cab driver took hundreds of detours with George and Nini—each settled in. Solange and her daughter in their house, and the couple in 3, rue Racine, each officially in their own rooms. The engraver's studio and bedroom were on the fifth floor, and George Sand had started renting a small apartment on the third floor in May. Rue Racine ran from the boulevard Saint-Michel to the place de l'Odéon, in the heart of a neighborhood different from what it is today. Haussmann wouldn't map out the boulevard Saint-Germain until a few years later. The Latin Quarter was the students and bohemians' domain: cobblestoned back streets, cheap cafes, seedy hotels, bookstores, and reading rooms.[155] Sand occupied a room with a fireplace facing the street, a kitchen with a stove on the courtyard, Manceau was only two flights upstairs if she wanted to work with him or escape unwelcome visitors. Maurice wasn't fooled, though—it wasn't easy to convince him that the apartment would be perfect for none other than mother and son!

"Blue carpeting, a Louis XV chest of drawers, a Chinese folding screen upstairs, and four embroidered armchairs," she described to Maurice, who had stayed at home while they finished arranging the apartment. Everyone was bustling around: Manceau set up hat stands, the concierge tacked up oilskin toile on the walls in the bathroom . . . which leads to an example of the scatological humor that was in fashion in Nohant.

Manceau: If Lambert has the misfortune of bad aim in the toilet, I'll smack him into next week! Such a nice oilcloth! You'll see, Madame, this place will be so clean that you could use it for a dressing room.

Maurice's esteemed mother: Doesn't that ever happen to you?

Manceau: What's that, Madame?

Maurice's esteemed mother: Bad aim?

Manceau: Never, I can assure you! I label them for ease of recognition.[156]

Here, we can also see how Manceau addresses George Sand respectfully as Madame, while she is less formal. This difference illustrates their entire relationship, with respect on one side and familiarity on the other. Her "good Manceau," "the wonderful friend," as she calls him in so many letters, is also shown a gruff affection in a scene from the rehearsals at the Théâtre du Gymnase. He was being questioned on how *Victorine's Marriage* had been staged at Nohant, but he tried to evade the question, arguing that he didn't know how to talk to actors. "Come on, you ass, go ahead, because I don't remember myself," his mistress pushed, snubbing his concerns with a dash of sadism. Embarrassed, Manceau complied. With absurdity worthy of Eugène Ionesco, the resident fireman remarked, "Here is a well-spoken young man. I'll bet he's a fireman."

Alexandre Manceau, with his approximate language or Parisian slang, made Madame roar with laughter at his schoolyard humor. Beloved and teased, he never left her sight. He was a part of her everyday life, from the theater to dinner, from Solange's place to their friends' apartments.

The world of theater enchanted the author, and together they ran from one theater to the next wanting to better understand what made the public laugh. Would these Parisian audiences who favored "champagne" take to her "fresh water?" The director, Montigny, had no doubts. Irritated when she wanted to make cuts to the second act. But in the end, he finally gave in. Sand was totally calm on the night before the premiere, while Manceau was suffering from acute stage fright vicariously.

Success! Standing ovations, a stream of friends backstage and in the lobby, the place was euphoric, despite her upset stomach and the prediction that Emmanuel "Bignat" Arago had made: "The president would be daft to wait any longer for a coup d'état, for it won't get any easier than it is now."[157]

A coup d'état? Really? Paris had never been so calm. In front of the Elysée: "A heavy silence, the dingy light of the streetlamps on the slick and shiny cobblestones." Facing the garden on the avenue Marbeuf: "same silence, same gloom, same solitude."

"It won't happen yet, not tomorrow," George Sand giggled to Manceau as they returned home from the circus.

The next morning was December 2, 1851. The engraver shook her awake with the news: a state of siege had been proclaimed, the National Assemblée had been dissolved, and universal suffrage had been reinstated. Louis-Napoléon Bonaparte had prepared his coup d'état in the strictest secrecy and had succeeded.

Ten years earlier, no one would have taken him seriously. He was the son of Louis Bonaparte, Napoléon's brother, and Hortense de Beauharnais, Josephine's daughter from her first marriage to Alexandre de Beauharnais. Louis-Napoléon had been raised in Rome and Switzerland, where his mother was living in exile. His first attempt at insurrection in 1830 failed, then his brother lost his life fighting for unification of Italy. Six years later, a second uprising in Strasbourg got Louis-Napoléon arrested and exiled to the United States. Finally, on August 6, 1840, he sailed from England to Boulogne—where his attempted coup failed yet again. This time, Louis-Napoléon Bonaparte was sentenced to life imprisonment at the Fort de Ham. During his imprisonment, he wrote *The Extinction of Paupers* (*L'Extinction du paupérisme*), a satire inspired by humanitarian socialism, which claimed: "The reign of castes is over. Now, one can only govern with the masses." He also exchanged letters with George Sand before his escape in May 1846.

Convinced that he was destined for greatness, Victor de Persigny persuaded Louis-Napoléon to return to France from London to run for the Constituante. Elected in June 1848, he soon resigned. That November, the Assemblée drew up the Constitution for the Second Republic, which called for a legislative Assemblée, appointed for three-year terms, and a president elected through universal suffrage for four-year nonconsecutive terms. He could not dissolve the Assemblée, which in turn could not impeach the president. At age forty, Louis-Napoléon ran for the presidential elections of December 10, 1848, banking on both his reformed image and his prestigious lineage.

The rest of the story tells itself. He was elected with over 74 percent of the votes, far outstripping the other candidates. Rural France had voted overwhelmingly for him, but so had many urban voters, for different reasons. Persigny had once again played a crucial role in the victory, organizing a propaganda campaign throughout the entire country. Then, the legislative elections introduced a conservative majority who, in May 1850, worked to limit universal suffrage for males, requiring three years of living in the same county. Three million voters were eliminated at once, mostly laborers, who moved constantly from one job to the next.

It was in Louis-Napoléon's best interest to re-establish the original universal suffrage, which had benefited him so much, and to strengthen his power as president of the Republic. Thus followed, in quick succession, several petitions, opinion campaigns, and political manipulation of men like Thiers, who was convinced that "the uncle's nephew" was "a complete moron who had to be led around." But the vote for the repeal of the May 1850 law was pushed back.

The coup d'état loomed large.

George Sand hadn't grasped the severity of the situation right away. Her friends' pessimism, tears, and panic now left her skeptical. She remained calm, listened, and tried to understand. Every evening, she sat by the fire, writing her *Journal*, ears perked for any noise from the street. It wasn't easy to sort out the rumors from eyewitness accounts. And besides, news was given in the conditional, because freedom of the press had been suspended. Unlike her friend Pauline Viardot, who retained her egotistical "artist's superiority," or the hotheaded and coldhearted Solange, she fretted constantly about Maurice, who had stayed behind in Nohant. Chaos reigned. Barricades went up in Paris. The first arrests were carried out. The Ministry of War plastered posters everywhere: "ANY INDIVIDUAL SEEN CONSTRUCTING OR DEFENDING A BARRICADE, OR FOUND WITH FIREARMS, WILL BE SHOT."

December 3: "People start dying." Suspicions run high. Couldn't the friendly coachman be a spy? He "pops out from behind every corner." George Sand is one of the most recognizable figures from the Revolution of '48, isn't she in danger? Manceau urges her to leave, "feeling somewhat responsible for [her] safety." "The good soul" pressures her so much that she surrenders and promises to leave Paris that very evening. "Oh, if only I were a man," she sighs, gazing out the window, "I would not leave." Maybe she's remembering the days of 1832, when she joined the uprising on the quai Saint-Michel with a young Solange. But Manceau, who stepped out for a moment to buy some soap, stops her from even sitting at the window! This time, there is no doubt: She has a protector looking out for her, and she is grateful for it. She settles in, waiting for any news from the outside. Shots ring out on the rue de la Harpe, and servants and laborers run down the street. Cannons fire in the distance, voices shout, more guns, then deathly silence in the city.

Moments later, trunks packed, she waits for a passport to allow her to travel. But a car is ready for them, so too bad for the safe-conduct! They fly past Pinson's house to pick up Solange and Nini, then whip the horses into a gallop. Solange argues with Manceau. They all laugh, to defuse the situation. The army is occupying the train station. No one asks to see their papers. The little band rides across the sleeping countryside in frozen darkness. Nini recalls how she had once eaten peas in Orléans. They arrive at Châteauroux at four in the morning, where the police inquire what was happening in Paris. The news hasn't reached Berry.

Exhausted and chilled to the bone, they reach Nohant at dawn. Manceau had ridden in the cart with the trunks, crammed between dogs and a crate of rotting codfish. Maurice and Lambert are pulled from their beds, sleepy and puffy eyed. Everyone hugs each other and rejoices at being reunited, just like in a storybook.

The grace period was short. At least 200 people died on the barricades on the grand boulevards, Deputy Baudin had fallen in the Saint-Antoine slums with his famous cry of "See how we die for twenty five francs!" corpses were thrown into the Seine, thousands were arrested, and still more fled the city. The working class was unwilling to defend an Assemblée which had deprived them of the right to vote. The sporadic rural rebellion was crushed or headed off at the start. Arrests increased daily, and sentences rained down: Almost 10,000 were deported, banished, and exiled to Guyana or Algeria. Every republican was a suspect.

December 21, 1851: The plebiscite voted a resounding *yes*, granting the president authority to draw up the new constitution. "It is natural for a democracy to be represented by a leader," said Louis-Napoléon, laying the foundations for a new presidential regime in France. The constitution instated him for ten years as the country's sole authority. He appointed his own ministers. The State Council would introduce new laws, which would be voted on by a legislative body elected by universal suffrage, but who would lack any right of initiative or amendment. The Senate would ensure constitutionality. The president of the Republic was all-powerful, and only a thin line separated France from a new empire. The line would be crossed by a decree that November, following another vote. Louis-Napoléon Bonaparte became Napoléon III on December 2, 1852. He had already left the Elysée almost a year earlier, in favor of the royal residence in the Tuileries.

A new battle had begun for George Sand upon her return to Nohant.

To her, the coup d'état had taken seed somewhere during June '48, when the bourgeoisie had started shooting the working class instead of allying with them. An unforgivable action with tragic consequences. "Politics sicken me more and more," she wrote to Solange in October 1851. This woman, who had proudly proclaimed, "My name is George Sand, and I am a communist"[158] in May, was losing hope, despite her general faith in humanity. The socialists had deeply disappointed her. She hated their sectarian views, their fanaticism, and couldn't handle the idea of a State dictator and direct governance. She believed in "labor associations" and in reconciling the bourgeoisie with the working class. Writing in her *Journal* on December 7-8, 1851, she reasoned that "the bourgeoisie should ask for, demand, and require a true, complete and universal suffrage. It should grant the fundamental rights of a *republican* society: the freedoms of press and speech and assembly, a progressive tax, free education, etc."[159]

Unfortunately, republicans, including her friends, were in no fit state to demand anything. Hetzel was forced to leave France on December 6 without any hope of returning. More and more of her acquaintances found themselves behind bars, in exile, or worse, deported. Sixty-six deputies, including Victor Hugo, the republican Raspail, and the former joiner Agricol Perdiguier, were expelled from the country in January 1852. Her former lover Victor Borie, her friend Alphonse Fleury, and her sculptor friend Luigi Calamatta followed Hetzel to Brussels. Marc Dufraisse, who she had helped nominate as the commissioner of Indre, was listed to be deported to Devil's Island. Emile Aucante and Ernest Périgois, regular guests at Nohant, were imprisoned. The motto "Liberty, Equality, Fraternity" was prohibited. The freedoms of press, assembly, and movement were suppressed. It was terror, George observed sadly. Even surrounded by her little circle, whom she couldn't live without—Maurice, Lambert, and Manceau at its core, as she wrote to Charles Gounod—she felt the pain of all those who paid so dearly for their ideas. Although she represented a strong republican figure for her contemporaries, even more so than Victor Hugo at the time, she wasn't really a militant like the school-teacher Pauline Roland, who worked closely with Pierre Lerous, or Flora Tristan, who died of exhaustion at age forty-one while waging a crusade for a workers' union. Sand was a writer above all else, who furthered her ideas through novels and plays. The interruption of 1848 had given her the opportunity to take action on the front lines, which resulted in such severe disillusionment. Her unique position had made her not only a muse but a free woman. She felt a "part of humanity." Simultaneously an idealist *and* a pragmatist, a woman of compromise *and* conviction, passionate *and* pensive, naïve *and* clever, she was determined to help her friends with admirable devotion, stubbornness, efficiency, and self-sacrifice. Under surveillance herself, she risked arrest. She was willing to take that chance and compromise herself. She drew harsh criticism for it, but she believed in doing everything possible to save whomever she could.

George Sand decided to intercede directly with her "half-wit ex-friend Louis-Napoléon,"[160] as she called him before the coup d'état. In her second letter seeking an audience, she pleaded: "I am no Madame de Staël. I have neither her genius nor her pride in fighting against the twin forces of intelligence and power. . . . But here my conscience orders me to relent, and if I must suffer every humiliation, every agony, I will do so, and with pleasure, with the certainty that I will never lose your respect for this woman's devotion, which a man understands and would never rebuke."[161] With great skill, she beseeched him to grant amnesty and renounce the unjust charges, stroking his ego, calling him a "genius of socialism," recognizing his victory as valid without foreswearing her own beliefs. She obtained a permit for transportation and left for Paris on January 23 with Manceau.

January 29: The president grants her an audience. The man hasn't changed from the one she once knew, still susceptible to appeals of human emotion. "You may ask for anything you wish, for whomever you wish," the future emperor allows.[162] What she is seeking is a general amnesty, not individual favors.

The situation was made even more uncomfortable when the men she sought to help criticized her actions. Some went so far as to refuse her aid, like her old friend Alphonse Fleury, the lawyer who had served as commissioner of the Republic in '48 but wouldn't return to France until 1859, after the amnesty. Worse still were those who accused her of surrendering her principles, like Marc Dufraisse, who had been saved from deportation to Guyana thanks to her intervention.

Louis-Napoléon Bonaparte granted her a second audience on February 6, 1852. She sent him eight letters from January to June of that year, drawing out official pardons for dozens upon dozens of convicts. Little by little, Sand was able to lower the deportation sentences of all the Indre deportees, and of her friend Pauline Roland, who would sadly not survive her deportation to Algeria very long. Working tirelessly, Sand remained in Paris until April 2, running with Manceau from the Ministry of the Interior to the Ministry of Justice, badgering the chiefs of staff and other officials who were hardly motivated to fulfill their master's promises. Above all, she had to convince her friends to accept the deals, which were sometimes only a permit, like Hetzel's, for a month-long visit to French territory. She begged Emile Aucante to accept the extension which she had managed to obtain for him, and work at her side to give Manceau a break from all the copying. With Aucante's assistance, Alexandre would be able to dedicate some of his time to engraving. Emile was a fine-looking lad in his thirties, originally from La Châtre, who had worked as a legal clerk. He shared George Sand's republican views and had been a long-time admirer of hers. She was instrumental in getting him assigned to house arrest at her home in Nohant, under her responsibility.

George Sand took criticism from all sides, from Louis Blanc to Michele Accursi, an Italian lawyer exiled in Paris, a friend of the republican patriot Giuseppe Mazzini. No matter that she claimed: "It makes absolutely no difference to me to be compromised, slandered, or insulted without any chance to defend myself.... Others are being imprisoned or exiled for their political views. I can certainly risk my reputation in the name of friendship."[163] She was "ready to put all her irons in the fire if necessary."[164] As the weeks dragged on, she was subject to slights from both sides: powerful propaganda that exploited her actions in the official press, and no thanks whatsoever from her friends and peers. By the end, she felt "disgusted with everything and almost everyone on this earth."[165] Still, she stood by what she felt was her moral duty, unfazed by her own weariness, her stomach problems, her choking fits, which could prevent her from writing a single letter, her exhaustion. *"Bled, syapsiated [sic], emeticated, morphicated,"*[166] she chalked up all her health problems to being of "the critical age!" As others fought, she negotiated. Manceau supported her in her battle, writing for her when she was too tired, accompanying her on her errands, serving as her secretary, keeping the *Diaries* up to date, "forgetting himself to help me live."[167] "He is so good, so devoted that I take advantage of him," she admitted. But that didn't mean she couldn't snap at him. She had always had trouble getting up in the morning: "Madame finally woke up the twenty-first time. Her first words to Manceau were 'Go to hell.'"[168]

After six months, George Sand sent Louis-Napoléon a summary of all the pardons he had awarded and all those which she was still waiting to see be carried out: deportees to Africa, temporary exiles— including Alphonse Fleury and Ernest Périgois, secretary for the prefecture of Indre in 1848—and incarcerated convicts.[169]

She wasn't satisfied with helping those who had been convicted, though. She also used her connections to help her cousin Augustine and even obtained a sinecure for Manceau's father, thanks to prince Jérôme Napoléon, the president's republican cousin, Prince Napoléon, whom she called "Plon-Plon," was the son of Caroline de Wurtemberg and Jérôme, Napoléon I's brother. Born in 1822, he was partially raised by Queen Hortense, along with his cousin, Louis-Napoléon. In 1848, though, he was the youngest elected member of the Constituent and kept his extremely leftist, anticlerical, democratic beliefs, in spite of his responsibilities under the Empire. Like another of George Sand's friends, Emile de Girardin, the patron of the *La Presse* newspaper, he represented the Empire's liberal branch. His resemblance to his uncle, Napoléon I, was uncanny. George Sand valued their friendship, which would prevail through it all.

Thanks to the imperial prince, Jean-Louis Manceau was made the warden of Luxembourg, then promoted to concierge at the Senate. George even went so far as to seek an award for him, as those given to his colleagues, for his thirty-eight years of good and loyal services in the military and as a civil servant. Alexandre's father had served in the Napoleonic army—had his son been raised in the Emperor's cult? One evening, when Prince Napoléon had come to sup with them in their "little den," with the workshop's pewter silverware, "Manceau nursed the nub of his cigar and the dregs of his small glass and said: 'Maybe one day, who knows? He does look so much like his uncle.'"[170]

Manceau, a Bonapartiste? Well, he hated the catcalls during the president's procession ("stupid and cowardly") that he had attended in October with George Sand.[171] Did his sympathies help to shape his attitude? It's a valid question—and the same could be asked of Maurice, who didn't hide his sympathies for the emperor, either. At any rate, Manceau's father would serve as their messenger to Prince Napoléon, who maintained friendly ties with her and cordial ones with the engraver.

Sand was in no way supportive of the current regime, but she realized that it was not the time for political action. That would have to wait. Anything to avoid violence and bloodshed. Every dictatorship, from 1793 to 1848 to the present government, believed that *the ends justified the means*. That was the gravest political error, even if the facts supported the theory. "Only morality, fraternity, and evangelism can save this nation from its decadence anymore,"[172] she stated in a long letter to Alphonse Fleury, defining her political beliefs. The people were not ready; they had to be educated on universal suffrage. She placed all her strength and hope in their love for the people, even in her moments of doubt.

Actually, she was working through a period of "despondent philosophy," as Hetzel called it, despite her best efforts—diving into her work, clinging tightly to her friends and family—to prevent it.

Too much time, energy, and money spent for this period of low productivity . . . In March, her play *Pandolphe's Vacation* (*Les Vacances de Pandolphe*) fell victim to a cabal. More and more disagreements and editorial difficulties piled up with Hetzel, still exiled in Belgium.[173] She signed a contract with Alexandre Cadot for *Mont-Revêche and the Goddaughter* (*La Filleule et Mont-Revêche*) and worked hard to find a good solution for *The Desert Chateau* (*Le Château des désertes*), which had appeared in *Journal of Two Worlds* (*La Revue des Deux-Mondes*) at the end of the previous year. George Sand still lived from paycheck to paycheck. Money had to come into the coffers regularly. "A dark cloud has passed over our dear friendship," she wrote elegantly to her publisher, who would still remain her primary confidant.

April 2, 1852: Alexandre and George finally begin their journey down the road to Berry once again, accompanied by the freshly liberated Emile Aucante and the lawyer Fulbert Martin, with their coachman, Sylvain, at the helm of the bagottoire. "Nohant is beautiful, fresh, plowed, and flowering. It shines as brilliant as paradise itself."[174] Spring has arrived. Everything is bursting into fragrant bloom; the weather is warm and clear. George Sand feels reborn once again.

Chapter Ten

"LET'S HELP ONE ANOTHER NOT TO DESPAIR"

What power was it that pushed her to dedicate months of her life to others' freedom, forsaking her own work, her health, and her peace of mind? Political issues were of great interest to George Sand in spite of her occasional disappointment. In 1848, she was encouraged to campaign for the presidential election by the People's Emancipation Club and *Women's Voices* (*La Voix des femmes*), founded by the feminist Eugénie Niboyet, but she refused to run. Well aware that women had suffered the most oppression of the day, she couldn't find her place in the still-marginal feminist movement. But at that same moment, she was heavily involved in the socialist left, both "secretive woman and a republican symbol."[175] No one had asked her opinion about becoming a feminist candidate; it hadn't been her choice. Overall, she felt that the time was not yet ripe:

before giving women a political responsibility. They first had to make some social changes, starting with marriage laws. Being listed on the ballot would be merely symbolic, as women were neither voters nor eligible to be elected. "It is social equality, equality in marriage, equality in the home—these are the things you can and must ask for and call for," she drafted in April 1848 in a letter to members of the Central Committee, charged with supporting the appointment of candidates of the left.[176] She denounced "the lack of education, the abandonment and deprivation and poverty of women, which is usually much more severe than men's."[177] Her priorities were for civil rights, divorce, education, and workers' emancipation as a whole. Political rights would follow.

Besides, despite her idealistic nature, Sand had her feet planted firmly in reality. She didn't believe in symbolic gestures. Writing allowed her need for imagination to take a concrete form. Pragmatism always had a ready answer for the here and now, which became more essential with age. Of course, she preferred practical action, thus she sought out Bonaparte's help.

It was of primary importance to save those who could be saved, innocent men from imprisonment, exile, and deportation. Had she imagined in her wildest dreams that she would be the savior of humanity downtrodden, that she would intercede with the most powerful authorities? Did this devotion have anything to do with women's devolved role, as she alluded to in her second letter to Louis-Napoléon? Whatever the cause, her defense of hundreds of men condemned by the coup d'état earned her widespread admiration. Marc Dufraisse, a one-time critic, named her "Our Lady of Succors," and the Count d'Orsay, a close friend to Louis-Napoléon, wrote her this: "You are a very dear woman, independent of being the greatest man of our time." George Sand's public image was evolving from the scandalous woman, novelist, romantic lover, and socialist to the great moral figure of France (before Victor Hugo's exile made him its ultimate symbol). Her concern for social justice, her devotion, her pseudoconjugal private life, and the moral—even moralizing—tendencies of her novels made her a kind of unifying icon.

She had also achieved international fame. The English poetess Elizabeth Barrett Browning insisted on meeting her while in Paris, although she was very ill. "I won't die, if I can help it, without seeing George Sand,"[178] she pleaded with her husband, Robert Browning. She was received at the rue Racine apartment, her heart racing. She was about to kiss George Sand's hand, when Sand kissed her casually on the lips. Holding court among young men, George Sand seemed to be "*the man* in that company,"[179] whom everyone listened to with the highest respect. Sitting by the fire with her feet on the andiron, her lady of the house appearance seemed to have vanished. Like a priestess surrounded by a circle of worshippers, she gave "no oracles, except with her splendid eyes." Her elegance, calm disdain, and melancholy solitude left a great impression on the visiting poetess. "She was George Sand, and that was enough."[180]

Everything about her look was something of a curiosity, even a phenomenon. The English visitor described all this to her correspondents in great detail. Her fashionable waistcoat and jacket did not detract from her femininity. She spoke in low tones at a rapid pace, never raising her voice. (Oh, how wonderful it would have been to hear the timbre of her voice!) Perhaps not objectively beautiful: George Sand was stout for her height, with olive-toned skin, a slightly receding chin, a slight overbite but with white teeth, and . . . her nose "of a somewhat Jewish character."[181] But her solemn face and her brilliant smile overshadowed everything else. Even a cigarette in George Sand's little hand seemed a feminine weapon; Mrs. Browning would have loved to see her smoke but would not get the chance. Smothered by the "society of the ragged Red diluted with the lower theatrical," who "adore her *à genoux bas*, betwixt a puff of smoke and an ejection of saliva," the poetess, more comfortable in salons than in bohemian Paris, dreamed of kneeling before her goddess. But sadly, as she determined, "she would not care for my kneeling; she does not care for me."[182]

As Elizabeth Barrett Browning put it, George Sand was all simplicity. She was devoid of any pretension. Sand turned the normal standards of proper society and genre distinctions upside down and had adopted the freer behaviors of men while remaining a refined woman. This shouldn't have been possible, but she pulled it off with style. Seeking neither fame nor fortune, Sand seemed unfazed by gossip, according to records. She stood firmly by her own beliefs.

And George was learning to understand herself. Beyond that, she figured out how to put aside her personal interests when the situation called for it. Paying attention to others made her more objective. To the accusations of "proselytizing, presenting herself like an angel," she replied, "I am not writing for saints."[183] On the contrary, the years had helped her become more concise and more modest in her goals: "Let's help one another not to despair."[184]

Alexandre Manceau was no stranger to this measured realism. She had once attacked Chopin for not accepting reality; the engraver, on the other hand, wove his life into the warp of reality—although was that not an integral element of his art? Not only did he help her with her daily tasks, taking charge of the most practical bits, from posting copies of her books to arranging transportation for their trunks, from writing some letters for her to doing carpentry work; not only was he a caring companion and an ardent lover but, starting in 1852, he also became her diary-keeper.

George Sand had kept a periodic *Journal* during key moments of her life, more to organize her thoughts than to keep a precise record of her days. She lived too much in the present to feel the need.

Alexandre decided to record his lady's activities, meetings, readings, works, and promenades every day, until his death. At first, the *Diaries* were written in the first person, as if Sand was dictating them, but they morphed into third person after a few weeks. Manceau would also make personal notes throughout the entries, creating an entirely separate character. The *Diaries* were his own work, even if George added her own details from time to time or occasionally took up the pen in his place.

Almost every day began with a health report: Madame is doing well. Madame is in wonderful health. Madame is suffering. Madame has a headache. In fact, the writer's worst enemy was the migraines that brought her to the point of blacking out. Analgesics did not exist at the time, and only *paullinia* (a caffeine-rich plant) or a couple grams of opium could overcome the pain. Sleeplessness, even insomnia, were by no means foreign concepts to her—for years, she only slept four hours a night. Her body spoke to her. Her migraines could rush up seemingly without cause, save merely the sight of someone. No theory of the unconscious could explain this mystery, which, for George Sand, went hand in hand with the close link between the physical and the mental, between the mind and the body. She spent hours wondering: Were her fits of melancholy due to her weak stomach, which she had inherited from her mother, or vice versa? She experienced periods of such intense stomach pain that she became depressed and even wanted to die. She subscribed to the antiquated theory, still popular at the time, of *fluids*: Black bile was the humor that caused melancholia. But her own thoughts went even further, and the knowledge that the body could have such an effect on her mental state taught her to pay attention to it. "All the sadness that I beat back, my body will pay for in *booboos* and pain,"[185] she remarked, foreshadowing psychosomatic medicine. Both her letters and the *Diaries* overflowed with physiological notes, running the gamut from monthly time to her chronic constipation and migraines. Perhaps the latter symptoms showed a tendency towards stress or even a higher level of anxiety. At any rate, she had no qualms about discussing these subjects. In her youth, she had learned about practical medicine with her friend Stéphane Ajasson de Grandsagne, who was Cuvier's assistant at the Museum of Natural History. She swore by Raspail's *Annual Manual of Health* (*Manuel annuaire de la santé*)[186]—he was a great biologist, the "poor man's doctor," pioneer of hygiene in prisons and among the working class, and founder of *Friend of the People* (*L'Ami du peuple*).[187] Updated annually, this manual was dedicated "TO THE RICH in the interest of the poor; TO THE WELL in the interest of the suffering." She used it herself to care for those who couldn't pay a doctor, like a little girl with such infected sores that she was forced to open the windows because of the stench. In an era in which a woman's body was denied freedom, gagged in modesty, suffocated by corsets, obstructed by crinoline, stuffed into narrow shoes, shamed by religion, ignored by medicine, George Sand raised it to a place of prominence. She engaged in regular physical activities, including walking, gardening, and ice baths in the river, until a very advanced age. "Feeling like an animal, vegetable, or mineral, and losing yourself in that feeling, it's not degrading—it's best to feel that way for your entire known life, to show it in yourself, and at the same time live a superior life which we can only dream of or predict" she wrote in 1852.[188]

The *Diaries*, these "George Sand, by an eyewitness to her life," created a priceless document and not just because of their "use as a daily report of Madame's actions and gestures."[189] The entries also shed light on the nature of the couple's relationship, both the inherent transparency and the role distribution. George Sand's superiority over Manceau was never questioned. She was the queen, and he her knight. It shouldn't have been so easy to follow after the likes of Alfred de Musset and Frédéric Chopin. Worse still, he should have been mixed in with the list of second-string lovers. But Alexandre Manceau existed, armed with his weapons of choice: love and generosity of spirit. Neither master nor servant—or, perhaps, both at once—he started to occupy a more central place in the Sand solar system. His devotion was also a form of power, which the other favorites could not mistake. Surrounded by her band of "kids," as she called them, by their jokes, their youth, their vivacity, the queen was sheltered from her tendency to withdraw into depression. They saved her from becoming despondent, from her own dark, pervasive thoughts. And Manceau was the most valiant of them all, fighting for her well-being with every last ounce of his strength. If a headache attacked, he reported thusly: "I still did my best to distract her. I brought her to the garden to plant flowers, I was witty, silly, high spirited, but nothing worked."[190]

But this was by no means a shy, timid love. Hotheaded, often funny, sometimes grumpy or sulking, "Manceau, this poor, perfect angel" wouldn't always submit to his lady's grumblings. Their love did occasionally include a playful aggression. Proud, Manceau was prepared to be eternally devoted, as long as his efforts were appropriately appreciated. He could not stand being criticized. He could be touchy about the most insignificant little details. Fortunately, though, his humor prevailed, as shown one evening when Madame "climbed upstairs at 10:30 for the great *combing*, and she parted her hair all askance but only found it better when Manceau had FINALLY made it beautifully straight!"[191] An intimate moment with Manceau brushing George's hair before devolving into a bedroom scene. These squabbles were the bread of life for the successful couple.

Still, the key to their relationship is missing: their letters. Apart from that, however, their playful dialogue traipses across the *Diaries'* pages. At that time, they preferred to do battle with dominos, a strategic game through which they met in fierce matches almost every evening. Manceau and Sand both kept track of victories and defeats, tallying up their points. "Let the bells ring out, for Madame has won at dominos!" To which George added: "Manceau is furious." The engraver soon had his revenge: "Madame has learned the same lesson as she did in Toledo," then, "I've taught Madame a lesson," adding, "Isn't Manceau just the most charming lad!" After all, self-portraits are always the most flattering. Another time, he took pride in having let her win without her noticing. Perhaps a sign that she only had the upper hand when he allows it.

But Alexandre was also a man of great tact, who knew exactly when to compliment his beloved on her pretty flowered dress, her green-and-white striped skirt, or the fantastic yellow hat she had recently purchased. And when Madame wore flowers in her hair or "a crown of moss and privet buds, it's too pretty!"[192] He was in love.

She would take over when he was away or ill, as she did on this February day: "Mild, gray, humid day, a pink sky near sunset. I'm well. I finished fifteen pages.... Manceau has a migraine and retired at 10:30, we had to stop reading the book he was so interested in. We went upstairs at 11, and I continued to work."[193] Again, in May: "A wonderful surprise in Trianon: *the snail rock*. Manceau was upset, because he had expected it to be better, but he was consoled by my admiration. I finished cleaning and worked like a dog until 2 on a few more pages of my *Mémoires*, but the headache I've had since waking up got the best of me. Now, I'll lay aside my inkwell and pick up my spade. I'm planting some gorgeous orchids. Manceau's helping."[194] She had plenty of admiration for his work, too, like his engraving of Thomas Couture's portrait of her: "delightful, a striking resemblance, yet pretty."[195] She wanted to distribute copies to her friends and print it on the covers of her own works.

The *Diaries* read as a coauthored musical score, showing pictures of a couple's life together: their days spent working at Nohant, reading books, walking in the countryside, their dinners for two at home on the rue Racine, their evenings out at the theater, their admiring guests, their evenings spent working next to each other, their arguments, the moments of sheer perfection as George read to Alexandre from her current manuscript, whispering secrets at three in the morning after all their guests had gone. The rest is silence. It belongs to them alone.

"The satisfaction of such a completely personal passion could be called *drunkenness*, or pleasure, there is no happiness there," she admitted at forty-eight in her *Journal*. "Happiness is tough and indestructible, otherwise it is not happiness. Focusing on drunkenness, and placing your joy in that, it's impossible. *Transports of pleasure* are out of the ordinary and will end up killing you, and any person given entirely over to this delirious state will burst. Fever in springtime, rest in autumn. Haze and sleepiness, an autumn evening. Calm, the golden age. This is happiness. The youthful don't possess it, they can only act it out in joys, drunkenness, strength, their springtime."[196]

Who knows? Loving a man thirteen years younger could be like conjuring up springtime in autumn.

Chapter Eleven

"THIS MOTHER HEN INSTINCT"

"Our Maurice is sort of the daughter here,"[197] George Sand had once admitted to her cousin. He was the one, for example, who handled her order for two summer dresses for the morning, as well as "a pair of elastic garters, plush, no clasp, size medium." However, Maurice's indifference started to irritate and even worry his mother over time. He was still under her care as he approached his thirtieth birthday. He had wanted to stay in Paris to study painting, but now, after being rejected from the Salon, he was planning instead to write a play with a friend of his. This time, he has gone too far. A few well-chosen words sufficed for her to show him that he hadn't the slightest experience in the field. It would be better for him to pursue his drawings, a field in which he had already shown his talent. He still had a lot to learn, and if his mother was going to bend over backwards to pay for him to live in Paris, he would have to take that advantage to learn something.

The young man obviously wanted to gain a bit of independence and sow his wild oats. He had decided to live on the rue Boursault, near the Batignolles, in the new artists' neighborhood, instead of staying with his mother and her companion on the rue Racine. He dawdled, preferring to "take his pleasure." He may well have used Alexandre's presence as a pretext to stay away from the house, or perhaps he really was jealous. Probably both. He also needed money. Manceau was supposed to be engraving some of his sketches, but Maurice was getting impatient and was anxious to sell them. George jumped on him immediately: "I don't think that would be in his best interest, and his interest in this matter counts more than yours. You only spend a few days working each year, whereas Alexandre puts in weeks and months of diligent work."[198] Besides, he was doing the work for free—Maurice was in no place to complain! George tried to show her companion's merits, making an awkward defense of his devotion and his desire to please. But her vehement defense of the brave, hardworking, generous Manceau hardly helped matters. In reality, her son was torn between his need for independence and his fear of abandonment, and Sand probably only fed his jealousy. Such is the eternal and classic dilemma of mothers who love their sons too much.

Within a few months, Manceau had taken over the work on Maurice's studio, drawing up plans, managing the workers, minding the smallest detail, recycling a buffet to turn it into shelves, creating boxes and labels for his butterfly collection. "He glues together, nails down, cuts up, he swears and sweats, he calls upon all the gods of engineering, and he is finally in *his element*."[199] Above all, he was worried that he wouldn't finish before the son returned. Which, of course, would merit a big hug. Still, the two men got along well. They shared the same taste in drawing, theater, and their favorite hobby, butterflies. But they also brought guns to their friendship.

Manceau needed constant demonstration of gratitude, perhaps to legitimize his place in Nohant. But George's children were parsimonious with compliments. He was sensitive, easily felt excluded, his personal social issues were certainly part of it here. The slightest criticism was taken to heart. Manceau was a hog, acted like a pig, was boorish, stuffed himself like a turkey: such were the remarks dotting the *Diaries* in his handwriting. "Teasing Manceau was a hobby like any other, the poor guy!"[200] He was especially hurt when Madame called him a "buffoon" one evening, just to make everyone else laugh. A bit of sadism on Madame's part, and, perhaps, masochism on his. Beneath his service to each and every person floated his desire to be liked, if not necessarily for who he *was*, then at least for what he *did*. This was worlds away from the nonchalant Maurice, oversaturated by his mother's unconditional love since his birth. "His mother admires him, like always. She finds him handsome, the poor woman!"[201] explained Manceau with wit and a bit of envy. Maurice certainly was handsome, with his large brown eyes and sweet face, which set off his lush black moustache. He bore such a strong resemblance to his mother that, for years, one of his portraits was mistaken for George, as she flitted about Paris in short hair and a gentleman's top hat on her head!

My Bouli, she wrote to her son on his birthday: it will soon have been thirty-one full years since I birthed you under the light of the heavens—you, the most perfect of all my works.

I immediately dressed him with a hem of green silk, so that he would never have another equal to him in anything, not even that.[202] So today, I present you with these garters lined with the same green silk, in memory of that distinctive mark, and a big kiss from me to you in thanks for giving me thirty-one years of happiness.

Your Esteemed Mother

June 30, midnight

1854

Nohant

For the moment, though, George had decided to take charge of her Bouli's career and left no stone unturned. She even offered to write the captions for his drawings herself. The artist Tony Johannot had recently passed away, so she badgered Pierre-Jules Hetzel to have him do the next drawings for her *Illustrated Works* (*Œuvres illustrées*). This populist edition was created from her "desire to have the poor and downtrodden classes read her works, many of which had been written for them."[203] She obviously didn't trust Maurice and his willpower: "It's a good thing that I saw him [Hetzel] and took care of this business, otherwise it will never work," she wrote to her son on his arrival in Paris.[204] No one resisted George Sand. Battle weary, Hetzel finally agreed. It was now up to Maurice to get to work.

Things weren't going much better with Solange. She was still complaining of being bored and constantly moaned about her lifestyle since she had separated from Clésinger. It would take a lot to keep her from sinking deep into vice! This time, George blew up— was she supposed to *kill* herself working so that Solange could live in luxury? Her true reply was found in a novel she wrote at precisely that time, between April and May 1852. *Mont-Revêche* tells the story of a family torn apart by the jealous older sister, Nathalie. This "heartless girl who hates and curses everyone else's happiness" eventually causes the death of Olympe, her young stepmother. A "cold jail cell" appears many times in the novel, an image that George Sand used many times to represent her own daughter. In *Mont-Revêche*, George Sand transposed her disappointment in her children, for whom she *killed* herself working into a novel. The young, "humble and hardworking" Amédée, the lover of the beautiful Olympe, who chased butterflies to make her happy, who served her as a "charming, helpful, and virtuous" knight, was probably an idealized representation of Alexandre. The writer didn't touch on Nathalie's fate, and she remained absent from the ending, as if Sand herself was left in the dark. The girl would only find redemption in the later 1864 edition. She becomes a better person and marries but is unable to have children. A truly terrible punishment, once the origins are considered. The underlying question was if Solange actually deserved her daughter.

The light of George Sand's life was Jeanne, whom they called Nini. She would also involuntarily cause her greatest sorrow. This willful, mischievous little three-year-old girl fell prey to the disagreements of the Clésinger couple, who fought over her custody. A half-crazed father and an indifferent mother: such was Nini's lot, tossed around between the two of them, witness to some violent arguments. George took care of her in Nohant as often as possible.

The nineteenth century was the golden age of grandparents, a necessary component of the heightened role of the bourgeoisie family.[205] Specialists of children's literature, from the Countess de Ségur to Zulma Carraud, were swept up in the cult. Victor Hugo himself would mark the height of the trend with his *Art of Being a Grandfather* (*Art d'être grand-père*) at the close of the century. The grandparents "spoiling" their grandchildren represented a perfect harmony within the family and their desire to see their line continued. For George Sand, it was more than just a literary theme, this living love was an everyday occurrence.

Jeanne was born on May 10, 1849, before George Sand had reconciled with Solange. Contrary to customs of the day, not only had her daughter not returned home to give birth at her mother's house but George didn't even meet her granddaughter until the latter turned two years old. The Clésinger home saw constant cycles of separations, and arguments followed by reconciliations—the word "home" would actually be a misnomer. George had long since given up on trying to intervene, or even understand. Both the husband and the wife were probably at fault. She was only interested in protecting her daughter, whose husband had become furious at her infidelity and had left her homeless and penniless. The Paris Courts pronounced a judicial separation on August 31, 1852, and Solange was temporarily given custody of her child. She had left Nini in Nohant a few days earlier.

Nini remained in Nohant for a year and a half under George and Alexandre's care, the source of their every joy and concern mixed in with the constant fear that her father would take her away, ignoring the judge's sentence. They even considered hiding Nini away in a convent! The child's health was also cause for concern, as she contracted a serious case of dysentery that was sweeping through the region, killing dozens. Manceau and George Sand took turns sitting at her bedside. Doctors prescribed a strict diet and Manceau had to decorate the syringe with flowers and ribbons, and whistle a little tune during the entire procedure! George watched over her day and night, monitored her, emptied her chamber pots, and tried not to succumb to exhaustion. The art of being a grandmother included trials and tribulations. The repeated cycles of remissions and relapses wore her out, especially when poor Nini "soiled" herself in the middle of the night. "It's now 4 in the morning," George wrote to her daughter a few days later, "I'm still in the library, listening for any movement from Nini. She hasn't stirred once. This is the first time she's slept through the night since I've had her."[206]

Another time, "Nini hurt her little front bottom,"[207] as Manceau explained in the *Diaries*, and the doctor had to burst an abscess. But most of the time, Nini was a little angel, and George Sand cooed over the mischievous little brunette's every step. The child was discovering the garden in different seasons, the flowers, the sun "when it put on its gray overcoat," the "golden footprints" of the stars, and the notion of time, which still confused her. She loved watching the "North-ern Wights," playing in the "picturesque" garden, and reading in the "library." George reveled in her baby talk, her endless questions about the sky and death—she watched and listened with interest. Nini told Manceau her dream in which she would be an angel with pink wings, her grandmother with gold wings. She was scared of wolves and of Bluebeard, and had trouble distinguishing her nightmares from real life. When George Sand left with Alexandre for Paris, Nini was left in the care of Emile Aucante, her devoted assistant, and George Sand recommended a firm hand and a stable, regular schedule, for the child.

It came with a list of detailed instruction: Nini should sleep for twelve hours per night; starchy foods were preferred, beans, and pota-toes, but she should also get used to meat; she needs to be washed in lukewarm water from head to toe every morning and evening; change her underwear every day; talc her bottom with rice powder to avoid chapping; cut her toenails regularly but don't take off too much at a time; and above all, don't give her anything unless she asks for it politely and says "please" and "thank you." Nini tended to be tem-peramental and bossy. "If she is naughty, you should reason with her face to face, very seriously. She loves four-pointed debates, especially when she doesn't understand them."[208] Temper tantrum? Leave her to cry and pretend not to hear her. Nini was a nervous child, who usually tossed around in her sleep. Her grandmother had the foresight to put armchairs around her crib so she wouldn't fall out. Ever practical, she also invented the "wiggler," a huge dressing gown so she wouldn't get cold as she fidgeted around. This was a far cry from the Countess de Ségur's moral education. While there were strictness and a regular schedule, they also appealed to the precocious girl's reason and intel-ligence. The rest was filled with games, laughter, love, and more love.

Solange stopped by Nohant about every four months to see her daughter. Alexandre didn't hide his irritation at how she destroyed their lovely organization, bringing her daughter to the dinner table completely naked, after she had complained just that morning about how cold it was in the country. The new theme of the *Diaries* was Solange's idleness while the rest of the house bustled about having fun. "Solange scrapes the paint off her fingernails at noon. At one o'clock, she files them; at two, she paints them with yellow polish; at three, she makes a garland for her hair; at four, she combs her hair; at five, she fixes it all up; and at six, she dresses. And she's bored! How shocking. She embroiders in the evening while we read. Reading bores her," George wrote to Maurice, in her normal jeering tone.[209] Manceau couldn't stand her and dreamt of seeing her dig in the soil with her pretty painted nails. If she occasionally read a passage from the novel George was writing, he beat a path of escape. Solange was the black sheep of the family, a victim of her own aggression. Mired in her marital problems, her romantic intrigues, her financial issues, her high society, her troubled narcissism, and her fragile health, the young woman paid little attention to her daughter, even though she obviously loved her.

As the days passed, Grandma and Nini's lives became more tightly woven together. "I'm becoming attached to her, even though I swore to fight this mother hen instinct; otherwise, I'll regret it later because either I won't be able to keep her or I'll take care of the obstacles and then she'll still be taken from me," George Sand wrote to one of Solange's friends, with a clear head.[210]

Her mother hen instinct had lapsed during her own daughter's childhood, though. How could it not, with Musset, Venice, Pagello, and achieving fame as a writer? Conversely, she had once cared for Pauline Viardot's daughter, Louise, when that girl's mother traveled around for her recitals. But she experienced Nini's childhood in a way she hadn't known, or been able to, with Solange. And this time, she had a man at her side who shared that love. Manceau was crazy about the child. He was the one who cared for her in the mornings, with George taking over from noon until nine at night. He adored her, as George wrote to her daughter. Nini terrorized him but followed him everywhere, and he played with her as though he were a little kid. "When Manceau knocked Nini over into the fresh grass on her bare bottom, she was furious and called him a bonehead and a pig. Two minutes later, she rushed over to give him kisses and hung around his neck enough to strangle him."[211] He babbled nonsense to her to the point where she asked her grandmother, "Grandma, do I babble more than he does?" In the evening after dinner, she took to falling asleep on Alexandre's lap. The man had a bottomless ocean of love to give.

"Manceau is my best friend, the most loyal companion in the world," George Sand wrote to Hetzel. "He is constantly working to benefit everyone, for me, and for himself. Even after he's been engraving for several hours each day, as long as he can still see straight, he'll do my accounts, monitor the workers, make copies for me, coddle Nini, submit to Solange's teasing, read to me, write sonnets for Monsieur Aulard, take care of me if I'm sick, treat patients in the village, make alphabet books for the children, boxes for Maurice, plans for the mason and painter and everyone else. I can't tell you even one one-hundredth of what he does. He is in constant motion and is constantly applying himself, indulging and devoted with pleasure and even a fury sometimes: basically, as good as the good Lord above."[212]

No less than the good Lord! In addition to everything else, he was also a fireman, which included duties to manage voting in general elections. In Alexandre, George had found the only man who equaled her own generosity. He helped her with her treatments, watched over Maurice when he got a bad case of hives, and tirelessly cared for Pierre Caillaud, their carpenter, who had fallen gravely ill. "He's spending more time than ever at Saint Vincent de Paul."[213]

The mature woman had learned to appreciate this man's goodness and devotion, so far removed from the normal self-centered artist. She saw it as a sign of the strength she had been looking for in a companion. As a girl, she had dreamed of loving a righteous man, as she described him:

"The righteous man is strong, calm, and chaste. He is brave, active, and thoughtful. The righteous man is always ready to appear before God.

"The righteous man has no fortune, nor house, nor slaves. His servants are his friends if they are worthy. He lends his roof to the wanderer, his purse and his clothes to the poor, his time and wisdom to all those who ask of it.

"The righteous man hates the wicked and despises the cowardly. The righteous man is proud but not vain. Above all, the righteous man is sincere, which demands an extraordinary strength of will, for the world is nothing if not untruthful, cunning, vain, treacherous, or prejudiced."[214]

Manceau was this righteous man, complete with his temper, his weakness, and his humor.

Overshadowing their differences was their shared need for activity and for giving of themselves to the causes in which they believed. Manceau became a Freemason in October 1854, in a "magnificent ceremony."[215] Women were not accepted as Freemasons at the time— the first would be Maria Deraisme, in 1882—but many of George's friends belonged to these societies, which influenced her ideas and her work.[216] She and Manceau complemented each other. They trusted each other. Nini was an extra link in their relationship, the child they would never have.

Alexandre Manceau celebrated his thirty-sixth birthday on May 2, 1853, as she reached "the ageist revolution," "the most physically difficult years in a woman's life." She unabashedly recounted the negative effects of menopause, from fatigue to hot flashes, to her old friend Hetzel, still living in exile in Belgium. But she didn't see this new phase as a burden. In fact, she had found a way to ward it off: physical exercise and working with renewed vigor. She worked furiously throughout the winter of 1853. In July, Clésinger came to take back his wife and daughter, but in December, "the queen of all Ninis" returned with her grandmother to Nohant. She squealed with delight at finding all her old toys and dolls, and declared that she never wanted to leave again, "never ever." "Oh, how I wish she only belonged to me," George dreamed, innocently expressing her great desire to poach her own daughter's child. Eventually, to her delight, Nini started calling her "Mama" and was most comfortable and tender when speaking to her—a tiny detail which Solange could probably do without. George got another chance to be a mother by proxy, a second youth just when she herself lost her fertility.

Was it an unconscious desire for healing, a copy of her own childhood memories with her grandmother in Nohant? Or identifying both with her own grandmother and with her young self that she saw in her own granddaughter? All variations of the same theme: Solange, much like Sophie Dupin, was not a very attentive mother and was not ready to sacrifice anything of her own for her daughter. George took it upon herself to provide the replacement for Nini, like her own grandmother had done. And the child, just like young Aurore, found herself caught in the middle of a family conflict.

She had started teaching Nini to read in December 1852. The three-and-a-half-year-old child had a reading lesson every day and was rewarded for her efforts: a game of lawn bowling, or lighting a candle, which would make her eyes dance with joy! And since the little girl had quickly learned to decipher some letters, this school of encouragement seemed to be working.

And then there was the fun of bathing, during which Nini was George's "prettiest decoration." She was just as daring as Grandma and loved to splash about in the river, no matter how chilly it was.

Yet the garden provided the stage for their favorite adventures. They dug caves in the woods, picked flowers, collected rocks and moss. "She is such a dear little thing, so pretty, funny, loving, and affectionate. I have to admit that I'm her slave," she wrote to her cousin.[217] But a slave by choice, who dug her anxiety away with a spade in hand, working like a maniac for several hours each day, in snow and frost, on Trianon, the garden of rocks, ivy, and shells that she was creating for the child. Nini helped her "like a little mule,"[218] carrying moss and shells. "She digs, rakes, and drives the wheelbarrow. She'll have little muscles of iron."[219] Manceau helped them, too, and the garden became their shared work. He even installed a pond and surprised them one day with a marvelous fountain!

"I'm doing just as much mental work as physical exercise,"[220] George observed. She had discovered the antidepressant virtues of gardening, the wonderful hobby that made up her physical activity. Her migraines could still knock her down beside her wheelbarrow, but they were starting to abate. "It's fantastic, all these rocks, stumps, barrows full of sand and earth, and watering cans that I'm carrying around, and all the daydreams I'm having of plays, novels, sweet nothings, and intellectual wanderings."[221] George Sand, unlike her contemporaries, toiled away outside for five hours a day in the middle of winter, in an age when women were imprisoned in their wire cages of crinoline. "I swear to you that *writing* doesn't give half as much pleasure as digging around in the garden."[222] A new dream was taking shape: have enough money to forget that she had once been an author, and "dive into an active life with a mental part for daydreams, contemplation, and specific chosen readings—one or two hours per day for the mind, ten or twelve hours for the body."[223] But she knew that this dream could not come true for her.

In fact, she was guardian to a growing list of charges: Solange and Maurice; Eugène Lambert, who had left to paint in Paris; Emile Aucante, whom she had taken in to care for her land and her work with her publishers; and Manceau, even though he was financially independent. George Sand is overwhelmed. When she had to pay a visit to the Indre prefecture, she had to borrow an outfit from her friend Eugénie Duvernet. "My old hat will have to do, but my coat has a hole in it."[224] A fair number of staff was required to run the house smoothly, especially when some guests lingered for weeks at a time in the summer. And then there were her numerous gifts to the poor. No sooner had she reached a settlement with a theater director, she donated all 2,000 francs to the charity office of her neighborhood on the rue Racine. She rarely turned people away empty handed. Without any social systems, she felt it was the responsibility of the wealthy to fulfill the needs of the poor, even though George Sand herself thought that "individual charity is not the remedy. It is not even a palliative."[225] Her reaching out was endless. She helped the wife of a roofer who had fallen on the job, paid the admittance for her tenant farmer's servant to enter a hospice, provided an allowance to a La Châtre girl, daughter of Alexandre Lambert, who was detained in Algeria. In Nohant, she opened her doors to a young child abandoned in the fields, whose mother was "a loose idiot who jumped around between thirty-six fathers making babies."[226] George Sand had "bought" the boy from her and put him in a boarding school run by other peasants. When his mother eventually left the country, George brought him to live with her. A sickly child, Joseph Coret was martyred at eleven years old and would serve as the inspiration for "slack-jawed Joseph," a character in *The Master Pipers* (*Les Maîtres sonneurs*), which she would write in the early months of 1853. In this coming-of-age story set in the Bourbonnais forest, the character played folk music (the "sonneurs" were bagpipe players), an art form she placed above all others, at the very highest level. Both rooted in history and revolutionary for its strange tonality and combinations of melody, folk music had inspired one of her greatest pastoral novels.

Nini's presence did not keep the author from her nocturnal work. After *Mont-Revêche* and *The Master Pipers*, which would be published in July 1853, George Sand provided the theater world with *The Pressing House* (*Le Pressoir*) at the Théâtre du Gymnase, which the emperor and empress praised and "cried much over,"[227] followed by the stage adaptation of *Mauprat* at the Odéon. Then she started a new play, *Teverino*, which would eventually open as *Flamino* at the Gymnase on October 31, 1854. Each play was an endless series of negotiations with the directors, the actors, and the publishers—Bocage and the actor Frédérick Lemaître were especially temperamental divas. On top of everything else, she wrote articles and prefaces, and drafted new projects, like *The Illustrious Lovers* (*Les Amants illustres*), of which she would only write one volume.

Most importantly, though, she had begun writing more of her memoirs, "a more difficult garden to plant" than Nohant's Trianon.[228] She had first worked on them in April 1847, on Pierre-Jules Hetzel's recommendation. The revolution in '48 interrupted her work. She picked it up again when she returned to Nohant in June. Charles Delatouche, an industrialist who had acquired rights for her work for a five-year period, had wanted to stall publication. She kept writing but still had no publisher as of 1853.

In October 1854, Emile de Girardin would at last accept *Story of My Life* for publication in installments of *La Presse*. The narrative breaks were determined by the review's schedule and journalistic format, and sometimes even censors, like when she had to edit out a portrait of Armand Barbès.

Lecou, another publisher, began publishing the work at the same time, as a book in twenty volumes. The first volume appeared at the end of October, and the process finished in August 1855. Then, Michel

Lévy bought back the rights for a new populist edition to appear the following year. George Sand would release the definitive version of *Story of My Life* in 1876, just before her death.

These details are, in fact, significant. First, they reflect Sand's huge undertaking of memory and reflection over a number of years. They also show the success of this author's living work, the public's curiosity as they snapped up each subsequent volume like a magazine, the interest garnered by this unique work of such an exceptional scope and depth. The book opens on her father's life and includes large excerpts of his correspondence. By linking her life story with her family's history, George Sand was not just reconstructing the historical context of her story. She was also going back to the source of her first traumatic experience, the gaping hole left by Maurice Dupin's brutal death when she was four years old, and simultaneously breathing life into his romanticized ghost. She handpicked his letters, put them in order, even rewrote some, shouldering some of his history, following in his footsteps. Through her writing, she became the man her grandmother had tried to substitute for her.

She had begun writing these memoirs just as her liaison with Frédéric Chopin was ending and Solange's marriage was brewing. They bear witness to the trouble George Sand was enduring. Her broken relationships in 1848 completely changed the tone of her works and linked them more to the French Revolution, evoked when she wrote about her family.

Thus, her personal story was deeply entrenched in a wider context, reflecting how every individual, like it or not, takes part in public events. George Sand's political aspirations and disillusionments fed into her thoughts and actions. Besides, the book's final chapters are dedicated to paying homage to the great historians of her time: Louis Blanc, Henri Martin, Edgar Quinet, Michelet, and even Lamartine. By deciphering the past, their works provided a way to prepare for the future. In her conclusion of June 1855, she added more names of philosophers whose works she had referenced: Leibniz, of course, but also Lamennais, Lessing, the socialist Pierre Leroux, and the mystic Jean Reynaud.

Story of My Life is a survey novel, reflecting its author's personality without ever claiming to cover every part of the story. It follows an exceptional woman's career but also records that same woman's universal emotions, experiences, joys and sorrows, and thoughts on marriage, relationships, love, motherhood, work, and friendship, with which thousands of readers identified. But George Sand separated her public and private lives, and refused to disclose her own intimate life or those of her close relations. Her idea of an autobiography was opposite that of Jean-Jacques Rousseau's, no matter how much she admired his *Confessions*: You should not tell everything. The public would have to deal with it. Musset is barely mentioned, while Chopin is presented as both a musical genius and a hypersensitive man-child with whom she had had a mostly motherly relationship. Manceau never appears in the book.

"Let no scandal-mongers rejoice, I do not write for them."[229] She would be criticized for remaining silent on certain subjects, taking sides on others, and completely inventing still more. But that ignored how every autobiography is a work of rewriting reality and transforming the author into a character. Autobiographies obscure and distort just as much as they reveal. What *Story of My Life* shows is the image George Sand wished to show of herself. And besides, she's telling us a *story*, as the title clearly states. The reader would have to interpret it—nothing is more fascinating than that.

During this time, Alexandre Manceau was also hard at work. After an engraving of Eugène Lambert's *The Magpie and the Rat* (*La Pie et le rat*), he received a large commission which would take eighteen months to complete: *Joseph, Sold by His Brothers* (*Joseph vendu par ses frères*), based on Horace Vernet's painting. The same artist's

Mountain Goat Hunting (*La Chasse au mouflon*) (Maroc) would require even more time, almost three years of work, punctuated by his tasks in Nohant.

Nohant experienced an industrious lull. "Everything in nature, or really, in the house, is resting. My turn to fall,"[230] wrote George Sand one May night before falling asleep. For in this dreary and damp spring, "you have to be as happy as we are here to not be despondent."[231]

Chapter Twelve

"MY DEAR CHILD, THEY HAVE KILLED YOU"

Nothing in politics was lifting George Sand from her pessimism, neither the emperor nor her socialist friends. She kept as much distance as she could from authority. Her mail was opened and often confiscated, her plays censored. "All I see is madness, shallow thinking, cowardice, crazy ambition, or idiotic thoughtlessness."[232] What provoked most despair in her were the socialists' apocalyptic assumptions. She still hadn't recovered from June '48, and admitted as much to her friend Louis Blanc. When the Crimean War broke out, pitting England and France against Russia, she stood alongside the patriots. As for Maurice, he was ready to enlist, were it not for his fear of hurting his mother who had bought him a replacement draft card when he had pulled an unlucky number for his military service. Only a few pure individuals still garnered her respect, such as Armand Barbès, recently freed by Napoléon III. She invited the former activist to live at Nohant for as long as he pleased, but he chose exile instead.

The death of Hetzel's daughter reminded George Sand how frail and precious human life was. In a wonderful but darkly foreshadowing letter, she tried to make some sense out of it all. She did believe in the soul surviving after death. But, as she confided to another friend in mourning, "I don't know how to console others. I only know how to suffer alongside those I love."[233]

Summer 1854: unrest in Nohant. Her friends had to rescue her from her "growing unsociability." "My true distraction is bathing in the river," she wrote, "in a foaming pool where I can dive and let the troubles of my aging body and the worries of my pondering mind be swept away by the surging current."[234] Bathing had cathartic virtues, which she desperately needed that summer. She had recently celebrated her fiftieth birthday. "At fifty years of age, I am exactly as I was then. I love reverie, contemplation, and work; but beyond a certain point, sadness takes over . . ." she thought back to her twenty-year-old self in *Story of My Life*:[235]

There were indeed plenty of reasons for sadness.

On May 3, Jean-Baptiste Clésinger found letters from one of Solange's lovers. Drunk and blind with rage, he stormed into Nohant, hurled abuses at his wife, and took Nini away.

The child would never return to Nohant.

Nini was bounced around from a friend's house to the Bascan boarding school, where Solange had been raised, to the Clésinger's family home in Besançon, then to Dôle. "My granddaughter, my pride and joy, has been taken from me," George wrote to the mason-poet Charles Poncy. She was overwhelmed by an unspeakably raw sorrow and worry. Jean-Baptiste Clésinger took the matter to court. A summary judgment granted him custody of the child in early August. At first, he allowed Solange to see her and decided to withdraw his separation request—then, twenty-four hours later, he changed his mind and took the girl back. Nini was given to Madame Saint-Aubin-Deslinières, who ran the Villeneuve boarding school in Paris. They considered making haste to pick her up and bring her back to Nohant, but George Sand advised Solange against it. Châteauroux was rife with cholera. And besides, no matter how much she wanted to see the child again, it was better to acclimate Nini to life in the boarding school. Solange would have to resign herself to visit her often. The hope was for Nini to get used to living with other children and behaving like them, too.

George would regret her wise words.

She was tormented by grief. When she visited Nini in October, the child appeared sad and not well cared for. Dark omens haunted George Sand. Only Maurice and Manceau's care kept her alive, she swore. Alexandre read to her during the winter nights, as her eyesight was deteriorating and she didn't like wearing glasses.

"My dear Manceau," she wrote, in a rare surviving letter, "please ask Emile to copy this review for me tonight, and make sure he inserts proper punctuation where it's lacking. I *can't see very well anymore.* Goodnight."[236]

She embroidered floral themes for the armchairs while Manceau read: Balzac (she hadn't enjoyed his *Lily in the Valley* [*Le Lys dans la vallée*]), Walter Scott, Eugène Sue, Fenimore Cooper (whom she loved), Hugo (she thought *Punishments* [*Les Châtiments*] was too hateful and even shallow), as well as Leibniz and Jean Reynaud, the latter of whom had written *Religious Philosophy* (*Philosophie religieuse*), which she loved. The Leibnizien theory was based on balance and was both rational and cautiously optimistic, which fit into George Sand's views. Leibniz's great clockmaker, which tuned the different mechanical workings of the clock so that they could work together, caused passionate debates. For his part, Manceau only aspired to the modest role of the watch.

December 15: The engraver hears his mother has suddenly fallen gravely ill, and leaves abruptly for Paris. He fears the worst. That same day, in a dramatic turn of events, the Paris Courts grant the Clésingers' separation and decide that "the child will be placed in the care of Madame George Sand." It had been a long shot, in spite of their support. The next day, though, the lawyer Berthmont urges the sculptor to appeal, and the verdict is suspended.

George had been ready to collect Nini herself, but she knew she had to wait for the official authorization from the courts. Still, if they managed to secretly remove her and "send her here quickly, as fast as you can," that would be safer. She feared a new outburst from her son-in-law. The only person she really trusted to take care of Nini and bring her back safely to Nohant was Manceau. She wrote to him straightaway.[237]

As soon as he received the letter, Manceau went to the boarding school. He was told that Nini had scarlet fever, a fatal disease at the time, and was not allowed to see her. Next day, same response. But as he passed by the Clésingers' apartment at 29, boulevard des Capucines, he spotted the child with her father at the window. Was the scarlet fever a lie, a pretext to prevent him from seeing her, or was the child truly sick and in danger of dying? Clésinger had taken her outside with just a thin dress on in the middle of December. The bundle containing her warm clothes hadn't even been opened.

Solange arrived in Nohant on the 20th, without her daughter. Manceau had sent comforting news, but George still worried constantly. Solange, on the other hand, had recently converted to Catholicism, and was swaddled in the knowledge of Thy Will Be Done. George missed Manceau terribly. He finally returned from Paris on the 31st, his heart heavy with the recent death of Pierre Caillaud from typhoid fever, in spite of everyone's desperate efforts to save him.

Two weeks later, an express dispatch from Châteauroux delivered a telegram to the door at ten o'clock at night: Nini was dead. She had passed away the night before, on January 14, 1855. She was five and a half years old.

Manceau lacked the words to describe his own sorrow. Instead, he wrote this: "Madame is grieving, and the entire house grieves with her. Rollinat had carried the news in his pocket and hadn't wanted to hand it over until tomorrow morning."

Although she hadn't been properly cared for, the child had seemed to recover from her scarlet fever. But instead of being kept inside the warmth of the boarding school's infirmary, she had been sent back to class. Solange had returned to Paris the week before and had been called over in an emergency: Nini was coughing, her whole face swollen. She just played quietly on her bed and sewed scraps of cloth together. "She had taken a small locket with a lock of her mother's hair inside from around her neck and gave it to her," a heartbroken George told Lise Perdiguier. "She tried to smile and then fell asleep forever."[238]

The doctor named neglect as the cause of death.

The notice of appeal arrived while they were preparing her for the burial. *The child will remain at the boarding school and is only allowed to leave with her father.* He had won, but it was too late. Appalled, Victor Borie folded the paper into the child's cold hand before closing the coffin.

Solange put on a brave face and accompanied Nini's body in the train. A grief-stricken Manceau met them at Châteauroux and drove them to Nohant.

George Sand buried her granddaughter next to her own father and grandmother, under the cypress trees.

She wandered through the house with a broken spirit, gathering the toys that Nini used to play with, the dolls that she had dressed in a different color every evening throughout the entire winter for the child to find under her pillow in the morning. "That was my life and livelihood; she was the joy and light of my house."[239]

Anger mingled with her despair, less towards Clésinger, who she thought was irresponsible, than towards his lawyer, Berthmont. She was convinced that the former minister of Cavaignac had only taken action because of his hatred for her. She bore a grudge, wanting to call him out publicly, or even take him to court. "They have killed you, my dear child, they have killed you!" she spat.

Every day, she went to the chalet where she had played with Nini to cry alone. "I am too old to be comforted," she wrote to Solange. She and Manceau sketched her granddaughter from memory on scraps of paper.

Slowly, however, her dismay ceded to fatigue. She had to be leeched twice. The hard winter blocked the roads with snow and ice. The entire house fell ill, including the servants. Alexandre had a cough and a fever. George was unable to react, sinking deeper into her grief. The evenings around the table, reading and correcting proofs, had restarted. She was trying to sustain that illusion, to fight the sorrow eating away at her heart.

Maurice was worried, and he and Manceau urged her to accompany him to Italy. All three made preparations to leave. "Italia, Italia!" exclaimed the engraver. Maybe the Italian light could chase away their despair.

Chapter Thirteen

"ITALIA, ITALIA!"

With his "poor little purse," Alexandre financed the trip. A dozen days in Paris to do a bit of shopping, including glasses and a pince-nez for George, a sign of her age, followed by the ritual of visits. On March 4, 1855, waking up too late, George Sand missed the appointment with realist Champfleury but managed to receive all of the following in a single day: the actor René Luguet, Marie Dorval's son-in-law; the actress Madame Laurent and her children; Victor Borie; Alphonse "Télémaque" Dumonteil, a regular guest in Nohant; Adolphe Joanne, the famous guidebook author; Louis and Pauline Viardot and their children; the bookseller Charavay; the surgeon Charles Phillips; the actors Dupuis and Berton; the insurance agent Jean Pichon, a fellow Berrichon, who was one of George Sand's confidants; the young Léon "Polognon" Villevieille, back in her good graces following a quarrel with Solange; Captain Stanislas d'Arpentigny, whose dyed blond hair tried to mask his age; the publisher Henri Plon; the pharmacist Henry Arrault, who pioneered the Red Cross; Madame Hetzel and her son Jules; the sculptor Luigi Calamatta; Collet-Meygret, the secretary general of the police prefecture; Madame Scheppard, the widow of a British journalist; and Maurice and Solange! Afterwards, she left to have dinner with Emile de Girardin and his children, where she ran into Prince Napoléon and his aide-de-camp, the Polish writer Charles Edmond, and many others. Delphine de Girardin did "table tipping," a hobby which Alan Kardec would develop into a pseudoreligion in the years that followed. Perhaps she had hoped to communicate with her granddaughter, as Victor Hugo had, but it was all in vain. Manceau picked George up at ten o'clock and accompanied her to the Viardot's place, where they and a few other guests heard Pauline sing Handel. The evening finished after a tea around one in the morning.

They were also still waiting for their passport. Because of George Sand's heated notoriety, the papal nuncio would not issue her a visa unless she traveled under her married name, Madame Dudevant. There were also the final instructions to issue to Emile Aucante, Nohant's guardian: Buy a burial plot alongside the garden in the cemetery; horses, coaches, and books were not to be lent out to anyone; servants are prohibited from giving tours of the house or garden to passersby. And the last, most surprising instruction: She officially forbade anyone from cutting boxwood branches from the woods for Palm Sunday. George Sand had entered a staunch anticlerical phase.

They finally took the train out of Paris on March 11, 1855. Once they left Marseille for Genoa, the adventure began! An adventure allayed by letters of recommendation and friendly advice, of course. George Sand was recognized in the streets of both Marseille and Rome, something she hated but that confirmed her celebrity. According to Manceau, all of Rome knew that Madame was in town!

Since the seventeenth century, a journey to Italy had been an essential part of a painter's training. Following the example of Nicolas

Poussin and Claude Gellée, every self-respecting artist would do his or her own "tour," whether long or short. For both Maurice and Alexandre, this trip served as their apprenticeship. Each one filled up sketchbook after sketchbook, while the novelist took notes. While ostensibly distracting George from her grief, the change of scenery also served as a formative experience for the two artists. From March 15 to May 17, through chance meetings, inspiration, and the limits of Manceau's "meager purse" (they skipped Naples), the trio traveled from Genoa to Livourne and Pisa by water, then to Civitavecchia and Rome. They stayed at Frascati for three weeks, which served as their home base for further excursions. Then, to Florence, by way of Terni, Lake Trasimeno, and Levane, rolling along at the speed of an ox-drawn carriage, with horses hitched up to climb the mountains! From Florence, they took the train to Lucca and La Spezia before returning to Genoa and Marseille.

Travel conditions were often difficult, even risky. The driver, Alesso, got lost between Trevi and Perugia, and had to follow closely behind another coach. They navigated steeper paths with donkeys, which led to a couple of falls and arguments with the handlers. This Roman hotel had no toilets nearby; that Romagnan innkeeper offered them his own room, "the only one with a manageable stench,"[240] but with an unmanaged flea problem. Their hunting trophies were mostly snakes, scorpions, mice, and flies. Just outside La Spezia, they crossed a river by coach, bouncing around all day through water, over gravel and sand, the women with bare legs and feet—an unusual sight at the time—and the men with their shoes on. Lunches were sometimes at hotels, other times at private homes, like with Ida Ferrier, Alexandre Dumas' first wife, and her companion, Prince Edoardo Alliata de Villafranca. Or they would take their meals at their host's table, like in Rome. In Frascati, George Sand had rented the ground floor of the Villa Piccolomini, where they were looked after by Chiara

Allegrini, the cook of the Trattoria della Campana. Sadly, the unusual food—calamari, macaroni, wild asparagus, sturgeon, and olive oil salads—still provoked the anticipated intestinal distress.

Two decades earlier, George Sand had discovered Italy with Alfred de Musset. Venice was still colored by their passion, their highs and lows. Life had blossomed before her, her pen had flown across the paper, the world was hers to invent, to create. She had been thirty years old. Her memories were filled with the pleasure she found with the poet Pietro Pagello, the Venetian tears, or the shores of the Lake Maggiore on the way home.

This time, she was burdened with fifty years of sorrow. Her granddaughter's death had torn her asunder. She couldn't even write anymore, a sign of just how serious her inner crisis was, that her main distraction no longer worked. At first, the trip to Italy seemed like an escape, her last chance to break the dam of her life's vitality and desire. She would find the path to healing in the beauty of the land-scapes, the blooming wild flowers, the plants and insects and rocks, and in renewed physical exercise. Her instincts told her what to look for, what to listen for, where to move, how to open herself up to the wonders of nature, art, and the world, how to give herself over to the flood of new sights and sensations, how to refresh herself, sweep away the frozen tears of winter, and chase her depression away.

The springtime Mediterranean countryside was in full bloom, and she loved everything: red-stemmed orchids, myrtle, cyclamens, irises, anemones in every color imaginable, blue and white liverwort, laburnum, and the trees—olive, fig, and cypress. George and "her children" wandered off the beaten path in search of butterflies and rare plants, and spent hours exploring the Italian wilderness. But there was plenty of time to admire other things: the ancient splendor of the Villa Borghese; the ruins of the Villa Mondragone, where daffodils pushed through cracked mosaics; the waterfalls and grottos of Tivoli;

picturesque little Rocca di Papa, the village on a sugarloaf hill; the winding street of Porto Venere, damp from rain; the still-snowy slopes of the Apennine Mountains; the heavenly view over Lake Trasimeno at sunset.

Physical exhaustion brought sleep and a new appetite for life at last.

The travelers found an "Eden" at Frascati, a paradise where they would love to live, if only there were fewer Italians! For George Sand, as well as other travelers of the era, the scourge of Italy was its inhabitants. Burglary and begging were constant problems, she complained, as well as people's disgusting habit of relieving themselves wherever and in front of whomever they pleased. A tourist was constantly irritated by the fleas and filthy hotels, and bothered by the unpleasant smells and lack of comfort. Of course, these same complaints were made by foreigners traveling through France! La Spezia alone managed to avoid this judgment, and George dreamt of returning the following year.

Rome, on the other hand, was "horrific and dirty!" Many of her contemporaries shared this harsh opinion, claiming that the climate was unhealthy and the houses squalid. As for its ancient monuments and ruins, George Sand recognized that, "they're interesting, they're nice, they're intriguing, they're even amazing, but they're too dead." The first romantics, during the Empire, had enjoyed ruminating on chunks of column. But "that has become *tiresome*," she said, and "it's much better to live!" This 1855 traveler was breaking tradition with her predecessors, the Chateaubriands and Lamartines, and their deep thoughts about Palmyra's fate and mankind's fragile destiny. No urns, no tombs, no crypts or columbaria, no matter what they represented, could compete with the precious moment of the here and now and the glory of living nature. Less contemplating, more knowing and enjoying. This change in thought might have followed the shift

143

towards a new school of artists, who were moving from romanticism to realism, which *Madame Bovary* would soon illustrate brilliantly. Or perhaps this was just George Sand's personal desire to escape her past and her grief, as well as yet another proof of her anticlericalism, which had been much maligned in the Papal States.

But she and her companions did not, for all their groaning, miss the monuments and museums. They were the perfect tourists, eager to see and admire everything. After their journey through Spoleto, Assisi, and the gorgeous Perugia, Florence welcomed them "exuding health, appetite, and good spirits." Maurice, "Madame's little thing," her "lap lizard," "her great fool of a son," as Manceau called him (never short on compliments), had regained his fragile health after a bout of illness in Rome. Manceau had been forced to wander the streets alone while Sand cared for her son, which may have been his intent all along . . . All the hotels in Florence were full, and construction spanned the banks of the Arno, so they stayed in the Swiss boarding house on the Palazzo Strozzi. George found that her love for the Médici's city hadn't waned, and showed her "children" around the Palazzo Vecchio, Santa Croce, the Annunziata, the Pitti palace, and Santa Maria del Fiore, the Boboli gardens. The three artists visited the Uffizi Gallery together and fawned over the Pitti gallery filled with works by Raphael, Veronese, Andrea del Sarto, Titian, and Michelangelo. They ate ice cream at Doney in the Cascina gardens in spite of the rain. That night, they strolled along the Palazzo Vecchio and through dark streets by the light of the moon.

Nini's memory may have cast a shadow on George Sand's quiet moments alone, but she seemed to be successful in keeping it at bay. She pushed her sadness away like she always did when faced with someone's absence, a habit left over from her mother's abandonment and the tears she had swallowed at each new separation. Sometimes, this ability to overcome loss is due to a hard heart. For George Sand, however, the deeper the wound, the deeper she buried her pain, even to the point of seeming indifferent or forgetful. The wider the abyss, the more she came back to life, because of the intense "energy she spent to dismiss her suffering" and the "will to avoid being overcome by unhappiness as much as she could."[241] Maurice and Manceau also took it upon themselves to distract her and make her laugh, as they had been worried enough to encourage her to leave Nohant.

May 2, evening: They gaily celebrate Alexandre's thirty-eighth birthday with a poem from George that concludes with this declaration of love: "Manceau, my dear, we love you, with or without your hair. Let Venus cry for what she used to own. This heart will be faithful to you, love, alone." They had lived together for five and a half years.

The knight cared for his lady, giving her his own bed and watching over her when she fell ill, drawing her a flower when she was sad, giving her bangles and bracelets. Ever sensitive, he cringed when she teased him. George started to imagine her next Italian trip with all "the little friends:"[242] Eugène Lambert, Victor Borie, and Emile Aucante, too. True to her love of community, she could not find a perfect happiness except at the heart of her little band, the commune she reigned over as queen.

But for that, she would have to be rich! Henri Plon, one of her publishers, was waiting for her copy. Other ideas were sprouting, too. She had gathered mountains of images, sensations, and reflections without taking any notes other than those she sometimes added to the *Diaries*. Those would suffice to recreate Italy in a new novel, *La Daniella*, which she would start several months after her trip. Maurice took his leave from them at Genoa to travel to Torino, and George and Alexandre returned to France in a storm-tossed boat. The poor lad got sick and couldn't appreciate the exquisite Capri wine served onboard. They spent a few days in Paris, where the engraver learned of his acceptance to the Salon (although Maurice hadn't made it), before returning to Nohant. Manceau's instructions to Aucante preceded them, showing how attentively and thoughtfully he cared for his lady: "Make sure our rooms and beds are prepared, and lay out cool water and a modest breakfast for us: meat broth, eggs, lamb chops, and coffee. And between us, the house should have a joyful air, everyone should be awake, and the windows should be thrown open to let the sun in, so that my dear Madame can find a bit of happiness in her mournful house. Tell the gardener to put some flowers in the dining room and along the staircase, and make sure that if Madame wants to go to Nini and Caillaud's tombs that she finds fresh, new wreaths laid there. I will leave the rest to your imagination and good will. Let the table be set."[243]

A healthy and "sunburned" George Sand returned to Nohant, itching to experience a "second springtime" and get back to work.

Perhaps we can believe in Italian miracles, after all.

Chapter Fourteen

"MY SOUL HAS GROWN OLD AND WEARY"

T he coincidence between Nini's passing and the completion of *Story of My Life* was striking. The last words were addressed to the little girl, who was joined together in the same thought with George's, her friend Marie Dorval's grandson whose disappearance ended in death. Penned between two painful events, two fractures—the falling out with her daughter in 1847 and Jeanne's death—these memoirs provided George Sand with an opportunity for introspection. She created a character of herself in this fiction. By ending the *story of [her] life*, she marked the beginning of a period of time off, toying with the idea of an *after*. Besides the conclusion, written in June 1855, as she returned from Italy, *Story of My Life* came just before the long stretch of shock, silence, and creative paralysis that seized her after the death of her "beloved child." The girl had revived a part of what the woman had been, and her living memory was recorded in ink while the woman felt a part of herself become erased.

Italy had restored George to health. She had recovered her physical energy. She seemed happy. But only a few weeks had passed since her mourning period. The house in Nohant was still haunted by memories of the child, and she couldn't stand it. The months following her return would offer up scattered image after rippled image, trying to shake her life up enough to prevent the weight of her sadness from settling heavy on her shoulders. She only spoke of Nini with Manceau, who "had also been mad about her," and still not enough to make him sad, too. "My soul has grown old and weary in a year," she observed.[244]

As soon as summer ended, George and Alexandre were off to Paris again for the performances of *Master Favilla* at the Odéon. It was a mediocre play, as the ones that followed would be, stuffed with feel-good moments. It seemed to have more in common with Diderot's maudlin drama than with contemporary theater, even though it had been inspired by Hoffmann. They only stayed a dozen days, but returned to the capital in November for the entire winter. They wouldn't return to Nohant until the end of April 1856, in spring. Theater was once again their excuse for the long stay in Paris, as Sand was required at rehearsals for many of her plays. But nothing would go down in theatrical history: not *Lucie* or *Françoise*, both performed at the Gymnase; not her adaptation of Shakespeare's *As You Like It* at the Théâtre-Français, the first of the English playwright's works adopted by the Comédie-Française; and not the revival of *Mauprat*, either. The audiences were equally underwhelmed.

Still, she loved the theater passionately and felt drawn to it like "a magnet."[245] She was crazy about the actors and actresses, who made up her inner circle for those months. Perhaps she was drawn to them because they were the opposite of her taciturn nature, dragging her out from under her usual melancholy. Maybe they were a distraction for her, a permanent show. She was blind to their faults, but as she explained, "they seem more like children than people, and I love children."[246] She wrote to a chosen few constantly, showering them with a slew of compliments, and had them over to her apartment on the rue Racine, just down the street from the Odéon. Philibert Rouvière, a fiery brunette with a southern accent, won all of her attention. A talented painter turned actor, he was a rousing success in *Hamlet* and played the title role in *Master Favilla*. She saw him every day—quite a bit, which did not escape Manceau's notice.

By immersing herself in the world of theater, George Sand was able to regain her footing in the rest of her life, and work past this painful period. After returning to Nohant, she wrote a letter to the actress Sylvanie Arnould-Plessy in May 1856: "I have also rediscovered the child's presence here, whom it seems I will never be able to forget. In this house, in this garden, I cannot believe that she won't return to us one of these days. I see her everywhere, and this illusion breaks my heart over and over again."[247]

A few months earlier, she had fought a fierce battle with Solange over the anniversary of Nini's death. Her daughter had wanted to pray over her little girl's tomb and have a white marble cross erected there. First, her mother had tried to dissuade her from even making the trip. What significance would an anniversary have for such a loss? "Genuine sorrow . . . does not mourn at a scheduled hour."[248] She also prohibited her from entering the grounds of Nohant accompanied by any man and wrote the same warning to Emile Aucante, who was responsible for the property. She also instructed him to lock up every room which led to her own and take away the keys. She didn't want anyone rummaging through her drawers. Convinced she was play-acting, she also harshly forbid Solange from setting up any cross on her daughter's tomb. "She doesn't have to convince me that she has a heart. She would do much better to leave me alone, as overburdened as I am with work. She shouldn't go out and catch a cold; heaven forbid it would prevent her from attending a ball or a romantic dinner the night she returned, or the night after."[249] Such was her letter to Emile Aucante, who shared it with Manceau. Even the engraver was slightly shocked, although he tried to justify her behavior. Still, it was only a year later when George Sand grudgingly allowed a cross to be laid on Jeanne's tomb.

Beneath her anticlericalism shone her deep-seated aggression towards Solange. She refused to believe in the sincerity of her daughter's emotions, banishing her not only from her child's tomb but from her own house by locking up the rooms. Locked out from her heart, or from her place in the family, perhaps? It was a new wound for the young woman. George also couldn't stand her daughter's liaisons, her love of drinking, and her frivolity—especially after mourning.

All of this was fundamentally represented in the tomb, and in Jeanne herself. Just as her own grandmother had seized the young Aurore and shut out Sophie Dupin, George saw herself as a guardian of Nini's memory, of her grave ("the patch of earth where I will be sooner or later"), and of the right way to mourn her. Maybe, Manceau thought, Solange was going about it the wrong way. Or maybe George was actually tired and annoyed at the poor reception of her plays. Yet once again, it became a complicated game of identities. By rejecting her daughter in this way, George Sand behaved exactly as her own mother before her. Her letter to Aucante had ended abruptly with "Maurice is feeling better, he had been very ill,"[250] which says everything about where her priorities lied. When Solange came to pray over the tomb in January 1857, George shut herself up in her room and refused to even see her daughter.

Because of Solange's excessive behavior and marital spats, George Sand unconsciously held her responsible for Jeanne's death. She may even have considered herself as the child's true mother. In one of her texts, she describes a dream-like state, in which the child appeared to her as a young woman with the phrase "*Mother*, let's go see the kids' party!"[251] The girl then acknowledged the little garden that a woman, *a mother*, had planted for her (alluding, of course, to Trianon in Nohant's park).

It would also have been a matter of some importance at the time for her to read *Contemplations*, written by Victor Hugo following the death of his daughter, Léopoldine. The work appeared in 1856 and sold every one of its 3,000 copies in one day. George was deeply touched by its reception: "The poor man, to have experienced what we have and to have produced such a sublime work. Yes, Villequier's play is a masterpiece. *This is how it is*,"[252] she wrote to Pierre-Jules Hetzel, who had also lost his own daughter.

When Nini died, she was the same age as George Sand when the latter lost her father. Her grief for Nini was as though she had lost her own child. Nini had been the perfect daughter. The other one, the real one, remained.

Constantly seeking her mother's approval, Solange started writing poetry and sent it to . . . Manceau. He served as the arbitrator in the matter, but George couldn't help but share her opinions. "The form is nice, the meaning is a little shallow." Then, in the same letter, she once again tried to dissuade Solange from coming to Nohant. The daughter's reply shows she was not fooled: "Oh, my God, so many things stand in the way of my spending a week with you! No cook, no male servant, Pistolète in poor shape, Sylvain sick, Madame Caillaud hasn't done her work, Emile is away! How could I ever overcome all these obstacles. I'd best forget the whole thing, especially since you don't seem to be particularly entertained by the idea of my presence."[253]

In reality, George Sand's reluctance was partially due to her writer's incubation—she would finally start a new novel a few days later. The relief was immediately apparent: "Once my work has been *checked*, I can finally live again; otherwise, melancholy takes over," she explained triumphantly to her daughter, two weeks later, pressing her this time to hurry over for a visit.[254] Solange would stay at Nohant for the entire summer. That December, George would have a cross laid on Nini's grave.

She hadn't written a novel in three years, since *The Master Pipers*. The creative process was launched, her imagination ran wild, and a text inspired by her trip to Italy flew out: *La Daniella*.

With its complex setting, conventional characters, and twists and turns of plot, the novel follows normal conventions. This Bildungsroman was fed by her Italian memories, where she describes the social utopia that George Sand held so dear. The hero, a young painter from a good family, secretly marries Daniella, an Italian servant, whose natural artistic talent foreshadows a career as an opera singer. The child they're expecting avoids illegitimacy, too. The novel's themes were sometimes critical of the Church's morals and of Roman politics, which sparked a lively debate and earned both the author and *La Presse*, which published the novel in installments, a warning from the Ministry of the Interior.

George Sand had entered a new stage of her life. In a letter to Emile Aucante on May 11, 1856, her handwriting suddenly changed, smack in the middle of a sentence. She stopped using her right-slanting English-style cursive she had learned in the convent and adopted a straighter, rounded script, leaning slightly to the left.[255] To her contemporaries, this new handwriting would have seemed shockingly modern and feminine. A later letter to Pauline Viardot explains the change: "My dear Sweetie, you should get accustomed to my new handwriting. My hand had been stiff and broken, but I discovered that I could write much faster this way without smearing the ink."[256] This also shows how strong her flow of writing was, barely keeping up with her thoughts, that her hand would be "broken."

The most explicit goal of this change was comfort. "Our handwriting can be however we like, and we can change it without changing views or behaviors," she later argued to Abbé Michon, who wrote the highly popular *The System of Graphology* (*Système de graphologie*).[257]

Yet the handwriting on the paper still revealed a serious evolution.

In his graphology analysis, Frédéric Dubois explains that the change shows "a progressive liberation of the physical act of writing, correlating to a reduction of her own inconsistencies." Concerns of form fade before freedom of movement, a greater harmony between her impulses and her self-image, a calm self-affirmation, and a recognition of her femininity.[258] After years of often bitter experiences and the death of some very close friends and family, George Sand had finally come to fully accept herself. She stopped hiding her true self from others. Her change in handwriting, as her earlier name change, could have signaled a significant evolution in her personality. Writing *Story of My Life* was probably another important component, as well as her relationship with Alexandre Manceau.

This more mature woman had finally reached the path to serenity.

Chapter Fifteen

"MANCEAU OWNS A *HOUSE!*"

"I still yearn for *absence*. My own space. Absence, for me, is the little corner where I take refuge from everything, every concern, every irritating relative, every domestic problem, every responsibility in my entire life."[259] Along with a *deserted house*, the dream of absence, from herself and others, was a constant one for George Sand. It had not been an easy winter: exhaustion, migraines, colds, coughs, arm pain, renal colic attacks preceded by persistent back pain. But still, nothing had prevented her, after *The Snowman* (*L'Homme de neige*), the story of which took place in Sweden, from writing *The Gallant Lords of Bois-Dore* (*Les Beaux Messieurs de Bois-Doré*), a seventeenth-century swashbuckler. She was weighed down by her household responsibilities and by everything everyone expected of her. Her family, friends, servants, tenant farmers, guests, passersby, neighbors, not to mention the impoverished and other solicitors . . . It wasn't enough for George to withdraw from Paris, from business and modern life. Absence, withdrawal, shifting out of the day-to-day, these things make up the space necessary for dreams to unfurl, for a return to one's essential inner self. A room of one's own, to borrow Virginia Woolf's dreadfully overused phrase, helps to dissipate the constrictions of reality. This is what George dreamt of for so long, and Manceau would be the one to present her with such a gift.

It all began when Alexandre hiked along the Creuse river with the naturalist Depuizet at the end of July 1857. The sun was shining, and the entomologists picnicked on the grass before hunting for rare specimens. The village of Gargilesse sat at the end of the road, "a sheltered nest built within a crater of rocky hills."[260] They walked to the village and fell in love at first sight. Manceau and Sand were both infatuated with the "petit-suisse,"[261] which boasted a climate that rivaled Italy's: the Algira lived there, a butterfly which was known to reproduce in southern regions. It was so warm that they ordered Panama hats from Paris for their next visit! They had discovered paradise three hours down the road from Nohant: a chateau, cottages lining the ravine, an inn, and friendly peasants. The rest of their evening was spent making plans.

George Sand had already spent a day in Gargilesse with Maurice, fifteen years earlier. But then, the village's charm had been shrouded by rain. And at the time, she hadn't been ready. Manceau and Sand set off two weeks later to verify their first impressions and make sure she had really found her ideal village. "Every artist who loves the countryside has dreamt of spending his or her last days living the simple life. It bordered on an idyllic existence."[262] George Sand wondered if, perhaps, she was just romanticizing rural life, an accusation she had often heard. The issue was just as relevant as realism in 1857, especially since *Madame Bovary* was published that April.[263] She felt pressured to have to defend a point of view viewed as romantic, even dated, to the new waves of thought. Peasants were neither as coarse as realists believed nor as angelic as idealists argued. But they could no more be lumped under the same heading as any other member of society. Still, she claimed, there seemed to be less corruption in the true countryside than in the cities.

Gargilesse was located in the department of Indre, about ten kilometers southeast of Argenton-sur-Creuse. George Sand marveled at the beautiful countryside and the supposed purity of its inhabitants, living well away from the road, protected from the vices of civilization. Old-time hospitality reigned in this Rousseau-esque Eden along with simple values, accurate speech, and the joy of nature. "Everyone here takes to the water like ducks. Every Sunday evening, the entire population swims and bathes, showing the kids how to jump from the highest rocks into the deepest pools and fishing by hand from the rocks in the river."[264] Even women bathed in the river! The catch was divided up evenly, and all returned to their homes for dinner. Such a description wouldn't seem out of place on a Pacific island. In Gargilesse, George Sand found the change of scenery she sought: an exotic paradise populated by friendly if rough locals, a mere few hours from home.

She started nurturing the idea of finding a house there, but Manceau was one step ahead of her. On July 12, he bought the thatched cottage they had stayed in, a tiny little house next to the village, across from the school: "For Manceau, it becomes *his attorney, his building*, as he writes to his attorney. Manceau owns a *house*![265] He wasted no time to work on it straightaway. "I am unable to prevent him from arranging his shacke [*sic*], more for us than for himself," George wrote to Maurice, always careful to handle her son's jealousy as best she could. "He's parsing out a ship's quarters to the centimeter, making certain all have their own little area, their own nail for their own hat, their own chamber-pot, a place for each boot, everything....The whole thing is quite amusing, and he's satisfying his two passions: caring for others and decorating. I say this only to calm myself down when I see him spending all of his small income."[266] Those final words show the difference between their revenues, and their social statuses. Manceau, of humble origins, from a working class family, had never owned any property. This new home—his—was a huge step up. Now, Sand was in his house and not vice versa. A proud man: Manceau would no longer feel obligated to her. George couldn't ignore that she was the beneficiary of all the money he was pouring into his little cottage. Alexandre Manceau was the first man (and the last) to give her anything.

The summer was spent coming and going between Nohant and Gargilesse. The couple had not spent time apart from each other for years. When Manceau left for his cottage by himself to oversee renovations, Sand would join him the next day. "We would kiss as if we hadn't seen each other for a whole year."[267] Sometimes, they made the trip together, as a couple or with friends. Monsieur Moreau, a heaven-sent local, served as their guide. They would take day-long hikes along the Creuse ("our legs are begging for mercy!"[268]), have whitebait and wild cherries for lunch, snack on goat's milk and cheese at the mill, and dine on crawfish omelets at the Malesset inn. She even recorded the recipe: "Boil the crawfish without seasoning, peel and cook them in butter. Slide them into an omelet, three-quarters done. Fold omelet over and serve." It's a gourmet dish worthy of the grandest epicureans."[269]

Manceau worked hard to equip his house with the latest comforts of home. "In Gargilesse, everyone knew of this Monsieur Manceau who has an English-style flush toilet in his bathroom," the new homeowner boasted.[270] He also had two bedrooms, iron-wrought beds, wicker chairs, and a white poplar table, all of which made a tidy, yet simple home, a far cry from chateau living. Chickens pecked around the front door, schoolchildren shrieked, and the neighbor woman knitted on her front steps. George Sand loved that there she was neither the lady of a manor nor a man but merely a visiting woman, "an *outsider* who *isn't from around these parts*, but who is very nice all the same." Instead of taking the dirty main road to the inn, she would scale the sheer rock face behind the house! She also dived headlong into her latest hobby, mineralogy, and became convinced that the water and air in Gargilesse worked miracles. George Sand walked several hours each day, letting her skin become tanned "like an Etruscan vase." She was "as good as the new Pont Neuf," she wrote to Solange, in spite of her fifty-four years.[271]

Back in Nohant, George and Alexandre fell back into hosting, and this time, more guests than ever. Trees on the lawn were cut down to make a better view. Sand installed an indicator board for the servants with bells in the kitchen. With new energy and Manceau's help, she would redecorate her own room in three days the following year. Prince Napoléon turned up one day, accompanied by his aide-de-camp, something that triggered alarm bells for the informers spying on George Sand for the emperor. She discovered that one of her valets had been bribed by the local authority. He was passing along information. Furious, she protested to the local police about their methods and their new governing-by-informing on people.

Theater, baths in the Indre river, lunches on the terrace, political literary discussions alternated with escaping to their "Jan Mayen Island," where she dreamed of spending the depth of winter. Two separate worlds, light-years apart.

Despite the whirlwind of her life, she never lost sight of her work, and published a *Letter from the Village* (*Courrier de village*) about Gargilesse in the journal *Le Courrier de Paris* while putting the finishing touches on her novel *The Gallant Lords of Bois-Dore*. She had been "scratching away like a galley slave" but had miscalculated the time for her deadline. "No more doodling, I now must put wind in my sale" the novelist moaned. You think you're done with the novel in your head, she said, but alas, you forget that that novel needs to be written—the least fun part of the job. In May 1858, though, she broke her own record: 620 pages of her new novel, *She and He* (*Elle et Lui*), in twenty five days. And 200 of those were after her long strolls in the countryside from the cottage! "It's a nice little final push for the novel. I've never taken as much pleasure in working as I do at Gargilesse," she mentioned, completely satisfied.[272]

That winter, the village was awash with fog, and the Creuse "fell down and twisted through dams of ice" like a Highlands landscape painting. They were happy to find their house nice and warm, and attractively decorated. Manceau, she wrote, was taking care of his caterpillars. The couple's peaceful evenings were filled with games of bezique, dominos had been replaced, and Manceau and Sand battled each other fiercely in matches which could last as long as five and a half hours. Come wind, rain, or hail, each parting was such sweet regret. As lady of an organized house, she made lists:

"In Gargilesse, we still have: four or five packages of cigarettes, Guéritois shoes, Fontainebleau shoes, wooden clogs *without slippers*, gray ankle boots, old skirt/jersey, a neutral petticoat.

"*We don't have much ink left if there's only the little bottle.*

"Bring towels and sheets. Madame Malesset doesn't always have some, and she doesn't wash her towels very well, they're very dirty and smell of grease. There weren't any at all the day we arrived.

"Nothing else to bring besides a wide-toothed comb and the bandeaux brush."

The countryside was enchanting, and she had fun with life in the dollhouse. "My life circles around Gargilesse with an irresistible attraction. This village life, jumbled up with true *rustic* living, seems more normal to me than chateau life, which is quite complicated. Not having to worry about anything in the world with regards to material things, this has always seemed to be the ideal life, and I've found such an ideal here in my little room, where I have just enough space to sleep, bathe, and write,"[273] she wrote to Solange, whose life was a million miles from such simplicity! Years later, she would even return on her own. "I make my own bed, sweep, unpack my bundle, clean up, prepare my dinner: eggs, potatoes, thick soup, apples, sugared almonds, and coffee, all cold, but nice and fresh, right out of the crate. I serve *myself*, I take *my* time, and I write to Maurice and Mancel,"as she nicknamed Manceau.[274]

Did the author of *The Devil's Pool* see herself as Marie Antoinette in her little hamlet in Gargilesse? Not really, but she did catch whiffs of her pastoral novels in the air. George Sand was delighted to play the Little Fadette.

Manceau had his beloved all to himself, or very nearly. How would he not be thrilled to see how well she took to his house, to the point that she didn't want to leave? With Gargilesse, he had transformed one of George Sand's deepest, most genuine wishes into reality. She would make regular, quick visits to their solitary retreat until 1863, writing a good part of many of her novels during that period.

Chapter Sixteen

"THE TRUE STORY OF SHE AND *HIM*"

Manceau was George Sand's first reader, and not a very critical one at that. Each new creation was hailed as "wonderful" or "charming" in the *Diaries*. One evening in June 1858, however, George found him absorbed in reading *She and Him*, the novel she had finished fast as lightning in Gargilesse. What would the knight think of his *adorée*'s romantic past? Nothing of his reaction would be recorded. Manceau would also never give any indication of his reaction to the circus that resulted from the book's publication. The novel told the story of her love affair with Alfred de Musset and would reintroduce it to the public. *Story of My Life* had only touched on the subject briefly. But on May 2, 1857, the poet passed away. Perhaps his disappearance had given George the desire to revisit the past. Or had she finally given herself permission, remaining faithful to her refusal to write biographies of the living? Maybe it had been her visit to Fontainebleau months earlier with Manceau, as part of her ritual pilgrimage to her lovers' haunts. Or was it the desire to tell her side of the story, years after Musset's *Confession of a Child of the Century* (*La Confession d'un enfant du siècle*), which had set their story in stone as the epitome of romantic passion? "Our names will go down in history with the other immortal lovers who have become one person from two, like Romeo and Juliet, like Heloise and Abelard. No one will ever speak of one of us again without mentioning the other," the poet had predicted.[275]

Musset had quite elegantly shouldered responsibility for their downfall upon himself. He hadn't written a word on George's liaison with Pietro Pagello in Venice. Octave is that recurring figure of a two-faced hero, more fit to suffer and to spread suffering than to love. Presenting himself as a victim of the times and prisoner of his own inability to be happy, he is both narcissistic and clear headed, obsessed with purity and debauchery, cheating and jealous, loving and cruel. By the end of the novel, he ends up fading away before Smith, a simple character, devoted but weak. Brigitte, on the other hand, is torn between her passion for a man who makes her miserable, and her drive for life and need for stability. Now, twenty-five years later, George had once again chosen a "good, honest, and kind" companion, but so many lovers had come in the meantime!

George had become very emotional when reading *Confession of a Child of the Century*. "From the first hour to the last, from the *sisters of charity* to the *puffed-up madwoman*, every tiny detail of the miserable intimacy are recorded so faithfully, so meticulously, that I started wailing like a dog as I closed the book," she had written to Marie d'Agoult.[276] But she had not been nostalgic in the least and had no desire to rekindle the flame—she had lost faith.

What would this mature woman think of the young novelist, "this time, seriously enamored"[277] with a twenty-two-year-old poet, a dandy in blue trousers and velvet jacket, sitting next to her at the dinner François Buloz, head of *Journal of Two Worlds*, had hosted for his collaborators? The poet would pay her a visit at her apartment on the quai Malaquais a few days later. She lounged back on throw pillows in an oriental negligee, smoking a long, cherry wood pipe. Alfred de Musset, down on one knee and very aristocratic, feigned admiration of her embroidered Turkish slippers, brushing his finger along the tip of her tiny foot. They gazed into each other's eyes. The desire was immediate and reciprocated. They both knew they were made for each other.

Now, her children were older than she had been when she and Manceau had climbed into a stagecoach bound for Italy. He had cheated on her in Genoa, then in Venice. She betrayed him with Doctor Pagello, who had been called to treat Musset's brain fever. Still, she cared for him faithfully. Then, he returned to Paris while she stayed in Venice, only to follow with her Italian lover, six months later. They saw each other again, fell back into each other's arms, broke up again, got back together, left each other. ... Their waves of passion, lies and deceit, tears, insults, vows, blows, laments, threats, and promises had once held the entire literary world spellbound. Yet she still felt the need to stoke the embers. They would prove to burn hotter than she expected.

Musset was George Sand's great passion, her soul mate and her antithesis. "No one will understand you better than I," Octave tells Brigitte as he leaves her. The opposite was also true. The poet's friends didn't expect him to ever recover from their love affair, but George had known how to turn the page. On March 6, 1835, she left Alfred definitively, without a word, and took refuge in Nohant. "I have suffered greatly, I have made some mistakes, but I have loved. I have lived my life and not some imitation fashioned from my pride and idleness," she had written to him.[278] Musset would recall the letter in *You Don't Mess Around with Love* (*On ne badine pas avec l'amour*).

As time went on, they shared less and less in common, to the point of nothing at all. In spite of their promises, they didn't manage to transform their love into friendship. They ran into each other randomly in the Théâtre-Italien in 1841, as described in the poem *Souvenir*. It would serve as the final sentence of their passion, which, according to Sainte-Beuve, had been the highlight of Musset's poetic career.

They did frequent some of the same locales: Prince Napoléon's house, or actresses' salons, such as Rachel and Rose Chéri. But the events in 1848 drove them further apart. Musset had set the Académie française in his sights but lost his post as librarian to the Ministry of the Interior, the same place where Sand assisted Ledru-Rollin. According to George's account, they saw each other once more in those years. "He was very emotional and was crying; but alas, he was drunk!" she admitted to Sainte-Beuve.[279] Musset would eventually be accepted to the Académie, but all for naught. His brilliant corpus preceded him. Nothing remained of the curly-haired, blond poet of twenty, save his hair. He had squandered his genius. An alcoholic of forty-six, he looked older than his years: his body sickly, barren, embittered, and devastated by age. No one would have suspected that his plays would be the only ones from the entire romantic period to rouse modern audiences, two full centuries later.

Ever since they met, they had gone through witnesses, confidants, and seconds, like two duelers. Everything snowballed as years progressed, like a never-ending divorce that divided every acquaintance into separate camps, of friends or enemies. The public has always been enamored by celebrities' love lives. Readers of the time had waited impatiently since *Story of My Life* had been published, but they got their fix with *She and Him*. So much, in fact, that George Sand's novel caused a satirical, vengeful reply from Alfred's brother, Paul de Musset, called *He and She* (*Lui et Elle*), which was followed by *Him* (*Lui*), an offshoot penned by Louise Colet, another ex-mistress of Musset. As soon as the novel appeared in installments of *Journal of Two Worlds*, from January 15 to March 1, 1859, the press went wild: Debates recommenced everywhere, a Monsieur de Lescure wrote *They and Them* (*Eux et Elles*), and *They by Me* (*Eux par moi*) was signed by Gaston Lavalley, a Normandy scholar and head librarian at the Bibliothèque de Caen. The Venetian lovers have never fallen out of favor since then—they still inspire novels, movies, songs, and other romantic stories, some that are far removed from the violently sad actual story.

Despite protestation to the contrary, George Sand couldn't deny that she had a lot to do with her legend. Their relationship essentially resided in letters. She was known to be a great and prolific letter writer, with an estimated 45,000 letters penned in her lifetime. Publication of her intimate correspondence would be a serious consideration of hers. It hadn't been the first time.

1851: Alexandre Dumas fils is detained at the Russia-Poland border, awaiting a visa. By extraordinary happenstance, he finds himself entrusted with George Sand's correspondence with Frédéric Chopin, from a Polish aristocrat, who had received the letters from the musician's sister. The Pole suggests that the young man copy them, thinking the task would amuse him. Dumas père alerts George Sand, who recovers the letters and destroys them, keeping only the last one, depriving history of an incomparable record of her relationship with Chopin in one fell swoop. Dumas fils would also destroy his copies, which makes Sand eternally grateful.

"Never give a deceased's letters to anyone who asks them of you," she advised her protégé, the mason-poet Charles Poncy.[280] Descendants had the final say on their publication but were most often opposed to the idea, either because of speculation on or respect for the deceased. One "would not always be happy to see the entirety of their letters published, letters that had not been destined for the public eye."[281] So, what to do? Edit? Correct? But then, letter holders would oppose that, trying to guarantee the authenticity of the letters. In short, she warned, you're looking for trouble in any case, including legal problems.

"My letters may become what they will; I do not wish to think of it. I've convinced myself that the most intimate letters will not be shared beyond the protected, intimate circles,"[282] she reasoned a few months later.

It was no coincidence that she was pondering this dilemma at that moment. Sand and Musset exchanged their first letters in June 1833, a few days after they met, which was about a month before their actual affair began. Their passion burst with lust and frenzy, which their correspondence only nourished, tracked, and intensified. It was a dialogue, or sometimes a double monologue, which laid out the script for these two great artists' harmonies and dissonances. Like in every romantic drama, the letters were filled with tears, daggers, poison, unspeakable happiness, blessed friendship, hair chopped off or pulled out, unconditional love, and betrayal. This correspondence made a daily journal of their love and, as such, could serve as testimony for the prosecution or the defense, depending on the point of view.

After they separated, the lovers agreed to hand over their letters to Gustave Papet, one of George's Berrichon friends, a doctor and the owner of the Château d'Ars. He was entrusted with two anonymous packages, sealed with wax and tied with black ribbons. In 1854, Musset wanted to burn his letters, and Papet promised to return them to him on the condition that George Sand also recovered her own package. They remained in limbo until December 1856, when Musset's lawyer, Jules Grévy, restated his client's request. By that time, though, the laws of correspondence ownership had been set: The physical object belonged to the owner of the letter, and the content to the writer. In January 1857, François Rollinat suggested, on George's behalf, that all parties meet together to burn the precious valuables. He declined to mention that Papet had already turned both packages over to Sand. On May 2, Musset died. So it was his brother, Paul, who made his own request for the letters two weeks later, thinking he could get everyone to agree to save a couple from the fire. Sand had always enjoyed a good relationship with him, and invited him to Nohant for such a ceremony. He never showed up.

George's good faith in this whole story leaves room for debate. Firstly, she claimed to have burned the entire correspondence. Then, the press announced a publication date of April 10 for a book by Paul de Musset "which apparently contains letters from Madame Sand."[283] Perhaps he already had some in his possession. She left no stone unturned to find out, even resorting to thinly veiled blackmail, threatening to expose him for what she knew he was. The elder brother was less talented but more stable and had the reputation of always caring for his younger brother. Of course, their relationship had many more layers, but it was all embodied in Paul's marriage to Aimée d'Alton, his brother's former mistress, after the latter's death. The man who championed Alfred de Musset had not always been so devoted to his scandalous younger brother, if Sand and Hetzel were to be believed, and became exasperated with the poet's extravagance. But the publisher didn't spare his feelings, either, for the poet he knew so well: "He is a rotten lover, a worse friend, and an even more terrible citizen. ... You say that he was not evil. No, he wasn't wicked, he was worse than that! He was poisonous from birth, naturally rotten. ... There never was a good word that could describe him. He may have spoken of good things, but his actions were bad."[284] George, who had seen her own brother change under the grip of alcohol, implored for leniency. Surely a man who lived off of absinthe and rum and suffered multiple bouts of brain fever would lose his sanity. Yes, he was mad, and a violent liar in his madness. But that was the tragedy of alcoholism, which, she added, wreaked more havoc throughout France every day.

In reality, Paul de Musset had taken extracts from George Sand's *Intimate Journal* (*Journal intime*) and copied them word-for-word in his book. Nauseated, she decided not to read it.

But she took it upon herself—and this was most likely why people criticized her—to edit some passages of her own letters, even told Sainte-Beuve as much: "I'd like to cut out every criticism from *her* to *him*, even though I wanted you to read everything. I've made all the necessary cuts in the part I copied myself, and I even took scissors to my writing for everything that could harm or compromise outside parties."[285] One of her envelopes, addressed in ink, even enclosed a letter written in pencil in a much later handwriting.[286] After all, she had changed her handwriting in 1856. It wasn't difficult to spot the modifications, which were, of course, offered as favors for Musset and others. Afterwards, she returned the letters to Emile Aucante, whom she trusted completely, and with good reason. He fulfilled her every request exactly. In spite of her desire to publish "the true story of *She and Him*,"[287] she took Sainte-Beuve's advice and demurred, but requested that her trustee keep them as evidence: "I recommend that you publish this correspondence *after my death*, and give you every power to do so."[288] Thus, modern audiences can read the exchange between the two, so filled with love and symbolism that it continues to be relevant today. The letters first appeared in *The Paris Journal* in 1896, then in a bound edition in 1904. They haven't gone out of print since then, and the so-called erotic texts have attained the level of scripture.

It seems unlikely that George Sand had imagined, during the twenty days it took to write the 625 pages of *She and He*, "the whirlwind of reactions it would provoke." Sand had to write the thoughts and feelings of each person as she remembered them and as she saw them from a distance. These were no memories that she dug up from the past, this was a novel. "This was retrospective emotion, and her own emotions," she wrote to Sainte-Beuve.[289] Let the one who has never rewritten past loves, not even in his or her own head, throw the first stone! The debate about autofiction is an old one: As soon as text passes from autobiography to novel, the author must take full responsibility for the creative liberties. The transposition was quite clear—two painters took the place of two writers, brown hair replaced blond, Venice gave way to Florence, memories came from her trips with Manceau to La Spezia—but Sand had reasons for her choices. Thérèse's only fault was giving in to the passionate Laurent, who was unstable and prone to hallucinations, like when he thought he saw his double at Fontainebleau (Musset himself described the scene in his *Nuits*). An adolescent and perverse weakling, the character of Laurent suffered from Musset's own later years' depression, basically an extended, drawn-out suicide. The romantic, moving outbursts were replaced by a simple, sincere compassion for this boy, so young and talented, but who had no ability to control his anxieties and impulses. "Laurent possessed a certain charm that she was fatally attracted to: weakness.... And as soon as his weakness had claimed victory, his strength returned to make others suffer, like all beloved children," George Sand analyzed retrospectively. The story ended like real life, with the young woman's flight. As for her affair with Pagello in Venice during Musset's illness, she would chalk it up to the poet's hallucinations, worsened by fever and delirium.

Paul de Musset took it upon himself to refresh her memory. *He and Her* switched the responsibilities. The little dagger that Olympe wore in her belt the night that she met Laurent would become symbolic. Paul de Musset made Olympe a phallic woman, whose natural generosity was swallowed by her pride. That character trait pushed her to lay claim to both her modest birth and her mother's tumultuous past, making Edouard a victim of her manipulations. Beneath the surface of the modern Jacobin artist—a musician, this time—with a masculine pen name, hid a dangerous predator who destroyed her men, leaving behind a "parade of ghosts." Even worse, after she betrayed them and sent them away, she would publicly disparage them and tarnish their reputation, too proud to ever admit the slightest wrongdoing herself. Paul de Musset went on a crusade to right the wrongs done to his brother, and contributed hugely to George Sand's reputation as a praying mantis.

And then there was Louise Colet, the queen of opportunists, who went a step further. She sketched George as a bossy, self-righteous hypocrite, and Alfred as a spineless crybaby with no will of his own. This writer had certainly figured out how to get herself noticed. Her sometimes lover, Gustave Flaubert, who had made her his confidant while writing *Madame Bovary*, also appeared in a highly unflattering light in *Lui* after permanently breaking off their affair.

By returning to past loves, George Sand opened Pandora's box. With no power to close it again, she resorted to her tried and true methods: silence and work.

Chapter Seventeen

"IMPERSONALITY HAS SAVED ME"

The end of the world was announced for June 13, 1858, when the comet was due. The year had already started badly. The economic crisis had hit France directly after the United States. Two Italian refugees, Orsini and Pierri, had attempted to assassinate the emperor and his wife. That had prompted a General Security law, to imprison or exile any former political prisoners. A fresh wave of arrests led to 375 deportees, including some of George Sand's close friends: Ernest Périgois was forced to flee to Italy, and Jean Patureau-Francoeur, a former winemaker and mayor of Châteauroux, for whom she had finagled a pardon after the coup d'état, was deported to Algeria. After negotiating with Prince Napoléon, they were eventually allowed to return to France. Patureau, though, would choose to remain in Algeria, as a colonist in Constantinois. Under his short-lived Ministry of Algeria and the Colonies, Prince Napoléon encouraged organized rural colonization under civil administration.

A few months later, he married Clotilde de Savoie, the daughter of the king of Piédmont-Sardaigne, the future Victor-Emmanuel II. His mistress, Sylvanie Arnould-Plessy, George Sand's actress friend, fell by the wayside. True to his "left-leaning" ideas, the prince tried to counsel his cousin, keeping a delicate balance between authoritarianism and his liberalism, which he had learned as a child and which was necessary for the business development and modernization of France.

In August 1859, general amnesty marked the new regime's transparency and allowed all political convicts and exiles to return to France. George Sand entreated her republican friends to return, but some refused: Pierre-Jules Hetzel, in Belgium; Louis Blanc, in England; Victor Hugo, in Guernesey; and Armand Barbès, in Holland, had chosen voluntary exile after being freed in 1854. She wrote a suspiciously modest letter to Hugo, saying, "History will remember your choosing exile. It will pass over my simply resigning myself to my fate."[290]

She was a separate player from the opposition, as a friend of Prince Napoléon and in her role as a mediator. She had long kept her distance from authority without necessarily fighting it, calling upon one friend or another to help her cause. For her, it was always a matter of compromise without surrendering her principles.

Manceau and George Sand had discovered Baron Haussmann's recent developments during their last visit to Paris in 1857. They walked through the Bois de Boulogne, explored the Jardin des Plantes and the Jardin d'Acclimatation, and shopped at the Magasins du Louvre, which were almost as luxurious as Boucicaut's Bon Marché. It was the era of *Lady's Pleasures*. But neither the *Diaries* nor any of her letters mentioned anything about the huge construction projects in the capital nor about the resulting speculation. Most likely, this absence was because of how short their visits were, or how they stayed almost exclusively in the "artist" neighborhoods, or perhaps how ambivalent they felt towards Parisian life. Yes, the new railway lines cut the journey from Châteauroux to Paris in half, to eight hours. But this was nineteenth century Berry countryside, truly another time and another world. Letter writing was still integral part of George Sand's life, something that had recently been improved by railway mail transportation and the invention of the postage stamp. She had ample time in Nohant to write long letters. Many she simply *had* to write in order to stay in touch with the faraway literary world, publishers and authors, theater directors and actors, and political figures. Her entire professional life was handled long distance. She stayed up to date with current events through her subscriptions to journals and newspapers, her books, and other Parisians' regular visits to Nohant.

The couple had not set foot in the capital since 1857 and would only return for a couple of weeks in 1859 and 1860. For the latter trip, George ordered a new black dress from her seamstress, a far cry from the elegant high fashion house, Worth, that had just opened on the rue de la Paix.

On this trip, she went three separate times to cheer her "dear little girly," the singer Pauline Viardot, who was playing in Gluck's *Orphée* to wild acclaim at the Théâtre-Lyrique. It was the first time the role was interpreted by a female voice, and the public was enthusiastic. The young woman was physically unattractive, had an exceptional voice, and was a talented dramatic actress. In that production, she achieved the pinnacle of her career and of all of lyric art. Once the inspiration for George Sand's *Consuelo*, she had briefly caught Maurice's eye, before George married her to the journalist Louis Viardot. The painter Ari Scheffer adored her, as did Ivan Turgenev, who trailed closely behind her. She had proven herself worthy of her "Mama's" undying affection and admiration. But her nomadic diva life led her all over Europe, and the women saw each other less and less often, even with their shared— and abandoned—project to adapt *The Devil's Pool* into an opera.[291]

Each time they traveled to Paris, both Manceau and George fell ill. "My God, I am so sick and tired of being here!!"[292] lamented the Parisian-born Alexandre. These excessive visits irritated him: "too many people, too much noise."[293] Their many visitors included Hector Berlioz, Eugène Fromentin, Maxime Du Camp, and Gustave Flaubert (whose name he wrote as "Flobert," referencing a famous gunsmith from whom he had purchased his hunting rifle). This was *Madame Bovary* author's second visit, the first having happened the year before. The Normand found George Sand to be "a charming woman,"[294] but he was hardly entranced by her writing. George, for her part, praised *Salammbô* as a "capital book" and defended its virtues to the press. With Hugo, her exchange had been as one power to another, not without a healthy dose of respect and deference; with Flaubert, she became much more personal very quickly. In just his second letter, the novelist asked George for her portrait to hang in his study.

Manceau and George Sand still lived on the rue Racine but had moved into two larger apartments on the fifth floor. George's studio served as her salon and parlor; the engraver worked in his own. They had frequented Magny's, the restaurant on the rue de la Contrescarpe (now the rue Mazet in the 6th arrondissement), for many years. Starting in 1866, this would be the site of the famous dinners during which the Goncourt brothers, Alphonse Daudet, Emile Zola, Ivan Turgenev, Gustave Flaubert, and others would meet along with her, the only woman. These dinners would establish Sand and Flaubert's friendship, which would give birth to one of the greatest correspondences between writers.

Maxime Du Camp had recently met George Sand for the first time, and he saw her as a "fine bourgeois woman" in secondhand silk and last season's boots, with an olive complexion, flat cheeks, and too-long teeth, but whose overall look retained its beauty. The password "Shibboleth" gained him access to the rue Racine apartment, which was guarded "by an unsettling man, with a thin face, wandering gaze, and hands betraying manual work."[295] Du Camp added, "She has quite the raggedy engraver trailing along behind her, who seems to watch over her with great concern." The author of *Souvenirs littéraires*, Gustave Flaubert's childhood friend, was known for the slightly malicious intent of his portraits. Those can be set aside, however, to find a not uninteresting outsider's perspective of Manceau. His hands were stained or gashed from engraving tools, he appeared skinny and sickly, and the description of his concerned look matches his portrait by Auguste Lehmann. There is also some underlying social contempt, which the ultrasensitive Manceau would have felt quite clearly. Despite ten years of cohabitation, Du Camp did not recognize him as official companion. But Sand herself was hardly treated any better: She was said to be blessed with "the tranquility of the brooding animals whose lulling eyes seem to reflect the vastness of space."[296] This was the hierarchical Second Empire society. Even in cultured circles, the "humble engraver," as he liked to call himself, was deemed inferior, and he knew it. No matter, when George Sand was invited, and she was asked everywhere, Manceau went with her, including to the Prince Napoléon and his wife, Clotilde de Savoie.

Two years later, the brothers Jules and Edmond de Goncourt penned the report of their first visit. Manceau was a "small man, average looks, just like anyone else," and he presented them with a smile to "a gray, drowsy shadow" sitting backlit in the corner. She answered their questions in monotone, like a statue which automatically relit cigarettes. Her placid nature was once again compared to a brooding animal. Manceau took it upon himself to steer the conversation along, showing off her literary prowess like a "freak show ringmaster." He proffered a relatively poetic explanation: "Really, we're disturbing her. ... Say you have an open faucet at your house. When someone comes in, you shut it off. That's what it's like for Madame Sand." She rose to walk them to the door, and they saw "a bit of her calm and sweet face, with features drawn lightly onto pale, peaceful, amber-colored complexion."[297]

Money was tight in 1858, approaching a *breakdown* (Manceau's words). He had taken to secretly paying the rent for George's Parisian apartment from his pocket. Sand placed her hopes in *She and Him*, whose subject had possibly been conceived more out of practical concerns than sentimental considerations. "We've been living on credit for three weeks. This must be dealt with quickly, so see to it that the greatest possible sum of money is withdrawn, for Maurice will undoubtedly need it for his use, as I do for mine," she wrote to Emile Aucante.[298]

Smothered by financial difficulties, she considered taking a loan. The Second Empire was developing credit, thanks to the new banks. But Sand didn't trust bankers, who, she claimed, charged exorbitant interest. She preferred to use a private individual, who would offer a favorable rate. "My children will not forgive me for being poor," she admitted to Emile Aucante. The price of wheat had dropped, and the summer drought in 1858 had increased the price of feed. She barely managed to pay her tenant farmers.

Aucante had his own problems. A year earlier, young Marie Caillaud had given birth to a little boy, his son. Manceau had taken it upon himself to give him almost daily reports on the mother and child. Marie had given birth on her hands and knees, the new trend, and the child was given to a nurse. Emile had been a natural child himself, and he recognized his son at birth by proxy. He would marry Marie a few years later to legitimize the child. He worked at a fire insurance company in Paris and was trying to start his own literary agency. But in spite of George's support, it would never get off the ground. Two problems, she explained: Either authors were not *sellable* and no money would come in, or they were, and they didn't need the help!

And who could trust publishers with reprinted titles, anyway? She advocated for state-protected, taxable copyrights, the "poverty law." And for no other reason than to bring in those who represented the impoverished, to help regulate the publishers' accounts. The foreign rights that Aucante considered were equally hopeless. She had never, not even with all the translations, seen a single cent from abroad.

Most of the time, she sold her texts to a journal for a fixed sum. The journal would retain exclusive rights until the end of the publication, which, because of her massive production of writing, wouldn't always be easy for her.

For example, the agreement she signed in 1858 with François Buloz, the publisher of *Journal of Two Worlds*, for *She and Him* was as follows: She would receive a total of 4,500 francs for publication in the journal and in a separate volume.[299] The text would belong to the journal for two years, during which it could do with it as it liked. If the issues or volumes sold during those two years brought in more than 2,000 francs, the author would earn the balance. She was also prohibited from publishing a novel anywhere else during those two years, but the journal would pay her at the same rate as *She and Him* for any book she wrote during that period.

But she could also sign other contracts for previously published texts, such as a new edition of *Pastoral Novels* (*Romans champêtres*), for Hetzel, at the rate of two francs per copy for the copyright, up to the 5,000 francs she owed him after dissolving the business they had started together. That rate was especially high; Normally, she had been receiving thirty cents per copy. Buloz would eventually prevail upon Hachette and Michel Lévy to pay her at the rate of fifty cents, which the latter was giving to Prosper Mérimée and Octave Feuillet.

Years before, she had protested against Captain D'Arpentigny. "The captain is overly anti-Semitic," she wrote.[300] But even George

Sand, with her clever strategies and incessant negotiations with her publishers, was not exempt from the era's prevailing prejudices. "The wandering Jew symbolizes for me the entire Jewish people: rich and banished since the Middle Ages, with its eternal five cents which never dry up, constant work, their lack of goodwill for those not of their race. I see them on their way to ruling the world and recrucifying J. C., that is, attaining the ideal place. That is how it will go for intellectual property, and fifty years from now, France will be Jewish."[301] These were her claims in a letter to Victor Borie, her former lover, whom she had playfully mocked as a "capitalist." In another letter, she recommended to Aucante to "Never do business with Jews." Frédéric Chopin, bound by his Polish origins, most likely influenced these ideas in Sand. Still, it seems that these comments are more a reflection of the distrust of general commerce by some socialist thinkers, such as Marx or Proudhon. Also of note, the first part of Gobineau's *An Essay on the Inequality of the Human Races* (*Un Essai sur l'inégalité des races humaines*) had been published in 1853.

The new Jewish bourgeoisie had sprung up in this third generation and were granted French citizenship in 1791. That minority became a scapegoat. So it was more shocking for Alphonse de Rothschild to be the governor of the Banque de France than for Charles Germiny or Eugène Schneider, who held the same post. And there were the Pereire brothers, devotees of Saint-Simons' writings who founded the first commercial bank in France. Their Crédit Mobilier bank funded new railroad companies—the future Compagnie générale transatlantique, the Compagnie des omnibus de Paris, the Compagnie des salins du Midi—thanks to savings from individuals, the famous French nest eggs. In 1857, they paid up to 40 percent dividends to their small stockholders. These shares garnered even more hostility than the traditional business investments of a certain Achille Fould, who had financed the recent coup d'état.

Meanwhile, while George Sand would rail against her publishers, Buloz or Hetzel, never attacking persons or origins, it wouldn't prevent her from entrusting her collected works up to "that Jew,"[302] Michel Lévy, in 1860. The contract ran for ten years and would guarantee her 75,000 francs paid in monthly installments. A five-year contract was also signed with Buloz at *Journal of Two Worlds* as well for three novels per year for a total sum of 82,500 francs.[303] The agreements benefited George Sand hugely, ensuring her a stable, steady income. These two contracts, however, caused a brief falling out with Pierre-Jules Hetzel.

Michel Lévy's sudden death at the age of fifty-four upset her greatly—they had become close friends. His brother, Calmann, would take over his publishing house.

Social differences became more pronounced under the Second Empire. The frenzied spending of the court along with that of investors clashed with the bleak poverty of workers, the rise of alcoholism, and unemployment. George Sand continued to distribute aid to those in need. She put her network of connections at anyone's disposal and gave freely of both her time and money. In 1862, she began a regular and close epistolary relationship with the financier Edouard Rodrigues-Henriques, a man renowned for his philanthropy. As their friendship grew closer, her prejudice against Jews would melt away.

"God bless those who are rich and are kindhearted!" George Sand exclaimed in a letter to her new correspondent, whom Alexandre Dumas fils had introduced to her. The former stockbroker personified the Jewish bourgeoisie in the Second Empire, eager to integrate French society: A music lover and protector of artists, he was also the owner of the vast Beaupréau estate in Rueil. Despite a strict religious life, his four daughters married non-Jews. A third of his fortune was dedicated to philanthropy, which he crafted into a mission and a philosophy. Philanthropy was one path to social justice in a society in which the poor had no rights. Everyone debated the responsibility of the rich, from stoics to the Bible, from Bossuet to Lamennais, from Saint-Simons to English utilitarians, from philosophical and religious domains to economic and social spheres. Clearly, it played a large role in George Sand's life. She eventually became a victim of her own generosity and had to make her donations anonymously. But her funds were modest. Edouard Rodrigues opened up a whole new philanthropic world for her. He deeply admired her. "Madame Sand has made me better," he repeated time and time again, as if echoing Bakounine's words to his brother, "I become a better person every time I read her works." Rodrigues offered to make a fixed sum of money available to her each month to help whomever she wanted. This "piggy bank" could be replenished if necessary and provided the main funds for George Sand's charity.

Eventually, she would recommend Manceau's son, Auguste Guy, to Rodrigues. She would also entrust the philanthropist with the future of Francis Laur, a penniless boy who had entered her friend Charles Duvernet's service at fourteen, before going blind. Thanks to Rodrigues' help, Francis would finish his studies and become an engineer, a journalist, then a deputy! There was no middle ground for Jews, she observed: When they were generous and helpful, they were more so than anyone else.

More importantly, their correspondence led her to reflect further on the role of the wealthy in society. Did it consist only of individual generosity, of moral duty, means of justice? She suggested that they organize their dialogue as a "socialist doctrine:" he would ask questions, and she would try to respond. Sand's depth and views were developed in two letters of dozens of pages each.[304] She supported equal rights and responsibilities for all, provided that they work towards general progress. To the question, "How can we reach perfection?" her response was: "Freedom is as necessary to the individual as air and light." Freedom alone could guarantee the path to equality, through every business and association which contributed to the development of a fraternal society, not one based on the strong devouring the weak. Everyone would have to commit to self-sacrifice. This foundational freedom also condemned dictatorships as well as revolutionary violence. The former Robespierre administration didn't excuse the crimes of the 1848 revolution.[305]

Lamennais's social Catholicism, as well as Pierre Leroux and Louis Blanc's socialism, had all influenced her views. The latter's motto, "To each according to his needs," seemed to her to be the golden rule for a more just society if "needs" included not only food and work but also education and personal development. Literacy was necessary for a fully fledged and true citizen who took responsibility for his or her own choices.

Sand was ridiculed with a bit of misogyny for her philosophical pretentions. Critics pointed to her flights of passion, her lack of intellectual rigor, and her idealism. But until the end, she pondered the meaning of human life, an individual's responsibilities within a society, and possible human advancements. She had discovered a prime discussion partner in Edouard Rodrigues. Like her, he was generous, and he took action. Thanks to his "piggy bank," she was able to aid the peasants in her area. They weren't in dire poverty, she explained, but if they fell ill, their families could no longer care for themselves. The commune's funds went to help the truly impoverished. The bourgeoisie wouldn't dream of loosening their purse strings. "The Center campaigns have been abandoned. This is truly the country of slumber and death."[306]

"Oh, if only you were here, my good Jew, you would rouse these Celts, still stuck in their daydreams of Gaule, and stir them to action,"[307] she exclaimed (in a puzzling manner to modern readers). "You are right to take pride in your race."[308] She assailed him with her requests to aid her friends and close acquaintances, also appealing to the financiers Emile Pereire and Edouard Salvador on his recommendation. Speaking to Edouard Rodrigues stimulated and comforted her. She rejoiced in the "friendship of golden years." She reciprocated by helping him furnish the perfect populist library, including the complete works of Walter Scott and Fenimore Cooper, as well as Corneille, Schiller, Goethe, Shakespeare, Hoffmann's *Fantastical Stories* (*Contes fantastiques*), and Musset's *Comedies and Proverbs* (*Comédies et proverbes*). And that was just the beginning. She would soon write a new novel, *Antonia*, which she would dedicate to Edouard Rodrigues.

She also went so far as supplicating the empress, an active Catholic, on behalf of a needy old weaver poet, and a shipwrecked fisherman from Toulon. Each man would receive 1,000 francs. She approached the Indre prefect to help a poor woman get readmitted to a hospice after being mistreated by her daughter and son-in-law, offering to pay her fees if necessary. The list was long: She went to Baron Haussmann to help open a theater for her actor friend, Bocage. She represented her former maid Catherine Labrosse who had also been abused by her children. She recommended Edouard Plouvier, a former tanner turned dramatist, to François Buloz, and Emile Aucante to Ferdinand de Lesseps and Ludovic Halévy. The former received not only 700 francs from her pocket (a sizeable amount) but also her support at the Ministry. That was a bit surprising, considering that he had already had over forty of his plays produced in Paris. Surely some of those had profited from her involvement, too. And the list goes on and on. Many benefited from her generosity and management. It never mattered from which side she sought help. The end result was all that counted. But never, under any circumstances, would she ever ask anything at all for herself.

And yet, she was going through a difficult period. The publication of *She and Him* had caused a sensation, sparking a two-year-long tidal wave of reactions. Another event led to a trial, which she hated. In August 1858, Monsieur Breuillard, a private school headmaster, unleashed a diatribe against romanticists. One especially harsh paragraph attacked her personally: "Only this old woman, worn out by a debauched body and spirit, could attempt a heretofore unknown love in her novel, the carnal love of a prostitute for her illegitimate son." He seemed to allude to *François the Waif*, but Madeleine wasn't a prostitute, and François wasn't her illegitimate son. Breuillard would only be fined 100 francs.

George Sand was convinced that he had been influenced by Louis Veuillot, the ultra-Catholic figurehead and head of *L'Univers*. He was so extreme that bishops forbade their congregations to read his works, and even the pope was forced to denounce him. Veuillot took every opportunity to decry the novelist's harmful influence. George Sand is no longer mentioned as a moralist. Quite the contrary, in fact: Her moral freedom, her declared beliefs on marriage and divorce, participation in the revolution of 1848, socialist and anticlerical ideas, friendships with Freemasons (Manceau, too, was a member, starting in 1855), and her gender, of course, made her the primary target of self-righteous and Catholic France. The Church was historically royalist and had rallied around the prince-president, who had supported the Falloux Laws, which favored private schools and Catholic teaching. The empress also used her influence to support the Church, which benefited from an increased budget, a flood of new schools and parishes, and a nearly direct censorship on the University. Pope Pius IX would later publish an encyclical which condemned Protestantism, reason, freedom of expression, tolerance, divorce, socialism, progress, and modern civilization.[309] The battle between republicans and the Church became a central issue of the day, and George Sand was right in the thick of it, lambasting clericalism and any religious influence over civil life.

Then, in December 1859, the Chinon scandal broke. Sixteen-year-old Angélina had given birth to a servant's child, and she and her mother were brought before the court, charged with burning the child to make it disappear. The headlines were horrible and revealed the nefarious moral influence of the time. While under oath, the young woman had reported, "I had read George Sand's novels. I was torn between the despair of my failure and the joy of having raised a servant up to my level." The public prosecutor seized the idea and denounced "these most dangerous and detestable novels that this young woman devoured happily every day." He added, "It is well understood that social laws are scorned in the lofty novelist's school." France fell in love with the Lemoyne affair. Fights broke out over copies of the newspapers which reported from the courtroom. Once again, Louis Veuillot took advantage of the occasion to criticize George Sand.[310]

But the left didn't spare her their venom, either. The anarchist philosopher Pierre-Joseph Proudhon went a step further than Breuillard had, accusing her of advocating "spiritual incest" in *François the Waif*. He also devoted an entire ten pages in his *Of Revolutionary Justice* (*De la justice dans la Révolution*) to criticizing her, reproaching her defense of gender equality as a source of "unquenchable lust." He protested the deplorable images circulated throughout her novels. "Devolved to her wanton nature, the emancipated woman can no longer resist her obscene thoughts." He felt this sharp repulsion for the author even before reading her works. It would be laughable, if his pages didn't boil over with such a strong hatred, much like other insults from Nietzsche, Baudelaire, Barbey d'Aurevilly, and more. "The Sand woman," as Baudelaire called her, was the incarnation of everything these men feared and loathed.

"Must I accept this?" she wrote calmly to Aucante.

She had reached the age of "impersonality," as she explained, the moment when one distances one's self from oneself. After all, these people were less attacking her personally than as a symbol of progressive ideas. One of the benefits of growing older, she said, was becoming indifferent to these blows to her ego, and opening herself more to other people, to nature, to all of life. "I have suffered so much in life, and I have surrendered so many battles to avoid becoming overly bitter that *impersonality* has saved me," she wrote in a moving letter to Hetzel. But impersonality did not mean insensitivity. And while she managed to protect herself from outside attacks, the same could not be said of her depression and her mourning over Nini's death. "Would you believe that my granddaughter still lives in me? I don't feel her death, I can't believe it. She is in my thoughts at every moment, as if she were still here. I watch her grow up, I hear her voice changing, and every day, I say to myself that she would be so many years old. She is just absent, she can no longer comfort me, she has gone."[311]

Nothing about that time made her optimistic. She didn't see herself in the "feverish *je ne sais quoi*, constantly eyeing something small and selfish, jealous, false, and base, which used to be hidden, but is now flaunted."[312] This new public seemed beyond her reach as an author. How could she be useful to her contemporaries? She became more sharply pessimistic, as this bitter letter to Edouard Plouvier shows: "What can I say? Evil walks upon this earth." Attacks, slander, problems, and to top it off, Vaudeville's rejection of one of her plays had shattered her optimistic nature. "I'm too old to delude myself," she decided.

But a more serious concern was plaguing her, one she had tried to ignore over the years: Alexandre Manceau had been having a chronic cough for the past three years now. She was worried. She urged him to consult their friend, Doctor Vergne, who prescribed him some iron. All too familiar to Chopin's companion. She feared this frightful symptom of consumption, this cough which was bringing down her "wizened angel?"

Manceau had also been devastated by the news he received of his younger brother's death, two years after the fact. Henri, the little, seventeen-year-old brother, sailor had succumbed to yellow fever in Port-au-Prince. In his play *A Simple Heart (Un Coeur Siimple)*, Victor, a young sailor, dies in Havana: Flaubert would dedicate the play to George Sand. "Poor Mancel is sad, and so am I," wrote George in the *Diaries*. She thought he had been "fantastic" in the Italian farce they were performing at the Grand Théâtre of Nohant, but "he's tiring himself out, which adds a sad note to my laughter."[313] These worries would never leave her.

After three years of work, the engraver had finally completed *Mountain Goat Hunting*, based on Horace Vernet's painting. His devotion to George Sand and to Maurice's butterfly collections had kept him away from his personal work. One can't help but think that he sacrificed a good part of his promising career by committing himself wholeheartedly to Madame and her son. Even so, he fired off another order for his dealer, Goupil, before undertaking a new job: *Masks and Clowns (Masques et bouffons)*, one of Maurice's projects. This close collaboration with Maurice and George would occupy his time from the end of June 1858 to April 1859. A careful comparison of the engravings with the original drawings shows Manceau's great skill and the improvements he made to Maurice's drawings.[314] The *Diaries* tell of his grand efforts, which deprived him of even spending time with the one he loved: "I wake at the crack of dawn, and it's like I don't live with them anymore." After dinner, George and Maurice discussed their work together around the table, so Manceau had to return to his studio. Completely worn out, he retired at ten thirty, writing sadly, "This is my life, and not a very fun one at that."[315] Was he hoping that Madame would decipher his message? This time, she spared no effort to ensure her son's success: She translated texts from Italian for him, read and corrected his works . . . that is, she rewrote them.

April 2, 1859: Relieved, he finally completes his work. "Manceau has finished and packed up the last plate for the Comédie Italienne. Tra la la!!!"

Masks and Clowns would prove to be a huge publishing success. Maurice was finally earning money, and he received the Legion of Honour (thanks to his mother's intervention, as Solange pointed out). He was praised for the success of the collaborative work, and in the meantime, Alexandre Manceau had the immense pride of seeing twenty-four of his engravings exhibited at the Salon in May 1861. Finding a new commission proved problematic, however, since his usual publisher, Goupil, hadn't approved his working for a rival. He was worried, he confided to Aucante in strictest secrecy. It was the first time in his professional life that he found himself without work. "Oh, and I so wanted to be a millionaire . . . what about you?"[316] Eventually, Goupil gave him Louis Matout's painting to engrave, *Ambroise Paré Performing an Arterial Ligature (Ambroise Paré pratiquant la ligature d'artères)*. In it, the doctor sits enthroned on a battlefield, showing a crowd of admirers the bloody stump of an amputee who was the first to receive the new surgical procedure.

George and Alexandre had also begun a new teaching project. Each one had taken in a student: She took Marie Caillaud, whom they called Marie des Poules, or just Bélie; he took the valet, Jean "Henri" Brunet. They had applied maternalism à la Sand to their daily life. Yet, there was no hesitation to fire a drunk servant, like Auguste "Jardinet" Lureau, Nohant's alcoholic handyman, "glassy eyed, wooden legged, with a tongue as thick as raw sausage."[317] Or Michel, whom Manceau had charged with not leaving Madame's side, not even for an instant, during his absence, who nevertheless managed to get to La Châtre three times in three days![318] It could take weeks to find a good fit for the kitchen. But once hired, the domestic help became part of the household. The little peasant girl, Marie des Poules, had entered into

George Sand's service at the age of eleven as a barnyard girl, which was how she got her nickname.[319] By eighteen, she had been promoted to chambermaid and been welcomed into the family. She attended readings, offered her opinions, and acted onstage in the Grand Théâtre of Nohant. She made "extraordinary progress from one play to the next. She has presence, and confidence, and always *speaks* in such an adorable manner,"[320] her mistress reported.

To each his own method of teaching: classical for Manceau, modern for George Sand. After just a few weeks, Marie could read and understand a randomly chosen sentence. She jumped directly into *Little Fadette*. Manceau's student, on the other hand, could figure out how to write but not how to read. Much like with their dominos or card games, the two instructors enjoyed the competition, which defined their relationship, even such a competition at arm's length through their respective pupils.

Their shared passion though, was still their work. "I am becoming a country woman and an impassioned *novelist*, two things which can, fortunately, go together very well,"[321] she wrote to her actress friend, Rose Chéri, for whom George Sand's life probably appeared to be quite dry. Without the means to travel as much as she would like, she asserted her "complete resignation to graze in [her] own backyard."[322] She rose at nine o'clock every morning—quite a feat—ate lunch with Manceau, gardened, did some sewing, worked on her novels, and went to bed at one o'clock. "There's not a soul here, so we're working a lot." In 1859, George Sand published *Narcisse, She and Him, The Green Ladies* (*Les Dames vertes*) (a ghost story), *The Snowman*, a fantasy, *Promenades Around a Village* (*Promenades autour d'un village*), and the preface to *Masks and Clowns*, in a single year. That wasn't counting two leaflets, *The War* (*La Guerre*) and *Garibaldi*, and a play produced at the Gymnase, *Marguerite de Saint-Gemme*.

She had already tackled fantasy in *Rustic Legends* (*Légendes rustiques*), which Maurice had illustrated. The stories borrowed heavily from Berry legends, from the same oral history as she explored in *Visions of Night in the Country* (*Les Visions de la nuit dans la campagne*). The stories showed her serious interest in popular culture, treated more as poetry than as folklore.

In May and June of 1859, her trip to Aubergne with Manceau and the young actress Bérangère planted the seed for three new novels: *Jean de la Roche*, *The Black City* (*La Ville noire*), and *Le Marquis de Villemer*. She rediscovered the pleasure of walking and climbing through the still wild countryside, although it didn't prevent her, a few months later, from complaining, "My life is as sheltered as an oyster!" She wrote a letter to Hetzel, still in Belgium, saying, "We are old now, and ugly. Maurice is putting on weight, Manceau is balding, and I'm a hundred years old. But what does that matter if we love each other enough to enjoy each other's company? The good part of growing older is that we all age together."[323] She yearned for sunshine and wanted to accept Charles Poncy's invitation to Toulon, but as she explained to him, she couldn't travel alone anymore "without my wonderful Manceau, my other half." Instead, she contented herself with the springtime morels and sent off the 936 pages of *Le Marquis de Villemer*, her latest novel.

A few days later, on May 5, 1860, Garibaldi and his Redshirts left Genoa to land in Sicily. This time, George Sand didn't suppress her enthusiasm: *Evviva Garibaldi!*[324] She dedicated her essay *War, La Guerre* to Italy and the hostilities with Austria, the central issues of the day. The Franco-Sardinian victories in Magenta and Solferino had paved the way for the Zurich treaty in July 1859. But the issue of Italian unification was far from resolved. And it provided a new subject to argue about with the perpetually skeptical Solange: George, like all republicans, followed with feverish interest Garibaldi's landing in Marsala, the conquest of Palermo, and the Redshirts' entry into Naples. Eventually, Garibaldi would give up his march to Rome in October 1861.

At fifty years of age, George dreaded falling ill and not being able to write; signing contracts in early October 1860 with Buloz and Lévy was of great relief to her. Meanwhile, Manceau's brother, Emile, after a fourteen-year-long absence, had unexpectedly arrived from Valpararaso to Nohant in June. The "Zindien" shared his drawings from Haiti and Chile with the ever-curious George Sand, regaling them with stories of his journey to the Marquesas Islands. This shy lad of thirty-five, with but a few pennies in his pocket, was looking for a job. Like Manceau, he could draw well and had dexterous hands, but little practice. As his brother explained to Aucante, he would be satisfied with simple jobs: wooden facsimile reductions or ink on stone tablets. Maurice recommended him to his publisher, Bouju. George approached Adolphe Joanne, the publisher of the famous guidebooks. Two years later, she would try to help Emile gain entry as a designer at the Sèvres factory. Sevres did not hire the young man.

It was a rainy summer, but that didn't prevent "the stronger sex, the brave and intelligent sex"[325]—meaning women, of course—from bathing in the freezing river. The house overflowed with guests well into autumn. Play after play ran at the Grand Théâtre. Manceau acted, directed, and handled the scenic design. George wrote the plays and took care of the costumes. She also split her time between card and board games with her guests, lawn bowling, botany, mineralogy, and pruning her garden, where she wasn't afraid to get her hands dirty with her groundskeeper to chop down branches with the billhook. And she wrote, of course. She still owed *Journal of Two Worlds* three novels per year! Where did this woman, who had become portly with age (even if she bragged of being the same "circumference" as the year before), find the energy? Perhaps in the passion she found in everything she did. As she explained to François Buloz, she didn't know how to stop learning once she found her source material. But this nonstop activity had its price: migraines, exhaustion, rheumatism, stomach problems, and nausea.

Overnight, on Sunday, October 28, 1860, she came down with a high fever and became delirious, and was diagnosed with typhoid fever. Poor Manceau was beside himself with worry. He moved into her room to watch over her day and night. Trousseau had identified this as a bacterial infection. Today, she would be treated with antibiotics and rehydrated intravenously, but the nineteenth century didn't have these resources. One after the other, doctors came to care for the patient, prescribing fever-lowering baths, quinine, herbal teas, mustard-based poultices. Borie and Lambert sent a professor of medicine from Paris—who charged 1,000 francs for a pointless consultation. George Sand hovered between life and death for several days. On November 5, her sturdy constitution finally pulled her out. It took several weeks for her to recover strength and start writing again, much to the chagrin of her friends and family. She had overworked herself, but she protested: "Nothing of the sort. I was going on vacation enjoying myself, I lived like a true peasant from Auvergne."[326] She started a new novel on December 20. Still quite fragile, she began a new novel and suffered a relapse. She eased her stomach pain with opium. "To sum it up," Alexandre Manceau concluded on New Year's Eve, 1860, "terrible year for health, huge literary successes, awful weather, zero harvest."[327]

The doctors encouraged her to stay in Midi. The idea of a trip south excited Manceau. As George wrote on the night before their departure, he was "like a chestnut on an open fire: jumping, snapping, catching on fire, and setting everything else on fire around him. He's doing the books, paying people, climbing upstairs and down, talking and shouting, exhausting himself, and he doesn't grumble." They took the road to Tamaris with Marie Caillaud, passing close to La Seyne-sur-Mer in Var. After meeting Maurice, they remained in Tamaris from February 19 to May 28, 1861. They had rented a remote house with a magnificent view that dominated the valley. The countryside was ravishing, but the rugged climate of Var, with its mistral, torrential downpours, and blistering heat made daily life difficult. George Sand hadn't fully recovered. She still suffered bouts of nausea, abdominal pain, fever, and joint pain. Barely leaving the house during the first month, she took advantage of the situation to correct the proofs of *Valvèdre*, which she had to send to Buloz. While Manceau waited for his engraving tools to arrive, he fished for oysters and octopus from a barge, lying flat on his stomach. He was still coughing, though, and had little appetite. Despite everything, the trip would prompt at least one Sand novel, *Tamaris*, whose main character, a doctor, extolled the therapeutic virtues of that region.

It was during this trip to Midi that she learned that she had been selected among several other candidates for the Académie Française Prize, a coveted prize which came with a sizeable sum and had never before been bestowed upon a woman. She refused to take one step towards Paris. However, as she wrote, "If the Académie awards me this prize, I will of course accept it. Despite Sainte-Beuve's high recommendation, Victor Cousin, Désiré Nisard, Prosper Mérimée, and Alfred de Vigny, the Academie would bestow the prize on Adolphe Thiers. That seemed fine with George Sand—she hadn't felt herself ready for "*their literary benediction*," as Manceau called it. Afterwards, the emperor offered her an equivalent sum to that of the Académie, at the behest of Princess Mathilde, Prince Napoléon's sister. Sand declined the offer. No one would buy her. Upon learning this, the empress suggested that the Académie could "at least" grant a seat to the greatest female novelist of their time. The world would have to wait until 1980 to see a woman, Marguerite Yourcenar, elected to the Académie française.

They were finally able to accept François Buloz's invitation to stay in Savoie by returning through the Alps. This enchanting region had only been French for a short time. A true disciple of Rousseau, she loved the mountains. It seemed that the high altitude could heal anything. She was three years from her sixtieth birthday. "My feet will not always carry me into the clouds, so I must allow myself this chance!" she wrote to her lawyer.[328] Above all, she got the chance to visit Charmettes, the house of Madame de Warens and Jean-Jacques Rousseau. After the revolution, the little cottage near Chambéry had become the site of many a literary pilgrimage and was almost worshipped, although only the ground floor was open to the public. George Sand was a Rousseauist to the core, and this was a way for her to pay homage to this writer. As she wrote in *Journal of Two Worlds*, her generation owed him a love of nature, a bliss of righteousness, a contempt for an artificial life, and a dislike of the world's vanity. Shortly after this visit, she would begin a novel (unfinished), *Rousseau's Son* (*Le Fils de Rousseau*).

"May 31, 1861, in a tropical heat. All the snow had melted around Chambéry, and Savoie was opening like a flower. This land and this precise time of year are so beautiful by themselves that, reaching the end of my pilgrimage, I had forgotten about Jean-Jacques in spite of myself. I took so much pleasure in the outside world that I didn't care any longer for where I was or where I was going. But as soon as the cottage door opened, some humid odor brought me back to the past, as if the place had remained locked up, silent, and empty, between then and now."[329] Manceau wasn't nearly as affected by the magic of the area as he was by the heat, and he succumbed to an hour-long dizzy spell. George Sand would return for another visit on June 2.

Back in Nohant a week later. Berry seemed very flat to them after Savoie. She became depressed and fell ill upon their return. For the first time in her life, she didn't seem happy to be back in Nohant. "It's incredible how quickly a sickness can destroy such a strong and lively person,"[330] wrote an astonished and irritated Manceau. George wrote about her poor Alexandre, "who forgets himself when I am sick."[331] She worried more and more over her companion's coughing fits, his loss of breath, and his fainting spells.

They both wrote in the *Diaries* that had become a form of correspondence between two people who rarely separated from each other. Their joys, complaints, teasing, worries, and concerns were all written to share things that they dared not speak aloud. "Let us try to stay young and trembling until we are old, and to believe until we are at death's door, that our lives have only just begun," wrote George to Alexandre Dumas fils.[332] A fine wish! This age of *impersonality* was also a fresh youth. There was so much to discover and learn! And besides, she was sure of this: You love better at sixty than at thirty.

Who ever said that George Sand was old?

Chapter Eighteen

"I SO LOVE MY NEW DAUGHTER"

About her daughter, Solange, Sand wrote, "The more she turns on her charm, the more I feel her claws tearing my heart, and her hatred in my life!"

What a tangled web between a mother and her daughter, between the extraordinary artist and a thirty-two-year-old woman, whose fascination had dissolved into a rivalry, her admiration into frustration, her need to be loved into despair at being pushed away. So much misunderstanding, injustice, tactlessness, intolerance, and dishonesty.

As for the father, Casimir Dudevant, what became of him? He lived in his Guillery home in Gascogne with his servant and their daughter. Maurice and Solange both paid him regular visits. He wrote them letters reminding them of his affection and sent Solange presents from his farm: melon jam, goose-leg confit, and wine by the barrel. He never lost interest in his children but played a marginal role in their lives, as often happens when couples separate. His daughter lived in fear that he would leave his entire inheritance to his illegitimate child.

Solange was the dark side of George Sand. She was a harsh, unfair, merciless, and distrustful mother, but one racked with concern whenever her daughter fell ill. Her legendarily calm demeanor vanished. George could no longer stand her daughter, plain and simple, who "kills [her] with her follies and whims."[333] Solange retorted: "My mother loves me because I am her flesh and blood, but she doesn't like me. Any instincts that we share will clash with each other. Ideas, thoughts, and appreciations differ from each other and only deepen our feud." Well said.

Solange symbolized these children who burn their wings in the glory of their star progenitors. She became a bad caricature of her mother. Married at the same age, they both separated from their husbands. Solange wanted to be free like her mother but became a woman kept by a string of rich lovers. She wanted to write, and even researched and penned two novels and assorted columns, but she had neither the talent nor the dedication for the craft. As a side note: George had forbidden her from taking "Sand" as her penname, while her son signed his work "Maurice Sand."[334]

Finally, what was probably the nail in the coffin for George Sand: After Nini's death, Solange converted to Catholicism, professing her own faith as fervently as her mother was preaching anticlericalism. She loved fashion, parties, social events, and luxury. This stunning brunette whirled from the arms of one dance partner to the next, from ball to high-society ball. She expanded her own web of contacts. She was constantly looking for herself and losing herself, superficial and clairvoyant at the same time.

Early on, her husband, Jean-Baptiste Clésinger drew her with lowered eyes, hair pulled back, dressed in a sensible dark blouse with a white collar.[335] At twenty-three, she has all the traits of a young girl, with her round eyes framed with thick lashes, her long nose, and her mouth lined with a half-smile. Taken side by side, the two portraits seem to tell the whole story of Solange's personality: Underneath the mask of a woman, drunk on the ease of her success, lives a little girl, as unloved as she had always been. She never bloomed mentally, and it turned against her and everyone around her. Over the years, Solange had developed a hard outer shell of skepticism, slander, irony, and, admittedly, malice, even downright nastiness. George Sand was always on her guard and tried hard not to wake up the demon inside Solange, but often she could not help but provoke it.

Solange lived extravagantly and required endless sums of money. Her husband gave her an allowance, as did both of her parents, although she would accuse each one of the contrary. After her mother's death, she would pressure her brother to pull a large part of George Sand's correspondence from editors. But while she lived, George would do what she could to ensure that her progeny could sustain her lifestyle. "Live frugally, or learn to work,"[336] she wrote, exasperated. She especially hated when Solange shrugged off responsibility for her actions onto others and used her trials and tribulations and past sufferings as an excuse to act however she wanted. "When did unhappiness suddenly become an excuse for depravity?"[367] George wondered. She had her doubts but wasn't cynical. Solange fairly boasted about "sinning" with the first man who would come along, just for fun, collecting one lover after another. But this had nothing to do with her mother's version of freedom justified through love. She couldn't stand such a twisted copy of her own behavior. That was how Solange spoiled her life and the lives of others. "When you finally believe in yourself, then I, too, will believe in you," George concluded, before adding, "Oh, if you loved me, you would also love yourself! Instead, look how you are killing us softly, both of us, so slowly."[338] An interesting interpretation, which could also be reversed. This biting letter cut directly to her daughter's core: "You never truly loved me. In fact, you often openly despised me,"[339] George accused.

One can't help but hear the echo of George's relationship with her own mother in these accusations, and the suffering, which could even manifest itself physically. "I'm sick from writing you all of this. My liver has swollen to the size of a head as this gulf widens between us." This comparison explains a lot about her hepatic complaints. She was very in tune with her body's language, but not with her subconscious—for good reason!

The idea that Solange was considering moving near Nohant was something George Sand was fighting as hard as she could. Did she fear that her daughter's many lovers would reflect badly on her? Solange's visit to Nohant in 1856, accompanied by her lover at the time, Lord Alfred Seymour, had been a bad experience. Then, there was her affair with Count Carlo Alfieri, a Parliament Deputy in Turin. A known libertine and ladies' man, married to the niece of Cavour, this Italian count was the love of Solange's life. She took countless trips to Italy to visit him. She also had liaisons with Wacyf Azmy, an Egyptian pasha who was smitten with French culture. This high magistrate for Joint Courts would remain one of Solange's closest friends until his death. There were also the intimate relations she was suspected of having with her lawyer. If that was not enough, Solange chose a male servant instead of a chambermaid. Of course, George was shocked by her daughter's behavior. Her own adventures, she persuaded herself, were radically different, in that they were at least sincere. Was she moralizing? Not that George Sand had become absorbed into the bourgeoisie. But she was older now, and she lived in the country. She wanted to avoid rumors and the negative effects of Solange's flings.

But she went even further, calling Solange's lifestyle a life of "prostitution." One that was inconceivable and unsupportable without the modest supplementary income from her mother. "She is a paid and kept woman,"[340] George wrote to Charles Poncy, the former mason and poet who had become secretary of the Chamber of Commerce in Toulon. "I do not condone prostitution, and I will no longer have anything to do with a person who takes that path."[341]

During the 1860s, Solange lived in a charming little apartment on the rue Taibout, where she received once or twice a week. The journalist Henry Fouquier reported on her literary salons in an article for *La Liberté* on November 7, 1899. There, one could find the future Third Republic: Gambetta, Jules Ferry, even Charles Cros. Very few women, though—flattery had little place in Solange's parlor. She claimed to welcome all male respects paid without any ulterior motives, reserving her real charms for her lovers. "Still, the lady of the house, in spite of her slightly rough edges, is a well-proportioned, seductive woman," added Fouquier. This was around the same time when Solange would meet both her Egyptian admirer and the sumptuous Khalil-Bey, the Ottoman ambassador. The latter was famous for his extravagance and was often found in Juliette Adam's salon.[342] Solange would have a villa built for herself on the Côte d'Azur a few years later, which she would quickly tire of. ...

George Sand dreaded her daughter's proximity. The possibility hung threateningly over her life. "I respect her freedom. If only she would respect mine!"[343] It seems to be more a question of survival than morals. Solange blurred the clearly drawn lines in Nohant and disturbed the balance of work, nature, and friends, all of which allowed George Sand to live and write. Maurice and Manceau belonged to this universe; the latter had figured out not only how to integrate himself seamlessly, how to oil the hinges and make the entire place run more smoothly. Solange threw a monkey wrench into the organization. She didn't follow the rules and didn't play the game, both literally and figuratively. She had slipped out of her mother's power and become uncontrollable. Not only did she not belong in their world but she endangered that world. All George wished for was freedom and a relatively tranquil life that would allow her to practice her art. Solange would reignite conflict, the worst possible threat to this writer who had spent her entire life avoiding it—maybe because she had been its hostage since childhood.

But she also didn't appreciate her daughter associating with their mutual friends, as if they belonged to her. So close to Ernest Périgois (oh, if only she had married such a man, Solange sighed, her life would have been so different!), to Charles Poncy, who had done the renovations on her Midi house. She stayed in contact with Emile Aucante and Eugène Lambert, the painter. Did George just not trust her, or was she a bit jealous, as rumor suggested? Shades of her daughter's role in the Chopin debacle.

Until that moment, Solange had taken two trips home each year, one in the summer and the other for the New Year. But now, in September 1861, she wanted to rent a house in the area. George Sand formally forbade her from making the move and resisted another trip planned for Nohant in the fall. She was expecting friends, she wrote, those towards whom her daughter had expressed the greatest aversion: among others, Alexandre Dumas fils.

This harsh letter, explicitly excluding her daughter, led to a two-year-long quarrel. Taking the hint, Solange replied with dignity and retreated into a long silence. George would write her letters in vain, but she would not receive a single reply except a quick note at New Year's.

A few months later, Solange fell seriously ill, suffering from hemorrhages. At first, her mother treated the news lightly. She often experienced the same illness, "which has only one necessary remedy: the opposite of what is happening."[344] Solange had suffered through several miscarriages, whether accidental or not. At any rate, George Sand never took her complaints seriously, no more than her depression or suicidal threats. Solange was always putting on *airs*. Yet she was still suffering from hemorrhages two months later, which Doctor Guérin, a "female malady" specialist, had not been able to cure. News reached Sand, indirectly, who immediately started paying for Solange's doctor fees, pharmacy bills, and childcare costs. Solange, for her part, was spreading rumors that she would end up in the hospital, the poor's last resort! When Emile Aucante wrote to George, trying to intercede on Solange's behalf, George Sand became furious, responding: "Finally, she sees how she is punished for her sins, and she is furious. She won't even write me a simple *thank you* for all the sacrifices I make for her, none of that matters. She continues to rant and rave about me, calling me the *monstrous mother* to her little friends."[345] Later, a telling Freudian slip: "You say that we should feel worry for her. No! The more we care for her and spoil her, the more she screams."[346] Worry instead of sorry. That says it all about George Sand's feelings.

What is she *worried* about? Maybe being a "monstrous mother," she who preaches goodness and family love. The sentence was passed with no chance for appeal: She will be punished for her sins. Really! This, coming from the one who relentlessly defended women's freedom and who herself had gone through a string of lovers! George Sand's enemies accused her of being exactly what Solange so blatantly modeled. In such a self-righteous century, a virtuous childhood leading to marriage and motherhood would have expunged her of all sins. But here was Solange, chasing men and clamoring that she would end up in the hospital like the lowest of the low!

All this made the lady of Nohant shudder, convincing her that Solange was doing everything to attack her. She stopped naming her daughter in her letters, writing instead "her" or "one." "One dreams up I don't even know what to torment me, as if it was my fault that one had taken ill and become bored."[347] She started writing directly to Doctor Guérin, who reported only an "effusion of blood in the lower abdomen," and she thanked him for giving her news of [*her*] *poor invalid*. Three months later, Solange was still bedridden and still losing blood. The doctors planned to treat her with leeches in her uterus. She would take ten months to recover from the diagnosed metritis. In the meantime, she asked her friends to stop giving news of her to her mother. Both Manceau and, in the end, George herself tried to see her when they visited Paris in March 1862. They found the door closed to them.

In trying to analyze the facts of this rift, one needs to concurrently consider the violence of this mother-daughter story, the consequential suffering on both sides, in spite of their joint justification. George Sand hounded their mutual friends for details, as Solange didn't hesitate to tell every single person her side of the story. Sand saw her daughter's spoiled life as "some form of suicide, hastened along by everything she does."[348] But she would still not budge an inch on the distance.[349] George Sand's renowned "mother hen instinct" had given up with her daughter. How could Solange not have felt abandoned?

Around the same time, George Sand gave Alexandre Dumas fils a humorous explanation for her mother hen tendencies. "That doesn't prevent me from my mother hen instincts, and whenever I think about it, I cry *cluck cluck*, which means come here, come back, my little chickadees, look out for that hawk! I don't know what else to do or think when I hear you cheeping out of sight in the underbrush."[350] Yes, Dumas *fils*, the son, whom she thought of as her own child. He called her "my dear Mama."

The thirty-seven-year-old was a successful author, and the bastard child of Alexandre Dumas père and Marie-Catherine Labay, a seamstress across the hall. His entire childhood had been affected by his illegitimacy. His parents hadn't legally recognized him until he was seven, and they continued to fight over custody of the boy until his father's eventual victory. Alexandre resented him for a long time and suffered from the abnormal character of "this big boy I had when I was very small," as he described him. The son worked for his father at first and made a few tentative attempts before finding fame from the theatrical adaptation of his novel *La Dame aux camélias* in 1852. It had been inspired by his affair with a courtesan, Marie Duplessis. His play was received with a thunder of applause, a shower of flowers, and a great deal of emotions.

Abandoned women, courtesans, and bastard children constituted Alexandre Dumas fils's focus for most of his plays as well as a strong defense for the normal family life, something he had so lacked as a child. He launched realist theater with a social message, *Half-World* (*Le Demi-monde*). His anxious nature, his depressive and hypochondriac tendencies, and his gentleness earned him first George Sand's friendship then her maternal affection. This solidly built, mustachioed man, an illegitimate child with mulato origins, with his bright eyes, frizzy hair, touched her very much.

He came into her life at the time Maurice was away. Bouli had crossed the Mediterranean Sea to journey through Algeria. She had become Maurice's "widow" (her word). He subsequently had accepted Prince Napoléon's invitation to join him on a long voyage to America. The thirty-eight-year-old boy had, of course, asked his Mama's permission, which she had granted with a broken heart. He was gone for five months, an eternity for George. She put on a brave face so as not to ruin his fun, but anxiety gnawed at her. Maurice's letters home came irregularly, even though the poor boy tried to write her every day.

It was the longest she would ever have to be separated from him. Quite the shock for this woman, who had lived close to her son and was a friend of his for years. They had taken trips together with Manceau and had lived in such intimacy that the two men's roles of son and lover might have been confused. Was Manceau the substitute for her too beloved son? Did she encourage the rivalry between two people dearest to her? How could these two very different men live in such proximity without butting heads? Their trip to Tamaris had undoubtedly smothered Maurice, who felt the need to get away for a while, like he had done previously, after Italy. Prince Napoléon's invitation couldn't have come at a better time.

Manceau tried to make up for the absence, bending over backwards to distract George with jokes, slaving away to create new plays at the Grand Théâtre, caring for Maurice's caterpillars (although, in truth, he had always been the one taking care of them) and his collections and, finally, his mother! Maurice's prolonged absence thrust the engraver center stage and bestowed him with added responsibilities. She sung Manceau's praises to her new substitute son, the other Alexandre: "He is all love and devotion! I swear, it is the last twelve years I have spent with him, each day from morning to night, that has given me back my faith in humanity."[351] This gratitude went hand in hand with her kindness. Dumas fils was about to adapt her *Le Marquis de Villemer* for the stage. In her correspondence with him, she made a passing remark about her own mortality but instructed Dumas not to mention anything about it in his response. Manceau read her mail alongside with her and hated the very idea. For the same reason, she hid her concerns about Solange from him, and he too seemed to do the same vis-à-vis her. They protected each other. Obviously, Maurice's absence only strengthened their bonds and cast Manceau in the lead role at Nohant: the master of the house. For a time, anyway.

They were hosts to many guests during the summer and fall of 1861, despite which George Sand found time to create four plays! A few months later, something entirely new occurred to her: She ran out of ideas and had trouble starting another novel. In order to find her "literary I" again, she made herself reread a couple of her old books in an effort to find their strengths and their faults. And just like that, the creative machine came back to life "like a river that runs without really knowing what it could reflect upon becoming still."[352]

Alexandre Dumas fils arrived for the first time as guest to Nohant with his companion, Princess Nadia Naryschkine, a "siren with green eyes." Their daughter, Colette, had been born a year earlier and had not yet officially been recognized, since the princess was still married. Alexandre returned for a second visit to Nohant a few weeks later, with Charles Marchal, a thirty-six-year-old painter. This overgrown child with bohemian humor won George Sand over. A later photo would show him with a paunch and a satisfied air. George Sand found him extremely funny and called him her dear heart, her old rogue, her baby. Marchal would live there for two months, paying his way in portraits of the lady of the house, her companion, her son, her maid, everyone. Letters to her latest infatuation show an immediate and joyful friendship between the two. Purely platonic. In her letters, we see her sometimes bawdy humor and a familiar tone. Marchal made her laugh and took her mind off things.

Meanwhile, the prodigal son had returned! His mother helped him to organize the notes he had made during his long journey. Together, they turned these notes into a book called *Six Thousand Quick Leagues* (*Six milles lieues à toute vapeur*), which Maurice signed. It was for her an opportunity to learn and reflect on American democracy, which she had previously treated quite severely. As she pointed out, Americans kept the "Liberty, Equality" part of the French motto but forgot about fraternity. At that time, she was concerned by the clerical party's progress, the "cockroaches."[353] [*sic*]. She wrote to Prince Napoleon, "I'd rather live with your friends the Hurons than with the odor of the sacristy."

George Sand's letter on March 31, 1862, to Lina Calamatta, her future daughter-in-law, became the talk of the town. That's right: Maurice, almost forty years old, had finally decided to marry! His mother would pen this exquisite epithalamium: "My dear Lina, happiness will come, *trust in him*, and trust in us. The sole thing in life is to love and be loved. There are two of us who will have no other thought and no other aim than to love and cherish you. ... Thus come to us, darling girl, and be welcomed." Note the "us"! Its echo would come later, after Lina's mother-in-law had passed away, and she would remark, "Oh, I truly married George Sand more than Maurice Sand, and I became his wife because in fact, I adored her."[354]

George Sand's vast correspondence had over the years contained countless references to finding Maurice a wife. She had asked every single friend and relative for help. Two promising projects had been undertaken, and failed, in the months leading up to the marriage. The families of the region with young girls to marry off weren't exactly lining up, though. In spite of her fame, George Sand was a scandalous woman, who lived with a companion and stirred up incendiary ideas. But Nini's memory haunted her, and she had all but given up hope of ever seeing grandchildren playing on Nohant's lawn. Maurice was a compulsive bachelor, and he didn't seem too pressured to change his comfortable life.

Lazy Bouli typified the gifted dilettante. He was driven by neither fear nor ambition. Perhaps, reasoned George Sand, it was his inner happiness and calm, the absence of any suffering in his life, that prevented him from becoming a great artist despite his talent and originality. He could have become a caricaturist, judging by sketches from his youth and his love of marionettes, but he lacked dedication for the difficult path of a Daumier or a Philipon. He lived a comfortable existence between Paris and Nohant, both free and sheltered, with his marionettes, his drawings, the caterpillar and rock collections that Manceau cared for, and the theater in which the engraver served as actor, director, and stage manager. He had a curious mind and the same excellent taste in art and natural sciences as his mother. He liked to travel. Plenty of actresses and seamstresses were his mistresses. The allowance from his parents plus a small income was all he needed. And of course, his mother's love and adoration completed his full contentment.

With such a fulfilled life, why marry?

To make his mother happy. Lina, the daughter of Sand's old friend Luigi Calamata, an Italian painter and engraver, also a republican, had enchanted both George Sand and Maurice. A follower of Ingres's, Calamata had separated from his wife, herself an artist and the granddaughter of the sculptor Houdon. He taught art in Milan, where he lived with his daughter, Marcelline, or "Lina." She wasn't even twenty. There was Maurice, with his protruding belly and graying hair, marrying Lina, almost twice her age. According to George Sand, she and her son had been considering the idea for three years, ever since Lina and her father had visited in September 1859. Maurice had seen her again in Paris, and then the Calamattas had spent two more days at Nohant in Maurice's absence. The son had made his decision in the middle of virgin American forests, proposed by post, and marriage negotiations had been made. After a short hesitation, father and daughter accepted.

Maurice "had the calm, satisfied air of *solid men*. His mother was beside herself with joy. To her, Lina combined all of the best qualities. It was not a marriage of money or convenience but one of love. And most importantly, Maurice would not fall prey to his new wife or in-laws. "The child is a pure-blooded little Roman, black as black, *nera nera*, like the song says. She is sweet and true, slender and adorable, with frizzy hair, a charming voice, and a classic face."[355] This girl was made to please George Sand: Italian but not religious, a forward-thinking patriot (a republican, basically), musically inclined, and overall a lively and joyful person. The mother-in-law-to-be spread the news far and wide, writing over sixty letters. "My new daughter is a sweetheart."[356] She would not waver from this position and would always get along well with Lina. Maurice's wife would now become her "true daughter."

The former daughter, Solange, no longer welcomed her brother into her house and would not receive an invitation to the wedding. She would find out about the marriage in the newspaper.

Once the financial arrangements and negotiations had been settled with the future in-laws—George would give part of her estate to Maurice, neglecting Solange along the way—they started planning the ceremony. As usual, Manceau was put in charge of updating the future couple's quarters at Nohant, including the installation of the most modern bathroom. They would move into the master bedroom on the ground floor, where young Aurore de Saxe had slept, then her husband, Casimir and George Sand, then their children, before being reserved later for most important guests. The adjoining powder room had once allowed George Sand, the newly married Aurore, to sneak through a hidden door at night and meet the handsome Jules Sandeau, while their friends stood watch outside in the park.

In the meantime, Manceau's health was declining, and George Sand called his doctor. He coughed constantly and was easily tired by his feverish state. Doctor Darchy seemed optimistic and prescribed him baths, iron, and ammonia tonics, as well as Fowler's solution, a strong mixture containing potassium arsenic that was used to treat equine emphysema. But George didn't trust the doctor's diagnosis— he said it was just a simple bronchial problem, nothing to worry about. "If one of us has to be sick, I would much prefer that *it would be* me, as I've had my fair share of time."[357] In a few days, Manceau would turn forty-five, on May 3, 1862.

This was a time for celebrating! George put the finishing touches to petite Lina's wedding dress (nearly a dwarf, was Solange's description, with her usual kindness). They signed the license in the presence of their lawyers, with Manceau as their witness. The next day, May 17, was a beautifully sunny Saturday. Freshly cut white flowers were gathered for the bouquets, and George Sand herself plaited the bridal wreath. Lina made an adorable bride. One could have mistaken her for a young girl ready for her first communion! The civil ceremony took place at four o'clock in the afternoon in the flower-laden dining room in the presence of Luigi Calamatta and a few friends. The doors were flung open. The servants wore their best clothes, and even the laborers, outside in their working clothes, attended the event. Manceau wore white gloves and a fine hat. Lina suppressed a few giggles at the deputy mayor's voice, but Maurice remained solemn. There would be no religious ceremony, of course, which was against the wishes of Lina's maternal relatives. The instant they uttered the last "I do," the room exploded in laughter and tears and embraces. "God with us," cried an overjoyed George Sand. "I so love my new daughter!"[358]

The next day, they celebrated a formal wedding dinner with fourteen of their close friends, with only the latest fashion in crinoline gowns permitted! Each woman's dress required three table settings, Manceau remarked. The table sagged under sumptuous desserts, and servants ceremoniously served each course instead of setting the dishes on the table to be passed, as was the house's custom. The only element out of place among all the fruit confits was a sad-looking boiled fish, noted Manceau, with his eye for incongruous details.

The engraver finally completed his work on a painting by Louis Matour, an engraving that had given him much difficulty. He hadn't coughed at night for a few days. Their doctor friend Gustave Papet, who had once cared for Frédéric Chopin in Nohant, after examining Manceau, found nothing serious and prescribed only exercise. An easy remedy, as the engraver rarely stood still! As for Lina, she "awoke bright and early, laughing and dancing." The marriage looked to be a success. The weather was perfect. Manceau was working on a new commission (which would be his last), Horace Vernet's *Le Zouave blessé*, and George Sand had started a new novel. *Mademoiselle La Quintinie* would be an "unmasking," radical novel, a role reversal from Octave Feuillet's devout romance in *The Story of Sibylle* (*Histoire de Sibylle*). Here, the pious heroine would marry a freethinker, who would snatch her from the clutches of her confessor. The book's success made her the anticlerical movement's figurehead.

They celebrated Lina's twentieth birthday at the end of June and George Sand's fifty-eighth the following week. Casimir Dudevant was recovering from a stroke, and the children made plans to visit him. There were also talks about an outing to the "Villa Manceau" in Gargilesse and about more workshops in the Grand Théâtre. The family was together again (except for Solange, of course). Summer in Nohant would be wonderful.

Chapter Nineteen

"LET US DEPART, MY OLD FRIEND, LET US LEAVE"

A mere few months after the wedding, young Madame Maurice was expecting. George Sand was beside herself with excitement! Almost ten years after Jeanne's death, Sand witnessed the birth of her grandson on July 14, 1863. "He is big and strong, and he looked at me with a conscious and attentive gaze when I held him in my apron. I feel like we already know each other, and he seemed to want to say, 'Oh, it's you!'"[359] The midwife dunked the newborn in a warm wine bath, where he wriggled around—she would become a permanent fixture in the house. Then, he was given to his mother to nurse. On this anniversary of the taking of the Bastille, as well as for George Sand's birthday, cannons were shot and songs were sung. Maurice wept. All was well.

"As for the grandmother, she is overjoyed. I see her smile, and that makes me happy," reported Manceau, deeply moved.[360] Letters streamed out of Nohant, heralding the news: "It's a boy!" They gave

François-*Marc*-Antoine Dudevant the legal last name of Sand and the nickname of Cocoton. George Sand had fathered a dynasty! She was never at a loss for advice for the young couple, and the entire family's lives revolved around the baby. Even "Manceau is taking the week-old kid for a walk in the garden and giving him his first entomology lesson. We've told him that it's a bit early for that!"[361] The weather was nice and warm, and Cocoton, rolling around naked on a blanket, "loved to show his bottom to the world."[362] Maurice became a veritable father hen and cared expertly for his son. He proved himself "a great nanny and an excellent *diaper-warmer*," as his mother wrote to Victor Borie, who was himself a new father. Times had changed. "In these years, many people have taken up the mantle of paternity. ... It's like a show about yourself, an exhibitionist production. In short, we are now fathers whereas we were once *citizens*, almost a century ago: with great fanfare," wrote the Goncourt brothers, who knew nothing of the wholesome joys of paternity.[363]

They fussed over Cocoton's first smile (so named after Lina's own pet name, Cocote) and fawned over his first tooth. His proud grandmother found him especially alert, happy, intelligent, and precocious. Drawing from her own rich experience (she had nursed both her children, a true disciple of *Emile*), she was full of praise for Lina's nursing skills. She worried over the slightest sign of colic in the child and the wine that he was given to calm him down in the evenings, and understandably so. Broth was fine, so was cow's milk, but wine, at six months old? Surely it would be better to avoid exciting him by playing so close to his bedtime and to give him calming oatmeal or tilleul baths.

Of the four childhood friends—Maurice, Victor Borie, Eugène Lambert, and Manceau—only one remained unmarried. Despite his continual coughs, fevers, and fatigue, Manceau continued to devote himself, body and soul, to the woman of his dreams. But his physical ups and downs, his energy and hyperactivity and grumblings and joys, his swings from exhaustion to overexcitement made George Sand more anxious than she'd have liked to admit. He didn't know how to slow down. He wouldn't follow his prescribed diet, munching instead on peppers and gherkins. He was suffering. George shared her concerns with Manceau's cousin, Louis Maillard, a former engineer, who had returned from the Ile Bourbon with his wife and two adopted children.[364] Maillard loved botany and was as kind as his cousin— and equally worried about his health. Sand would update him with news about Manceau and try to reassure him, "He's so lively!" she wrote. Manceau, for his part, read her Pushkin and immersed himself completely in the theater of Nohant, as usual, "as if nothing was the matter."[365] He started writing poetry again, reawakening bygone pleasures, even spending entire evenings writing while others played cards and talked. One April evening, he read the play he had recently finished to George Sand. She was moved to tears.

Those tears no doubt sparked Maurice's jealousy. He had never fully accepted the love between his mother and his former friend. Manceau's position in Nohant had become intolerable. The same thing had happened years earlier with Chopin, who had suffered the incessant "nitpicking" from the son of the household.[366] But Maurice had been a young man then, and Chopin a genius. According to many, the beloved son's attitude as well as the incriminating role of Solange were key in the musician's departure. Maurice's lengthy stays in Paris had left a place wide open for Manceau. But the marriage and his son's birth had reinforced his new role: master of the house. Granted, he still didn't pay anything and did no work around the house, so the running of the household was left to his mother and Manceau. To avoid any false situation, the latter had paid a sum of 1,200 francs per year and, according to George Sand, had poured his income back into Nohant for years.[367]

It was perfectly normal for two generations to live together in the same house, but the tension in Nohant kept building. Had Maurice's four months surrounded by aristocracy on Prince Napoléon's yacht given him delusions of grandeur? Manceau felt his disdain. "It's so easy to tire of one's old friends," Manceau wrote bitterly. "They become unpleasant to the eye, like old clothes."[368] The rivalry between the two men was becoming more and more apparent. Maurice had recently turned forty. The little boy of ten, whose mother had been stolen away by a lover named Musset, was ravaged by jealousy, which the ever-present Manceau only exacerbated. For years, his only well-formed drawings had been reworked by the engraver. Manceau had also cared for and added to Maurice's butterfly collection. He had redone the workshop, and his abundant energy was the sole reason why the theater—Maurice's new passion, which had replaced marionettes—still existed. Manceau had been responsible for making the theater run smoothly. This was what Maurice had predicted from his very first caricatures! He himself had introduced the wolf into the fold. Now, his former friend had taken charge over everything.

Manceau had not only taken over Maurice's passions but he had snatched away the love of his life, his mother. Manceau had replaced him. From then on, Manceau and George Sand's relationship would pervade everything. Manceau was not only her secretary, manager, confidant, and lover but he had become her best friend, a lifelong companion. He was part of the *family*, as George highlighted at the end of her letters to Prince Napoléon. And what's worse, he was encroaching into the world of writing, that sacred ground, which Maurice, much like his sister, had started to claim as his birthright. Maurice had made sporadic efforts in writing, for which Mama supplied the story, editing, and corrections—or simply rewrote the entire thing. As he was trying to send his work to publishers and theater directors, they were outdone by Manceau's new composition, a play in verse.

This was the final straw. Manceau's writing! Fromentin, Dumas, and Gautier had enjoyed his play, and the entire clan at Nohant had lauded him. Worse, it had even moved his mother to tears. At first, Maurice only criticized Manceau for "absorbing himself *in his literature*." "One act in fourteen years! What dedication!" the new playwright replied sarcastically.[369]

The house would be filled for the entire summer with guests, such as "young" Alexandre, Théophile Gautier and Charles Marchal, Louis Maillard, the actress Marie Lambert, the Fleurys (former Nohant boarders), and Eugène "Lambrouche" Lambert and his young wife (who would stay until January). Maurice was away at Guillery, visiting his father during Gautier's brief visit. Théo, as they called him, had once appeared on the front lines of the battle in *Hernani*, in his long hair, black beard, cape, and red waistcoat. He had already confirmed his distance from sentimental and social romanticism in his 1835 preface to *Mademoiselle Maupin*. "There is nothing truly beautiful except that which serves no purpose; everything useful is ugly," reads his creed, which lays the path to Parnassianism. His 1852 anthology, *Enamels and Cameos* (*Emaux et camées*), was praised by the likes of Baudelaire, Leconte de Lisle, Bancille, and Flaubert. His ideas were the exact opposite of what George Sand touted as a writer's mission, but he was a major presence in the artistic world and a good friend of Alexandre Dumas fils. She even visited him in Neuilly at his little house on the rue de Longchamp, where he lived with his companion, Ernesta Grisi, his daughters, and his cats . . . whose stench would follow George Sand down the street.

The Goncourt brothers were kind enough to provide a record of Gautier's visit: as somber as a Moravian monastery, breakfast at ten o'clock with a half-asleep George Sand, sexual prudence, Marchal's farts and dirty jokes, boules in the garden, dinner at six o'clock, hours of mineralogy, and of course, Manceau's unwavering care for his companion, fulfilling her every desire.[370]

Gautier's letter to Ernesta Grisi describes his visit: "My dear Nini, I've arrived safe and sound at Nohant, where I have received the most gracious welcome. Marchal and the young Dumas are also here. This place seems very isolated, even though it's just along the edge of the road. The small chateau is very pretty, with ivy climbing up its old gray walls within a large enclosure, part park, part garden. Everything is fairly unkempt, but only enough to provide charm. My room is large and very practical, with a nice bed, a dressing table, and everything I'd ever need. Today, I watched the game of boules and took a very relaxing walk among the trees, which I needed, as I was still tired from the parties. Madame Sand is the picture of tranquility. She rolls her cigarettes, smokes, and remains mostly silent, for she works until three or four o'clock in the morning every night and then is half-asleep until noon or one, when she starts to wake up and laughs at Dumas' jokes, although it takes her a while to understand them. It's quite impossible to be the best woman and the best guy at the same time."[371]

For this visit, Manceau served as master of the house, keeping Théophile Gautier company and talking with him. After writing the first act of *Le Marquis de Villemer*, a new play adapted from his novel, Dumas fils was helping George Sand with the framework. He also gave Manceau advice on his play, *Marceline*, which would become *A Day in Dresde (Une journée à Dresde)*. (Marceline was Lina's name . . .

At the end of October, La Rounat, Odéon's director, announced that he would produce Manceau's play at his theater. He also attended the four-hour-long reading of *Villemer*. Everyone crammed into the hall except Maurice. Both plays—first Manceau's, then George Sand's—would play at the Odéon within the year. Manceau was proud and overjoyed. And as for Maurice, his jealousy found no bounds.

He was known to have temper tantrums. "He's not my brother," Solange wrote to Emile Aucante, "he's a wet blanket. He can only really get mad once or twice per year, enough for an awkward and violent outburst."[372]

No one knows what set Maurice off so badly this time. Was it Marie Caillaud's refusal to follow Manceau's stage directions during the rehearsals for *Datura fastuosa*?[373] Her success on the intimate stage may have gone to her head, as well as her liaisons with the journalist and playwright Edouard Cadol, who had spent several months at Nohant. Manceau had already caused tears with a joke a few weeks prior, and Maurice had taken her side. Finally, the two men's rivalry came to a head. Maurice went to his mother and demanded that she choose between him and Manceau, as he had done with Chopin. True to form, George likely hemmed and hawed, and agreed with Bouli, trying to calm him down. He returned to Manceau triumphant and laid out his instructions.

Sickened, Manceau's shaking hand recorded the tone and content of Maurice's "awkward and violent outburst" in the *Diaries* on Monday, November 23, 1863. "After I don't know what conversation, I was informed to depart on June 24, at the next St. Jean's—a catholic, national holiday. It didn't take long. That was all, after fifteen years of devotion. I'd like to record it here so I shed no tears over it, and I hope to be smiling about it later. No matter. Humanity saddens me. I will go off and be free again, and if I so choose to love someone and devote myself to that person again, loving being my great joy in life, I will be free to do so."[374]

Maurice humiliated his former friend by dismissing him at midsummer, like a hired hand coming to the end of his contract. Manceau's sadness and decimated dignity was confronted by Maurice's stubborn hatred. After his mother's death, he would continue by scribbling mountains of notes in the margins of the *Diaries*:

[boxed] reread *Tartuffe*! Maurice

Tartuffe, that hypocrite who slid his way into Orgon's good graces to embezzle the family fortune. Worse than a simple rivalry, this had become classist contempt manifested as a servant's dismissal. What a completely unfair suspicion of motive, considering Manceau's generosity and honesty! This was no mere tantrum but a deep grudge rooted in years of brooding. Maurice's annotations to the *Diaries* proved it. George Sand's son would also censor every single reference to Alexandre Manceau in the first edition of *Correspondence*, published twenty years later. His instructions were so strict that they would even be respected after his own death. This may be the reason why the engraver's role in George Sand's life has been ignored for so long.[375]

But after a night of reflection and tears, George Sand responded to her companion via the *Diaries*: "I am not sad, and you know why? Because we knew all of this, we knew it was going badly. Because I, too, will go off and be free again. Because we will not part from each other; and because this change may be for the better; and because I was hoping for any such change in this bitter and unjust life. Therefore, let us take leave from one another, my old friend, without bitterness, without rancor. We will never part from each other. Let them keep everything, everything except our dignity. We will not sacrifice our friendship, NEVER EVER," (which was double-underlined in her hand).[376]

George Sand had a man for whom she was prepared to leave Maurice, *her* son. It would be difficult to find a greater proof of her love. In one night, she showed her companion all of her attachment to him and gratitude for fourteen years of devotion.

One week later, Manceau left for Paris. George was beset by nightmares, dreaming of being "sentenced to death without knowing why." He returned after a few days. "Tonight my brave, valiant Mancel returned, he is well, in spite of so much running around, so much cold and heat and readings and sleeplessness. Everything is well again."[377]

The end-of-year festivities were marked by sadness and futile arguments. Despite the truffle partridges, petit pois, meringues, candy, and embracing, New Year's Eve was spent without joy.

The crisis averted, the house fell into a calm but dreary state. George learned how to cook macaroni and gnocchi, and sewed costumes for the marionettes. Lina doted on her child. In January, George left with Manceau for Paris. She told everyone who asked that she had wanted to live more freely for a while, to relieve herself of the too-heavy burden of Nohant, which had been placed entirely on her own shoulders. But news travels fast in the countryside. Marie des Poules, the chambermaid, couldn't help but tell her own version of the story. She "rummaged through my wastepaper basket and snooped in my diary—go away," wrote a furious George Sand. To the questions about a suspected falling out, she reaffirmed that her entire family got along perfectly well. In fact, nothing in her almost daily letters to her son and daughter-in-law, in the presents she sent, in the showered affection, would have given the slightest hint of a disagreement. Each missive even included "best wishes from Manceau" at the end.

The couple took advantage of their visit to Paris to sit for Nadar. The famous photographer was the obvious choice for the portraits that George Sand's admirers requested of her. Born Félix Tournachon, Nadar was a former journalist and caricaturist, a fervent republican, and a long-time admirer of George Sand. His talent had already been fully recognized. In 1852, Richebourg had taken an early daguerreotype of the novelist, but the results were so catastrophic that she asked him (in vain) to destroy the negatives. Now, she arrived with Manceu at the photography studio at 35, boulevard des Capucines. Every wall of the building, inside and out, was painted red, and Nadar's glowing signature was lit by gas on the outside. Nadar himself was a large man, dressed in a red blouse, with fiery red hair and mustache. He squired them into the salon, where they would pose, taking turns. (He would later photograph Manceau at age forty-seven, withered away by the tuberculosis that would eventually take his life.) Mancea proved to be a poor model, according to Sand. Posing must have been difficult for an active man, living in someone's shadow. The photographs are quite touching. Wearing a frock coat and a silk cravat, Manceau has a serious, almost worried expression, with a wide forehead, wrinkles, and overall, a profound look. The opposite effect emanated from George Sand, with her thick, curly hair styled with a band of silk, her large brown eyes, and full lips: an astounding expression of dignity, goodness, and serenity. But that day, even she suffered coughing fits while modeling. The photographer took many shots, and Sand and Manceau would keep many series of negatives, including the famous portraits in her striped outfit, and set of amusing shots with her in a Molière-style curly wig. "Manceau can't look more handsome than I do, and we keep singing, *Oh, too bad if Nadar is ill!*"[378] The pictures were retouched with care, and she would be satisfied with the end result. George Sand would finally be able to send her photograph to everyone who had requested it, especially to Armand Barbes and Victor Hugo who had remained in self-exile.

A Day in Dresde premiered on January 13, 1864, at the Odéon. Its 2,000 verses reflected Manceau's admiration for the Napoleonic era. A French health officer imprisoned at Dresde falls in love with a young widow, Marceline, the jailer's stepdaughter.[379] He wins her love over a Saxon rival and is freed after the green French army's victory at Lützen in 1813. Love, honor, glory, and country! George didn't hesitate to tell Maurice of Manceau's great success. All their friends attended, along with every last one of the critics. Prince Napoleon sat in the box reserved for authors, overlooking Manceau who sat down with the musicians. Applause rang out. Prince

Napoléon loved the play and the performance, and shouted his praise across the house to Manceau. The author, suffering from stage fright, had come down with a bad cold and showed little enthusiasm for his own play—contrary to a few weeks later, at the opening of his lady's play, where he showed great admiration.

March 1, 1864: *Le Marquis de Villemer's* premiere explodes into the theatrical event of the season. Students start camping outside the Odéon at ten in the morning and storm over police barriers into the theater. Shouts, cries, and applause drown out the actors. The huzza-men are utterly overwhelmed. It's a full house, 3,000 to 4,000 people had to be turned away. The imperial family can't stop clapping, the emperor weeps without shame, even Flaubert is in tears. Prince Napoleon loudly yells his enthusiasm. It is a complete triumph. George Sand is swamped by two hundred people congratulating her in the lobby. The students escort her all the way back to her apartment, crying: "Long live George Sand! Long live *Mademoiselle La Quintinie*! Down with the clergy!" It will take all night for the police to break up the demonstrations.

The anticlerical protests were all the more surprising in that nothing in the play makes any reference to the subject. A strong melo-drama, with love triumphing over social prejudices, whose first act had been infused with Dumas fils' brilliance. It tells the story of two brothers. One is introverted, serious, and very close to his mother, and he refuses to marry. Eventually, he ends up marrying a young, virtuous, upright lady-in-waiting. The other brother is a forty-year-old libertine, amiable and witty, who marries an heiress fresh out of a convent. The characters were well designed, the plot had a good pace, and the entire play glowed with George Sand's aura. Every performance would be a triumph. The box office took in incredible receipts. The Odéon, once considered "grubby, deserted, and far away," had over-night been transformed with luxurious carriages cramming into the back alleys around the theater. Elegant ladies would be seen standing in line for tickets at the box office every morning.[380] Now, it was lit up and full every night!

Sand had recently read Ernest Renan's *Life of Jesus* (*Vie de Jésus*), which described the Nazarene as a simple human being. *Le Marquis de Villemer* crystalized George Sand's anticlerical opposition—after *Mademoiselle La Quintinie*, she had once and for all become the movement's champion. Her success had made her even more hostile to Catholicism. She could not accept Jesus' divinity, or their version of hell, or confession, and as for abstinence? "Abstinence! From what? Imbeciles. Abstain from what is bad, for all of your days. Did God make good things for us to deprive ourselves of them? Abstain from feeling the warm sun on your face and from watching the lilacs bloom."[381] With her staunch anticlerical parrion, she was constantly denouncing the Church's hypocrisy and intolerance.

When Maurice and Lina decided to have a religious wedding and baptize their son, for pure respect of social convention, they chose Protestantism. George insisted on a liberal minister. After carrying on lengthy discussions with the cream of the Protestant crop, she agreed to be the child's godmother. Jules Boucoiran, Maurice's tutor in 1829 and a journalist for the *Courrier du Gard*, would be the godfather.

Maurice and Lina's marriage and baptism reunited the family in Nohant. It also set the course for her future with Manceau.

Originally, the couple had considered staying at Gargilesse on the Creuse river. But the village was much too far away from Paris' theaters. Thus, they decided to move just outside of Paris and keep a pied-à-terre in the capital. They left their expensive double apartment on the rue Racine in favor of a terrace apartment at 97, rue des Feuillantines (now 90, rue Claude-Bernard). Thanks to Manceau's cousin, Louis Maillard, who had a residence in Palaiseau, they found a house there, with a garden. It was a charming location, one hour by rail from the Gare de Sceaux (now the Gare de Denfert-Rochereau). Manceau rented the house in his name and took charge of the renovations and the ordering of new furniture. Despite his fatigue, he also handled the move to the new apartment in Paris and supervised the twelve crates shipped from Nohant.

Later, thanks to earnings from the sale of a Delacroix's engraving, purchased by Edourad Rodrigues, they would purchase the Palaiseau house outright, in Manceau's name. Delacroix's reputation had soared, and his art was much in demand. Maurice would benefit from the sale of all the other Delacroix paintings in Nohant, except *Giaour's Confession* (*La Confession de Giaour*), the painter's first present to them, and *Centaur* (*Centaure*), which his mother wanted to keep. George also proposed that her son and his wife take in Nohant's revenues, against their assuming its upkeep.

But panic seized Maurice and Lina. How could they take responsibility for Nohant and live there alone, without Mama? They refused and planned to move to Paris, to George's delight. The family would almost be completely reunited. However, unable to find anything to their liking, they stayed in Nohant. To all those in Nohant who deplored her moving away, George wrote endless explanations about how happy she was. But her departure turned the Vallée Noire upside down. There were countless letters from laborers in La Châtre, letters of thanks and farewells. Old Monsieur Aulard, the former mayor of the commune, cried.

George Sand was reveling in her newfound freedom and independence. This departure from Nohant possibly made her recall her youth, a time when she had negotiated with Casimir Dudevant the right to spend six months of the year in Paris. First she left the father, now the son. And once again, she avoided any quarrel. The only regret for her was the thought of not seeing her grandson as often. Cocoton had now four teeth and had started gnawing on bread crusts. He could almost say "Daddy."

Packing had begun. The sun peeped through to the garden in between rain showers. On Saturday evening, June 11, 1864, Lina offered a brief after-dinner recital in her sweet, dulcet voice. Alexandre Manceau wrote the following:

"LAST NIGHT IN NOHANT

"It was a night to remember, for all of us. There is nothing left for me to write about this final evening. And yet, I can't help but think that in the fourteen years I have spent here, I have laughed more, cried more, and lived more than I did in the thirty-three years that preceded this.

"From here on, I will be alone with her. What a responsibility! What an honor! What joy!"[382]

They would leave, as Maurice had wished, at midsummer.

Alexandre Manceau and George Sand slept in Palaiseau for the first time on Sunday the 12th. "I adore absolutely *everything*," wrote George, "the countryside, the little garden, the view, the house, the furniture, the dining room, the maid, the silence. It's enchanting. My good Mancel has thought of everything. It's perfect!"[25]

She would celebrate her sixtieth birthday two weeks later. A new life had begun.

Chapter Twenty

"YOUR PART WILL NEVER DIE"

his new life started in a new house, a "picture of comfort and cleanliness."[384] The ground floor consisted of the foyer, kitchen, butlery, dining room, and a small parlor. Upstairs were two bedrooms, a washroom, and an office; the third floor had two more bedrooms and the maid's quarters. The slate roof, a tree-lined garden, and a pond—"a green platter with a diamond in the center." Furthest from the village, their house sat in the middle of the countryside. Like a candy box, it was a home straight out of a Ruysdael landscape.[385] The new environment enchanted George, just as the house at Gargilesse had. She loved the river, the fields of wheat and roses, the prairies and gardens and fruit trees as far as the eye could see, the woods and hills. She hadn't expected such gorgeous countryside to exist so close to Paris, with wildflowers lining the paths: lilies, violets, wild hyacinth, comfrey in pink and blue, and wild broom. The soil was rich and fertile, the people friendly, and an absolute calm pervaded everything. Unlike nearby, at Bois de Verriere, there were no Parisians strolling on Sundays, no dandies and their lady friends frolicking. Pure tranquility reigned here, in the little paradise she shared with the man who had become her official companion. She was truly sharing her life with another for the first time in her existence.

Manceau had barely finished setting up the whole place and her office when George Sand got back to work. They lived close enough to Paris to visit as often as they liked and receive city friends in their own home: their jack-of-all-trades cousin, Louis Maillard, Dumas fils, Marchal, and the Lamberts were frequent guests. George also liked their three-room apartment on the rue des Feuillantines. Her taste for Oriental knick-knacks shone through—although Nadar found the apartment to be overly decorated—fit for youthful romantics.

Everything was going well. An unsettling note, however, appeared in the *Diaries* about ten days after their arrival. "Manceau was coughing up a little bit of blood, but I'm sure it's nothing."[386] George's commentary was not necessarily reliable. Aware that Manceau read the *Diaries*, she was obviously sparing him her concern. "Manceau's health is not bad." The official diagnosis was bronchitis. Consumption, though, was the scourge of the century (the term "tuberculosis" hadn't entered the lexicon yet), the romantic malady which had become known as the "white plague."[387] No one mentioned it, but everyone knew it was fatal. It killed one in four people in the whole of Europe during the nineteenth century, before anyone had discovered how it spread. Medicine of the time was powerless to treat it or prevent it. In 1819, however, Laennec's work had made it possible to diagnose the disease through a stethoscope examination. Doctor Camille Leclère, a specialist in pulmonary diseases who had recently completed a thesis on lung perforations, had most likely recognized the symptoms when he started caring for Manceau. He might have shared his findings with her. At any rate, it's highly unlikely that George Sand, who had lived through nine years of Frédéric Chopin's disease, would not have recognized the sad truth. There was only one possible treatment at the time, the "healing water" from the Pyrenees, said to be beneficial for illnesses of the chest. Manceau drank the water.

George herself had adopted a meatless diet in an effort to ease her own gastrointestinal problems; the diet centered around *ReValesciere Dubarry*, a miracle flour made with grains and dried vegetables, which she mixed with lemon to taste. She remained active, taking walks and working on her novel *A Young Girl's Confession (La Confession d'une jeune fille)*. As this new stage of her life began, she had burned all of her failed and abandoned manuscripts while Manceau organized the rest of her papers. Nothing like a move to oblige one to tidy up one's affairs.

Maurice and Lina had planned to visit Casimir Dudevant in Guillery to introduce him to his grandson. They packed baby carriage, hats to protect him from the sun, and, his grandma hoped, "something for a clyster in case he overheats." The baby was fussy and colicky. He had also started teething, which often made him cranky.

Tuesday, July 5, 1864: George Sand celebrates her sixtieth birthday, under a brilliant blue sky. She receives a card from Bouli that very morning, Manceau gives her a beautiful bouquet of flowers, and the painter Eugène Lambert and his wife spend the afternoon with them at Palaiseau. A nice walk precedes a hearty feast.

A few days later, she received terrible news: Cocoton was suffering from dysentery. Absolutely no fruit, none, advised George, suggesting instead starch baths and infusions of poppy buds. But the local doctor had prescribed rhubarb and purgatives. Manceau tried to soothe her worries, but George was racked with concern. She asked Guillaume Maillard, the lawyer, to send a telegram to Nérac. Casimir's house was in the middle of the country, and they couldn't spare any horses, servants, or peasants. A telegram was the only way to contact. Distance made her anxiety worse. She barely slept. News arrived at staggered intervals. "No change" or "better." Gripped by panic, Sand sent letter after letter, telegram after telegram. Every day, she stood watch impatiently for the six-o'clock mail. On July 13, she wrote: "No updates on the baby today. I have fallen into the depths of despair. I dare not hope, but still I seek news."[388]

Cocoton's first birthday passed gloomily on July 14. George could do nothing. She dreamed of being with him, watch over the baby, support Maurice and Lina. An encouraging telegram from Maurice came at six o'clock: "Better, have hope." The improvement continued for the next few days, and she started to breathe again. Eugène Fromentin, who had written the novels *A Summer in the Sahara* (*Un été au Sahara*) and *Dominique* that she had so admired, paid them a visit between two downpours.

But on Tuesday, July 19, the news crashed in just as they were sitting for dinner. "Much worse, little hope," the telegram said. The child was dying. "Come if you want to see him," Maurice advised. Manceau and Sand threw their things together and hurried to the train station. The train to Paris ran late, and they missed the connection for Orléans by less than five minutes. They were forced to wait for the train to Bordeaux at 7:30 in the evening the following day. On Wednesday the 20th, they arrived at Orléans at midnight, accompanied by Doctor Leclère. They reached Agen the next day at 10:40 AM, and took the mail coach to Guillery, arriving at two o'clock. The baby had passed away at one o'clock in the morning. They were received by a distraught Maurice; by Casimir and Jeanne Dalias, his housekeeper and mistress; and finally by Lina.

George Sand tried her best to comfort her son and his wife, while Alexandre Manceau helped the doctor and Marie Caillaud with the final preparations for the coffin. "The child is all cleaned up. The sad, ornate little corpse is a very sad sight to see," wrote Manceau. Eternally devoted, he spent the night in Nérac to alert the minister, send telegrams, and order coaches. The funeral was held the next day in the parlor. Manceau accompanied Maurice to bury the body in the family vault, the resting place of Casimir's father and Solange's first little girl, who had also died at Guillery.[389] Manceau wrote with a heavy hand and a broken heart, "Maurice even cries while eating." George Sand saw her husband for the last time, with the family united, past wounds forgotten. They helped Maurice and Lina pack their trunks before seeing them off to seek refuge in Nîmes, with Jules Boucoiran, who had been Cocoton's godfather. George and her companion then got back on the road for Paris.

Both were terribly shaken. George Sand kept working on her novel, but her mind wandered. Manceau worked on casting *Drac*, a play from Nohant that had been performed at the Théâtre de Vaudeville, but he was exhausted. He took a day trip to Paris for her while she waited at home, restless.[390] "I am antsy. Dining alone is not fun. I've walked through the entire garden, it takes about 800 paces." George Sand could never bear being alone. Now, it was harder than ever. "You should never again wish me a happy birthday," she wrote to her cousin, Augustine de Bertholdi. "The poor child fell fatally ill on July 5."[391] She cried herself to sleep every night.

Manceau signed the official papers to buy the house in Palaiseau on August 5, 1864, for 26,000 francs.[392] Ownership of the house was in his name for reasons that became clear later. He exhausted himself renovating the house, overseeing masons and laborers. Despite his coughing and choking, he went out in the garden with the workers in the rain as they test-drilled the soil to find a water source to feed to the pond. Then the chimneys started smoking, and they had to be torn out and redone. More problems. The cook left suddenly and had to be replaced. They installed a state-of-the-art sink into the kitchen, but the house was a worksite, open to the wind and rain, and covered in dust. Manceau encouraged George to avoid the house for a few days. His devotion did not preclude a certain amount of masochism. He hadn't thought this one through very carefully, though. George decided to spend a week in Gargilesse with Marchal, the painter. Manceau made a sober entry in the diary on September 13: "Maillard and I drove Madame Sand to the train station. She was absolutely charming and intended to tease Marchal to no end. We bid each other farewell exactly as if she were leaving for the Bois de Boulogne. Now, it is 10 o'clock. Madame will undoubtedly continue the entries."

Therein lies so much sorrow.

Madame, in fact, made no entry in the diary during her entire stay at Gargilesse. The entries would only reappear in Manceau's hand on the 21st. George spent a night in Nohant on the way to a three-day stay in Gargilesse with "big Marchal" before returning through Nohant once more. While at the little house in Gargilesse, she wandered along the banks of the Creuse and climbed among the rocky crags, despite September rainstorms. "But, you might ask, why such an escapade to Gargilesse?" she wrote to Charles Duvernet, her longtime friend in Coudray. Good question, and one that has been posed by every one of her biographers. Everyone sees ample evidence of infidelity, her first and only towards Manceau. The silence in the *Diaries*. The cozy accommodations, three small adjoining rooms.[393] Her occasional liaisons with Marchal after Manceau's death. Everything supports this theory. And yet . . . It's true that they may have become familiar with each other. Any more than that, though, is highly unlikely. Not because of qualms about the adulterous writings or simply trusting in George Sand's morality, when she figured out long ago how to paint herself in an advantageous light within an ambiguous situation, but because if this affair happened, everyone would be forced to admit that she was cynical, on top of everything else. This hardly seems in line with her character. In fact, she spoke openly of this "escapade" with Maurice and Lina, Charles Duvernet, and Edouard Rodrigues, not to mention the countless servants in Nohant, including the always-charming Marie Caillaud. It seems much more plausible that she needed a bit of space to breathe, a respite from the weight of her grandson's death and dealing with Manceau's illness every day. As she wrote later, she needed to "forget everything with big Marchal. You look into this joyful man's eyes, and you forget all else."[394]

But the end result was the same: Manceau was made to suffer. His imagination ran wild. And therein, it seems, lied the infidelity. There was another man in his own house, a house he bought specifically for her, where they had spent such wonderful times together, a house he would never see again. But this betrayal, for which he had given his permission, would be the last. He awaited their arrival on the train platform. George saw how gaunt his face looked after just a week's absence, how terribly his illness was progressing. She would never again leave his side, not even for a day. They exchanged not a word on the matter. Marchal would visit both of them again the next Saturday.

Manceau and Sand were present for the rehearsals of *Drac* at the Vaudeville and attended its premiere on September 28. The play was not a huge success, but Manceau didn't feel that his reputation had suffered for it. And wasn't that what truly mattered?

Manceau filed his last will and testament with the Palaiseau notary on November 1, 1864. He and Sand had spent hours discussing its terms, and they had finally put everything in order. Then, the new year started with a chimney fire. Nothing serious, but the house was icy cold for a while. George Sand took sick with a cold and chills. "Without her cheer, without her smile, nothing else matters," Manceau wrote that January. George Sand herself could have said exactly the same thing about him.

The renovations took all winter. They spent their days planting the garden, and their nights taking refuge in Manceau's studio, where it was warm. George struggled with publishers, theater directors, and critics to convince them of her son's talent, that they could trust him. Maurice had seemingly abandoned his painting and marionettes in favor of literature. After *Masks and Clowns*, *Six Thousand Quick Leagues*, and *Callirhoe*, he dove into a new novel, *Raoul de la Chastre*. George was overjoyed at his lengthy stay in the Parisian hotel, and even if she didn't see him as often as she would have liked, she showered him with tons of advice. She asked Sainte-Beuve for help with Maurice's novelwriting, "Throughout my entire life, this has been the nearest and dearest thing to my heart."[395] That's the best that could be said. When Buloz turned the book down—a book she considered to be a masterpiece—she nearly flew into a rage. "He is enormously talented. He's more: He is a genius,"[396] she wrote. She worked endlessly to reassure Maurice, to encourage him, to push him. He was the love and the greatest concern of her life. This is undoubtedly why Maurice would only ever be but an overgrown child: talented but jealous and without focus. "Be a man," George would entreat without realizing that she was standing in his way.

As for George herself, now that *A Young Girl's Confession* was complete, she was thinking of adapting *Mont-Revêche* for the theater. But since she hated rereading her work, Manceau took it upon himself to retell her the story! Her main concern was not to imitate the novel too much. They worked on it together: She created the outline while he developed the scenes. Manceau was thus promoted to collaborator. After his death, Maurice would take over (oh, the irony), but the play would never see the light of day.

Manceau was not one to hold a grudge. He gave theater directors his support for Maurice's play, *The Brabant Woman* (*La Brabançonne*), which the latter had adapted from his novel with his mother's help.

But other sad news was yet to befall them at the end of January. Louis Maillard, the cousin, whom Manceau was deeply fond of, suddenly contracted peritonitis and passed away within two days. It rocked both of them to their cores. He had been their neighbor both on the rue des Feuillantines and in Palaiseau, and they had seen him almost every day. Louis Maillard had fulfilled countless little tasks for them, always selfless, obliging, and completely at their service. Once again, Manceau undertook the dreary funeral arrangements. A shattered George Sand wrote an eulogy to be read at the cemetery during his civil burial. Maillard had been a dear friend to many; Alexandre Dumas fils, Eugene Lambert, Victor Borie, Emile Aucante, and all their other friends were in attendance. The Society of Saint-Simon, an organization Maillard had belonged to, gathered contributions for his widow and their two children to move back to Bourbon Island. Sadly, Louis' wife died of consumption less than one month after her husband.

This new period of mourning must have had a terrible effect on Manceau's health and spirits. "I have a good and faithful companion at my side," wrote George Sand to Edouard Rodrigues. "We speak of friends who have gone and those who still remain."[397] Winter would not end, it rained or snowed constantly, the roads had turned to slush, and George avoided bringing Manceau to Paris as much as she could. Each journey by train worsened his condition and exhausted him. They mostly stayed cooped up in their house. She tried to convince herself that the late spring, whenever it came, would bring a change for the better. Until then, they worked together on *Montrêveche*, she wrote a story entitled *La Coupe* for Buloz's journal, and started working on a new novel.[398] News from Maurice and Lina came too infrequently for her taste, even though they lived in Paris, at 16, rue de Bruxelles. "My dear children, I'm starting to believe that you have forgotten that I exist. I haven't heard a word from you in so many days!" She needed so desperately to be comforted, to regain strength. She cried out for help, even from them.

She no longer hid the truth from her friends. "Just between you and I, my poor Manceau has had a rough winter, and I myself have had terribly depressing days. … I dare not leave his side, not even for a day. His condition is not worrying at the moment, but he is concerned and is becoming depressed. What I have written you *must not leave this letter*."[399] Such was the plea to everyone: Above all else, keep up appearances. Such was the constant refrain to her friends, her son, her daughter-in-law, everyone.

But was Manceau fooled? For this time, his pain was great enough to wretch cries of despair from his pen: "For goodness sake, I am sick as a dog. I can't breathe anymore!"[400] He oversaw the work being done in the garden in spite of the cold and snow, and wrote, "We're dead tired, but we'll finish it!"[401] and "I'm half dead,"[402] and "I'm quite useless. Rough night, bad day."[403] He couldn't stand that his own weakness restricted his activity. The slightest gesture was a struggle. A simple walk in the garden drained all of his energy. This man, who for so long had served others, ached to feel so useless, and saw his frailty as a failure. What else was he good for? On April 22, he managed to drag himself to Paris to deliver an urgent letter to Maurice when his father sold his property in Guillery. He only found Lina at home; Maurice had reportedly gone to his mother's. He returned the same day to Palaiseau, utterly exhausted. No Maurice.

He had little faith in doctors, and only begrudgingly put up with their treatments. First, carbolic acid. Then, on Doctor Demarquay's recommendation, a balloon of oxygen to help him breathe. Manceau's appetite diminished, he became anemic and irritable, and fell into depression. On May 3, the disillusioned man wrote: "Today is my birthday. It could be my last. What do you think, O Lord?" He had turned forty-eight. He suffered from exhaustion, his incessant cough, sometimes with blood, the daily bouts of fever, the shivers and sweaty shakes, shortness of breath, and an insurmountable weariness in every single limb. He felt a muted anger against himself, against his utter helplessness in the face of such an illness. Sometimes the anger would just fade into a deep melancholy.

Every doctor gave the same unconvincing diagnosis: nothing but an infection of the bronchial tubes.

But in those days, one did not disclose the truth of such matters to one's friends and family. "I've come to fear the effect that all the medications have on him. I no longer place either my hope or my trust in anything," wrote George Sand to Doctor Darchy, the local doctor. Manceau had reached a phase where he tried treatment after treatment without any change.

Thus, George's confession: "I will remain strong, but my heart is dying."[404]

She suffered just as much from her companion's suffering, always alert for his coughing attacks, always gauging his strength for a walk in the garden on nice days. On his good days, they worked on *Montrêveche*. George read the beginning of her new novel, *Monsieur Sylvestre*, to him. He wept.

But then, there were the days, the long nights of coughing attacks, practically hacking up a lung. "This afternoon, I seemed to cough up my very bowels and innards, my abdomen seized up completely."[405] The coughing fits could last for hours. The Boutets, their new neighbors (Andre Boutet was George Sand's business manager), checked up on him every day. When Manceau and George were alone in the evenings, she darned socks while they played chess. "Here I am, glued to my chair. How nice."[406] He had recently been prescribed iron iodide, Málaga wine, and cinchona for his anemia. "Apparently, I'm doing quite well," Manceau wrote bitingly. "I'm rolling with laughter."[407]

By the beginning of May, they were running out of options. They tried a treatment prescribed by Raspail's *Manual* as a last resort. The liquid sedatives, smoking, and camphor rubs managed to relieve a bit of his pain. Prince Napoléon had even offered to send them his personal physician, but George demurred so as not to upset Manceau. "I'm sleeping fairly well," wrote Manceau one day. "I could be doing very nicely without all the sweating." It was June 6, 1865. Those words were the last Manceau would write in the *Diaries*, which he had kept since 1852. He could no longer find strength to write.

From then on, George Sand herself kept up the accounts. It became a nightly summary of Manceau's close-quarters combat with his pain, of his everlasting agony, of their intimacy. She knew that he read her writing. She devoted entire pages to him, making a special note of the smallest improvement: a horse-and-cart ride under the warm June sun, a bit of appetite, a stroll in the garden, reading out loud without coughing, a joke to make her laugh, a little song. One day, even a small pas de deux in his studio. She tried to encourage him without actually denying that his illness existed, which would offend him. Most of the time, though, she had no choice but to record the slow but steady decline of his health. She rarely left him alone, always listening for his coughing attacks when he could no longer get out of bed, constantly checking his pulse to monitor his fever. She worked while he rested during the day. "I can't do a single blessed thing,"[408] she moaned. And yet, she still managed to write a review of *Story of Caesar* (*Histoire de César*), written by Napoléon III. She worked through her discouragement, her exasperation, even her anger. "I just keep crying, which solves nothing. He takes everything out on me: his health not improving, his doctors not taking it seriously, everything."[409] She blamed herself for not having the power to care for him, for being so depressed that she couldn't raise his spirits. She couldn't sleep, couldn't live.

Just when things seemed like they couldn't get any worse, George took a nasty fall on the front steps and seriously injured her leg. She was confined to a chair and hated it. Manceau was trying a new treatment based on raw meat and ice-water rubs. George had asked Doctor Fuster himself, the pioneer of this treatment, to come from Montpellier to care for the patient. Manceau screamed in pain during the treatment, but the doctor insisted that she continue, even to the point of him hating her. "My poor child! This massage makes him scream. It breaks my heart. I just want to kill myself, but I must not. I must care for him and save him from himself." But her martyrdom proved useless for them both. She tried to trick Manceau by projecting outward optimism, but her letters to friends revealed the truth. "The prognosis is disheartening. There is only one thing you can do, as our friends, which is to show that you're keeping up your spirits."[410] She kept Lina and Maurice, who had returned to Nohant for good, regularly updated, though the news was a little toned down, and she kept up the ruse of a summer visit to Nohant.

She lived the daily life of all those who care for an invalid: hushed conversations, her companion's extreme weakness and irritability, her own powerlessness and guilt. Her world was restricted to their little house. Her leg was taking more than a month to heal, but the physical pain it caused was almost a balm for her grief. At times, she would be gripped with sob-racking despair. She felt her love for him and saw the loss which was to come. "He is my strength and my life. His physical weakness is my emotional weakness."[411]

She spoke of him and his illness in almost all of her letters. She had help from their neighbors, the Boutets, and their former landlady, Madame Bordin, who visited them every day. Their presence was priceless in every sense of the word. Maurice wasn't coming to visit. And still, George spent her last scrap of energy to rewrite the very poor novel he had recently finished.

Manceau and George took their last few steps together in the garden at the end of July. He gave her his arm. Two days later, they sat together in the vegetable patch for half an hour. The weather was glorious. He wanted to laugh in joy and managed the ghost of a chuckle, just for her. After few days, though, he had no strength left, not even to get out of bed. George tiptoed up the stairs six times that evening to make sure he was still breathing. In the morning, he shuffled to her room and sat in her armchair while she remade his bed. Then, he went back to sleep. He had stopped eating. He would not get out of bed again. He was very weak but calm and quiet.

On Sunday, August 20, George made an entry in the *Diaries*, knowing that, for the first time, Manceau would not read it. She had known the truth for a month but had done everything in her power to hide it from him. Manceau was going to die. He slept, blind with an oppressive fever. He was fading fast. Around midnight, he opened his eyes and told George he wanted to go to Nohant. It was their last night.

Alexandre Manceau passed away at six o'clock in the morning on Monday, August 21, 1865. He mumbled a few nonsensical words, struggled once more for breath, and fell silent. George Sand sat at his side. She changed his clothes and arranged him on the bed. She closed his eyes. She laid fresh roses on him. His face had softened, regaining its youth and beauty.

Their friends rushed from Paris to surround her: Dumas, Marchal, Fromentin, and La Rounat, the director at the Odéon. Manceau's sister, Laure, arrived but did not want to see him, afraid of being too disturbed by the sight of him. His mother, however, didn't make the journey, because he had not received his last rites.

Night fell, and friends departed. The house fell silent. The second night of the vigil began. George thought of Alexandre. "Such a lively man, so impassioned, and now he seems carved of marble!"[412]At times, she thought she heard him coughing. She was spent, but did not feel tired. "Alone now, and him, here beside me, in this little room. I can't listen to his breathing anymore, and tomorrow night there will be nothing more, I will be even more alone. Now and forever."[413]

The next day was Wednesday, and they buried Alexandre Manceau in the Palaiseau cemetery. George Sand had chosen his final resting place carefully. Felix Nadar and George Villot, Prince Napoléon's personal orderly, laid him out in his coffin. George had sent for a surgeon to confirm his death with an incision—she had such a fear of being buried alive. She had only invited thirty people, but sixty came. Maurice was finally in attendance to support his mother. Over one hundred laborers in Palaiseau came to pay their respects to the engraver, wanting to dress him in a white cloth and lay flowers on his grave. After eating dinner with Elisa and Andre Boutet, George returned to her house alone. She sat down at her desk, opened the *Diaries*, took up her pen and dipped it in ink. "My son is a part of my very soul. I will live for him, and yes, I will love gallant souls. Yes, but you, you who loved me so much, rest easy. Your part will never die."[414]

Solange wrote a letter of condolences to her mother but never sent it. She claimed that she would have come if not for the fear of adding another pain to her mother's suffering.[415]

George Sand left for Nohant with Maurice on the following Sunday. She would rediscover the gardens and the animals, bathe in the river, and relax in the calm of the countryside. Life was sweet. Lina was expecting again. And yet, as she wrote in the *Diaries*, "I still feel like someone is waiting for me."[416].

EPILOGUE

Alexandre Manceau bequeathed his property holdings—the houses in Gargilesse and Palaiseau—to Maurice.[417] George Sand would live there for a while longer, alone with her companion's shadow. She missed him terribly, but she refused to wallow in self-pity, only letting a few hints slip out to her confidants. It broke her heart to see his empty bedroom and abandoned studio in Nohant. She had to relearn how to live alone, without his help: taking a hackney by herself, overseeing the renovations in her apartment, keeping her accounts, organizing her papers. At first, she drowned herself in evenings out at the theater. Dumas fils, Eugene Lambert, Victor Borie, and others surrounded and supported her. Charles Marchal spent one day per week at her side. She attended the literary dinners on Monday evenings at Magny's. She developed a close personal friendship with Gustave Flaubert, her "troubadour," and visited him in Croisset. Finally, in 1869, she ruefully put her little "candy box" in Palaiseau up for sale and moved back to Nohant for good. She devoted herself completely to Maurice and Lina's children, her two granddaughters, Aurore and Gabrielle.[418] Her life was far from over, and there were many joys ahead: family and friends, travel, nature, writing, and other pleasures, the constant pursuit of happiness and beauty. She would never stop celebrating all of her life. As she wrote reassuringly to Flaubert, her pessimist friend, "before long you will gradually be entering upon the happiest and most propitious part of life: old age."[419]

Alexandre Manceau was hardly as famous, as brilliant, or as talented as Alfred Musset or Frédéric Chopin, and he rarely graces the pages of memory. This devoted man, who chose to spend his years in the service of the queen of his heart, usually remains in the shadows. He adored this woman, he admired and served the artist in her. His own talent as an engraver disappeared with his death, along with his pride, his cheeky humor, his courage, his physical ability, his active life, his temper, his love, his insatiable goodness, and his secrets. Biographers allow him but a few lines. His room and studio at Nohant, where he lived for fourteen years, are forgotten. Now, he has no place set for him at the table, and his very presence has been erased.

George Sand alone retains the memory of the man who loved her in the secret corners of her heart. He had been her companion and her friend. A woman never forgets a man who was so good to her.

Ten days after Alexandre Manceau's death, she started writing a new novel. She called it *The Last Love* (*Le Dernier Amour*).

ACKNOWLEDGMENTS

My greatest thanks to Monsieur René de Obaldia, who sponsored my research at the Bibliothèque de l'Institut de France, where I was able to consult the rich collection of George Sand's works in the Lovenjoul collection.

My thanks also to the librarians and staff of the Bibliothèque de l'Institut de France, the Bibliothèque nationale, as well as the Bibliothèque historique de la Ville de Paris, where I found many documents bequeathed by Aurore Sand. All the information concerning the Guy family became available thanks to my research in the Archives de Paris.

Thanks to Chistiane Sand, who welcomed me to her house near Gargilesse, and to Christian Pirot, who showed me around the village.

Thanks to Georges Buisson, who knew how to care for Nohant so well.

Thanks to my friend Alice Kaplan for her "peer review" and our rewarding conversation.

Thanks to my daughter Lisa, who was my first reader.

Finally, special thanks to my editor, Manuel Carcassonne, and the entire team at Grasset.

TIMELINE

L isted publication dates represent the complete bound edition.
T = theater

1804

June 5: Maurice Dupin marries Antoinette Sophie Victoire Laborde
in Paris.

July 1: Amantine *Aurore* Lucile Dupin is born at 15, rue Meslay, Paris.
She would celebrate her birthday on July 5 throughout her life.

1808

April-June: The family lives in Spain, where Maurice Dupin serves as
Murat's aide-de-camp.

July 21: The Dupin family arrives in Nohant.

September 8: Young Louis Dupin dies at three months.

September 16: Maurice Dupin dies in La Châtre.

1809

Aurore's mother grants guardianship to her mother-in-law, Madame
Dupin de Francueil, in exchange for a pension.

1818

Aurore enters the convent of the Dames Augustines Anglaises in Paris as a student.

1820

She leaves the convent, returning to Nohant to live with her grandmother.

Her half-brother Hippolyte Chatiron starts teaching her to ride a horse.

1821

December 26: Her grandmother, Madame Dupin de Francueil, born Marie-Aurore de Saxe, dies. She bequeaths her entire fortune to her granddaughter, including Nohant and its grounds (200 hectares).

1822

September 17: Aurore marries Casimir Dudevant in Paris, under the dotal system.

1823

June 30: Maurice is born in Paris.

1825

Aurore meets Aurélien de Sèze, and they begin a platonic love.

1827

She leaves for Paris, where she meets her future lover Stéphane Ajasson de Grandsagne.

1828

Her tutor, Deschartes, dies.

September 13: Solange is born in Nohant.

1830

July 30: Aurore meets Jules Sandeau, seven years her junior. They
  begin an affair.

1831

January 4: As per the agreement with her husband, she leaves for Paris.
  She may live there for half of each year, and her husband will give
  her an allowance in exchange for Nohant's revenues.
December 17: *Rose et Blanche*, by J. Sand, appears in bookstores.

1832

October: She moves from 25, quai Saint-Michel, to 19, quai Malaquias.
  She changes her name to George Sand.
Indiana, Valentine

1833

March: She breaks up with Jules Sandeau.
Late June: George Sand meets Alfred de Musset.
August 5–13: Sand and Musset stay at Fontainebleau.
December 12: The couple leaves for Italy, arriving in Venice on the 31st.
Léila

1834

Early January: George Sand suffers from dysentery.
Early February: Musset contracts typhoid fever. Sand calls Doctor
  Pietro Pagello to care for him.
March 29: Musset leaves Venice for Paris.
August 14: Sand returns to Paris with Pagello.
Jacques, Le Secrétaire intime, Métella, La Marquise

1835

March 6: George Sand breaks up with Musset definitively. She flees to Nohant without a word.

April 9: She meets the lawyer Michel de Bourges.

October 19: She has a domestic dispute with Casimir Dudevant and asks for legal separation.

André, *Leone Leoni*

1836

February 1: Musset publishes *La Confession d'un enfant du siècle*.

February 16: The La Châtre courts announce the legal separation of Casimir Dudevant and his wife. A treaty is drawn up in July after an appeal. George Sand recovers her property in Nohant.

August 28: She leaves for Switzerland with her children, where she visits Franz Liszt and Marie d'Agoult.

Simon

1837

Liszt and Marie d'Agoult stay at Nohant.

Her affair with Michel de Bourges ends.

July: She has an affair with Maurice's tutor, Félicien Malefille.

August: Sophie Dupin, George Sand's mother, dies.

She has a brief affair with the actor Bocage, followed by one with the writer Charles Didier.

Lettres d'un voyageur, *Mauprat*

1838

Balzac stays at Nohant.

June: She begins an affair with the twenty-eight-year-old Frédéric Chopin.

October 18: She leaves for Majorca with Maurice, Solange, and Chopin.

December 15: They move into the Chartreuse monastery of Valldemosa.

La Dernière Aldini, Les Maîtres mosaïstes

1839

February 24: They return to France.

October 15: George Sand and Frédéric Chopin move to 16, rue Pigalle (now number 20).

Spiridon, the second *Léila, Les Sept Cordes de la lyre* (T)

1840

February: Maurice enters Delacroix's studio.

April 29: The first production of *Cosima* opens at the Théâtre-Français and fails.

May: George Sand meets the joiner Agricol Perdiguier, author of *Livre du compagnonnage*.

October: Solange enters a boarding school.

Gabriel, Pauline, Cosima ou la haine dans l'amour (T)

1841

July: She goes to trial with François Buloz, publisher of *Journal of Two Worlds*.

November: She founds *La Revue indépendante* with Pierre Leroux and Louis Viardot.

Le Compagnon du Tour de France

1842

Delacroix stays at Nohant.

September: She moves to 5, square d'Orléans, and Chopin to number 9.

Horace, Un hiver à Majorque, L'Orco

1843

Fanchette, a fifteen-year-old "simpleton," is abandoned by nuns in the countryside and found pregnant after being raped. George Sand criticizes the affair in *La Revue indépendante*.

Lettres à Marcie, Consuelo

1844

September: The first issue of *L'Eclaireur*, a local republican newspaper, appears, edited by Victor Borie and Alphonse Fleury. It supports radical ideas of education and equality, similar to those of Pierre Leroux.

La Comtesse de Rudolstadt, Jeanne

1845

Le Meunier d'Angibault

1846

March 17: George Sand gets in touch with the sculptor Clésinger.

Delacroix stays at Nohant for the last time.

"High-society theater" begins.

La Mare au diable, Isadora, Teverino

1847

January: Solange becomes engaged to Fernand de Preaulx.

February 18: George Sand and Solange visit Clésinger's studio.

April: George Sand begins writing *Histoire de ma vie*.

May 19: Solange marries Clésinger.

July 11: George Sand has a violent argument with Solange and Clésinger.

Late July: She writes her last letter to Chopin.

Le Péché de M. Antoine, Lucrezia Floriani, Le Piccinino

1848

March: George Sand arrives in Paris to take part in the political events.

March 4: She sees Chopin for the last time.

April 9: The first issue of *La Cause du peuple* is published.

May 17: She returns to Nohant.

François le Champi, Aux riches, Histoire de France écrite sous la dictée de Blaise Bonin, Lettres au peuple, Paroles de Blaise Bonin aux bons citoyens

1849

May 10: Jeanne Gabrielle "Nini" Clésinger is born in Guillery.

May 20: Marie Dorval dies.

October 17: Chopin dies.

November 23: *François le Champi* opens at the Théâtre de l'Odéon.

December 23 or 24: Alexandre Manceau arrives in Nohant at age thirty-two.

La Petite Fadette, François le Champi (T)

1850

She begins her liaison with Manceau.

Nohant welcomes many guests and hosts many plays.

Histoire du véritable Gribouille

1851

January: *Claudie* plays at the Théâtre de la Porte-Saint-Martin.

March: She signs a contract with Hetzel for a populist illustrated edition of her works.

May: *Molière* plays at the Théâtre de la Gaîté.

November: *Le Mariage de Victorine* plays at the Gymnase.

December 4: George Sand reaches Nohant after the coup d'état.

Le Château des désertes, Claudie (T), *Molière* (T), *Le mariage de Victorine* (T)

1852

January 29: George Sand is granted an audience with Napoléon III and pleads the case of many political detainees.

February: She meets Prince Napoléon.

March: *Les Vacances de Pandolphe* plays at the Théâtre du Gymnase.

August: The Clésingers separate, and Nini comes to live in Nohant.

September: *Le Démon du foyer* plays at the Gymnase.

December: The Empire is proclaimed.

Monsieur Rousset, Melchior, Les Vacances de Pandolphe (T), *Le Démon du foyer* (T)

1853

September: *Le Pressoir* plays at the Gymnase.

November: *Mauprat* plays at the Odéon.

Mont-Revêche, La Filleule, Les Maîtres sonneurs, Le Pressoir (T), *Mauprat* (T)

1854

May: Clésinger finds compromising letters.

May 26: Nini leaves the care of Nohant and is returned to her father, who places her in boarding school.

October 5: *Histoire de ma vie* starts appearing in installments in *La Presse*.

December 16: The Clésingers separate again.

Adriani, Histoire de ma vie (volumes I to IV), *Les Visions de la nuit dans la campagne, La Vallée noire, Falminio* (T)

1855

January 14: Nini dies.

March 11-May 28: George Sand travels to Italy with Maurice and Alexandre Manceau.

September: *Maître Favilla* plays at the Odéon.

Histoire de ma vie (volumes V to XX), *Maître Favilla* (T)

1856

February: *Lucie* plays at the Gymnase.

April: *Françoise* plays at the Gymnase, *As You Like It* plays at the Comédie-Française.

May 11: George Sand's handwriting changes.

October: The revival of *Claudie* plays at the Odéon.

Evenor et Leucippe, Comme il vous plaira (As You Like It) (T), *Lucie* (T), *Françoise* (T)

1857

May 2: Alfred de Musset dies.

Manceau buys the house in Gargilesse. They take frequent trips to the village.

La Daniella, Le Diable aux champs (dedicated to Alexandre Manceau)

1858

George Sand doesn't go to Paris for the whole year.

She visits Gargilesse (in Indre) often.

She reconciles with François Buloz and *Journal of Two Worlds*.

Les Beaux Messieurs de Bois-Doré, Légendes rustiques (illustrated by Maurice Sand)

1859

April: *Marguerite de Saint-Gemme* plays at the Gymnase.

May 28–June 28: She travels to Auvergne with Manceau and the actress Bérangère.

The Lemoyne affair unfolds.

Elle et Lui, *L'Homme de neige*, *Narcisse*, *Promenades autour d'un village*, *La Guerre*, *Garabaldi*, the preface for Maurice Sand's *Masques et bouffons*, *Marguerite de Saint-Gemme* (T)

1860

She stays in Gargilesse.

She signs contracts with *Journal of Two Worlds* and the editor Michel Lévy.

October: She is weakened by typhoid fever and stomach problems.

Jean de la Roche, *Constance Verrier*, *Le Marquis de Villemer*

1861

Mid-February–May: She stays in Tamaris with Maurice, Alexandre Manceau, and her chambermaid Marie Caillaud. George Sand and Manceau return through Chambéry.

The Académie française refuses to award its prize to George Sand, so the empress suggests that she be given a seat on the Académie itself.

Maurice travels to Algeria and America on Prince Napoléon's yacht.

She becomes friends with Dumas fils.

She has a falling out with Solange.

La Famille de Germandre, *Valvèdre*, *La Ville noire*

1862

March: *Le Pavé* plays at the Gymnase.

April: *Les Beaux Messieurs de Bois-Doré* plays at the Ambigu-Comique (a collaboration with Paul Meurice).

May 17: Maurice marries Lina Calamatta.

July: She stays at Gargilesse.

Autour de la table, *Souvenirs et impressions littéraires*, *Tamaris*, *Les Beaux Messieurs de Bois-Doré* (T), *Le Pavé* (T)

1863

July 14: Maurice and Lina's son, François-*Marc*-Antoine "Cocoton" Dudevant-Sand, is born.

November 23: Maurice drives Manceau from Nohant, and George Sand leaves with him.

Antonia, Mademoiselle La Quintinie, Pourquoi les femmes à l'Académie?, Les Dames vertes

1864

January 13: Alexandre Manceau's *Une journée à Dresde* plays at the Odéon.

March 1: *Le Marquis de Villemer* plays at the Odéon.

June: George Sand and Alexandre Manceau move into a villa in Palaiseau, which they eventually buy. They rent a pied-à-terre in Paris at 97, rue des Feuillantines (now 90, rue Claude-Bernard).

July 21: Marc dies in Guillery. He is one year old.

September 28: *Le Drac* plays at the Vaudeville.

Théâtre de Nohant, Le Marquis de Villemer (T), *Le Drac* (T)

1865

August 21: Alexandre Manceau dies. He leaves everything to Maurice Sand.

After a brief stay at Nohant, George Sand returns to Paris and Palaiseau.

La Confession d'une jeune fille, Laura

1866

January 10: Maurice and Lina's daughter Aurore is born.

George Sand starts attending the literary dinners at Magny's.

May: She burns her papers and organizes her manuscripts.

She travels to Bretagne with Maurice and Lina.

She stays with Flaubert in Croisset twice.

Monsieur Sylvestre, Promenades autour d'un village, Le Lys du Japon (T), *Le roi attend* (T), *Les Don Juan de village* with Maurice Sand (T)

1867

George Sand moves back to Nohant permanently, taking Manceau's old room.

Le Dernier Amour (dedicated to my friend Gustave Flaubert)

1868

She travels to the south of France.

March 11: Maurice and Lina's second daughter, Gabrielle, is born.

George Sand visits Flaubert again.

She moves to 5, rue Gay-Lussac for her stays in Paris.

Mademoiselle Merquem, Cadio (T)

1869

April: The house in Palaiseau is sold.

Flaubert spends the Christmas holidays in Nohant.

Michel Lévy publishes new editions of fifty-five titles.

La Petite Fadette (an opera with music by Théodore Semet)

1870

July 19: The war with Prussia begins.

September 4: The Empire falls, and a new Republic is proclaimed.

Paris is under siege.

Autumn: A hot air balloon named *George Sand* manages to cross
enemy lines to deliver mail to Normandy.

Malgrétout, Pierre qui roule, Le Beau Laurence, L'Autre (T)

1871

March: Casimir Dudevant dies.

March 28: The Commune is proclaimed, which George Sand condemns.

Journal d'un voyageur pendant la guerre, Césarine Dietrich

1872

She spends time in Cabourg.

Francia, Un bienfait n'est jamais perdu, Nanon

1873

Flaubert and Turgenev stay in Nohant.

She travels to Auvergne.

Impressions et souvenirs, Contes d'une grand-mère

1874

She suffers from poor health.

She works on dendrite drawings, done with paint-soaked rocks and touched up with watercolors.

She is seventy years old and writes to Flaubert, "Now I am growing old, and I'm starting to feel it."

Ma soeur Jeanne

1875

Lévy publishes a new complete edition of her works.

She visits the Corot exhibit in Paris. She signs a contract with Charles Spoelberch de Lovenjoul, which will collect a significant number of manuscripts to be kept at the Bibliothèque de l'Institut.

She writes the stories for the second volume of *Contes d'une grand-mère*.

Flamarande, Les Deux Frères

1876

She begins *Albine Fiori*.

Her health deteriorates.

June 8: She dies after suffering complications from an intestinal blockage. Her last words are "Leave the greenery."

June 10: She is buried in the family cemetery in Nohant.

Contes d'une grand-mère 2, La Tour de Percemont (the last novel to be published during her lifetime)

ENDNOTES

1. George Sand, *Story of My Life* (*Histoire de ma vie*), a group translation, edited by Thelma Jurgrau, State University Press of New York, 1991, pt. 5, chap. 2, p. 947.
2. Prosper Mérimée, *Primary Correspondence* (*Correspondence génerale*), edited and annotated by Maurice Parturier, Paris, Le Divan, 1946, vol. 5, pp. 303–304.
3. Alexis de Tocqueville, *Memories* (*Souvenirs*), Calmann-Lévy, 1893.
4. Elizabeth Barrett Browning to John Kenyon, February 15, 1852, in *The Letters of Elizabeth Barrett Browning*, edited by Frederic G. Kenyon, Macmillan, 1898, p. 56.
5. *Corr., op. cit.,* vol. 9, November 15, 1850.
6. *Story of My Life, op. cit.,* pt. 2, chap. 8, p. 376.
7. *Sketches and Hints,* May 1847, in *Autobiographical Works* (*Œuvres autobiographiques*), Gallimard, coll. Bibliothéque de la Pléiade, p. 626.
8. *Story of My Life, op. cit.,* pt. 3, chap. 9, p. 621.
9. The members of provisional government: Dupont de l'Eure, Lamartine, Alexandre Marie, Louis Garnier-Pagès, Alexandre Ledru-Rollin, François Arago, Isaac Crémieux, Louis Blanc, Ferdinand Flocon, Armand Marrast, and, the only member of the working class, Alexandre Albert.
10. "Art in 1848" in the journal *The Artist* (*L'Artiste*).
11. *Corr., op. cit.,* vol. 8, to Pauline Viardot, March 17, 1848.
12. *Corr., op. cit.,* vol. 8, to Maurice Dudevant-Sand, April 18–19, 1848.
13. *Corr., op. cit.,* vol. 8, to Maurice Dudevant-Sand, overnight, April 16–17, 1848, p. 411.
14. *Corr., op. cit.,* vol. 8, p. 423, n. 3.
15. *Corr., op. cit.,* vol. 8, to Maurice Dudevant-Sand, overnight, April 16–17, 1848, p. 411.
16. Her property in the countryside, where she was born and raised. [AMC]
17. Ibid.

18. Born in 1809, Armand Barbès was the archetype of a romantic revolutionary. Founder of several secret societies, he spent his life between conspiracy plots and prison. Sand held him in the highest regard. See Sand-Barbès, *Correspondence from a Republican Friendship (Correspondance d'une amitié républicaine)*, preface and notes by Michelle Perrot, Lectoure, Le Capucin edition, 1999.

19. Some were also elected through the supplementary election in June 1848, like Victor Hugo and Louis-Napoléon Bonaparte.

20. *Corr., op. cit.,* vol. 8, to Pierre-Jules Hetzel, July 4, 1848, p. 532.

21. In French, these are the masculine adjectives that George Sand often used when speaking of herself.

22. George Sand, *La Petite Fadette*, preface, new edition, Michel Lévy, 1869.

23. *Story of My Life, op. cit.,* pt. 4, chap. 9, p. 840.

24. Ibid., pt. 2, chap. 8, p. 376.

25. Ibid., pt. 4, chap. 13, p. 893.

26. Edmond Planchut, *At Nohant (Autour de Nohant)*, Calmann-Lévy, 1897, pp. 71–73.

27. *Story of My Life, op. cit.,* pt. 4, chap. 9, p. 840.

28. *Story of My Life, op. cit.,* pt. 5, chap. 13, p. 1104.

29. *Corr., op. cit.,* vol. 9, to Pierre-Jules Hetzel, December 29, 1849.

30. Ibid.

31. Françoise Heritier, *Masculine and Feminine: Thoughts on the Difference (Masculin-Feminin: la pensée de la différence)*, Odile Jacob, 1996.

32. *Corr., op. cit.,* vol. 9, to Pierre-Jules Hetzel, February 3, 1850.

33. *Corr., op. cit.,* vol. 9, to Pierre-Jules Hetzel, December 29, 1849.

34. *Story of My Life, op. cit.,* pt. 4, chap. 9, p. 840.

35. *Corr., op. cit.,* vol. 2, to Emile Paultre, June 25, 1834.

36. This painting can be found at the Musée de la Vie romantique, 16, rue Chaptal, 75009 Paris.

37. Edmond and Jules de Goncourt, *Journal, Memoirs of the Literary Life, 1851–1865 (Journal, Mémoires de la vie littéraire 1851–1865)*, September 14, 1863, Laffont, coll. Bouquins.

38. *Corr., op. cit.,* vol. 9, to Emmanuel Arago, January 12, 1850.

39. Ibid.

40. *Corr., op. cit.,* vol. 9, to Pierre-Jules Hetzel, February 3, 1850.

41. Ibid.

42. *Corr., op. cit.,* vol. 8, to Maurice Dudevant-Sand, March 21, 1848.

43. *Corr., op. cit.,* vol. 8, March 28, 1848.

44. *Corr., op. cit.,* vol. 9, to Pierre-Jules Hetzel, late April 1850.

45. The protaganist of Stendhal's *Le Rouge et le noir.* [AMC]

46. Ibid.

47. Edmond and Jules de Goncourt, *Journal, op. cit.,* March 30, 1862.

48. *Corr., op. cit.,* vol. 9, to Emmanuel Arago, January 12, 1850.

49. *Corr., op. cit.,* vol. 9, to Augustine de Bertholdi, January 15, 1850.

50. *Corr., op. cit.,* vol. 9, to Rozanne Bourgoing, March 21, 1850.

51. *Corr., op. cit.*, vol. 9, to Pierre-Jules Hetzel, April 15, 1850.
52. *Corr., op. cit.*, vol. 9, to Pierre Bocage, March 14, 1850.
53. *Corr., op. cit.*, vol. 9, to Lise Perdiguier, January 9, 1850.
54. *Corr., op. cit.*, vol. 9, to Pierre-Jules Hetzel, March 24, 1850.
55. *Corr., op. cit.*, vol. 9, April 15, 1850.
56. *Corr., op. cit.*, vol. 9, to Pierre-Jules Hetzel, April 20, 1850.
57. *Corr., op. cit.*, vol. 9, to Pierre-Jules Hetzel, late April 1850.
58. Ibid.
59. Ibid.
60. Ibid.
61. Ibid.
62. Ibid.
63. Ibid.
64. Ibid.
65. Ibid.
66. Ibid.
67. Anne Chevereau, *Alexandre Manceau*, Christian Pirot Editions, 2002. All details concerning Manceau's parents are drawn from this book.
68. *The Artist*, 2d ser., vol. 7, Paris, 1841, p. 381.
69. *Story of My Life, op. cit.*, pt. 5, chap. 6, p. 998.
70. *The Artist*, 2d ser., vol. 7, Paris, 1841, p. 382. "It's perfectly fair to give credit to the engraver. Monsieur Manceau used considerable skill in rendering this painting's effect, and his achievement is such that all engravers of this kind can respect it."
71. *The Artist*, vol. 8, Paris, 1841, p. 108.
72. He produced three pieces: *Battle at Fort Mackenzie, August 28, 1833* (*Fort Mackenzie, Bataille du 28 août 1833*), *Mandan Indians Bison Dance in Front of the Medicine Lodge in Mih-Toutta-Hang-Kouche* (*Danse du bision des Indiens Mandan devant la loge de médecine à Mih-Toutta-Hang-Kouche*), and *The Travelers Meet the Meunitarri Indians Near Fort Clark* (*Rencontre de voyageurs avec les Indiens Meunitarri, pres de Fort Clark*). The first two were exhibited in the Salon of 1842, and the third in 1843.
73. His engravings were inspired by Charles Mozin's *Launching a Fishing Boat* (*Lancement d'une barque de pêche*) (Salon of 1843), Guillemin's *The Fantastic Effects of the Fier-à-bras Balm* (*Les Merveilleux Effets du baume de Fier-à-bras*) based on Cervantes (1843), and *Hagar and Ishmael* (*Agar et Ismaël*) (1844) based on Murat. In 1847 and 1848, he exhibited engravings of two Dreux paintings, *War and Peace* (*La Guerre et la Paix*), alongside *Setback of 1812* (*Revers 1812*) and *Success of 1845* (*Succès 1845*) based on Philippoteaux.
74. List of Manceau's works is borrowed from Anne Chevereau, *op. cit.*
75. *Corr., op. cit.*, vol. 9, to Pierre-Jules Hetzel, July 7, 1850.
76. Ibid.
77. Ibid.

78. Baudelaire had asked George Sand to intervene on behalf of his mistress, the actress Marie Daubrun, with the Odéon's director. She did so but in vain, and he would never forgive her. See also *Corr.*, *op. cit.*, vol. 13, pp. 294 and 295.

79. *Corr.*, *op. cit.*, vol. 6, to Pierre Bocage, July 20, 1843.

80. To Flaubert, August 6, 1867, in *Flaubert-Sand, the Correspondence*, translated by Francis Steegmuller and Barbara Bray, Knopf, 1993, p. 82.

81. In *The Strength of Age* (*La Force de l'âge*), Simone de Beauvoir also highlights her priorities of life over writing, the opposite of Sartre: "I will never be a writer above all else, like Sartre," she writes in her journal (*La Force de l'âge*, Folio-Gallimard, p. 32).

82. *Corr.*, *op. cit.*, vol. 9, to Pierre-Jules Hetzel, March 5, 1849.

83. *Corr.*, *op. cit.*, vol. 9, to Pierre Bocage, June 11, 1850.

84. Ibid.

85. *Corr.*, *op. cit.*, vol. 9, to Maurice Dudevant-Sand, December 10, 1850.

86. *Corr.*, *op. cit.*, vol. 9, to Pierre Bocage, December 11, 1850.

87. *Corr.*, *op. cit.*, vol. 9, to Armand Barbès, August 27, 1850.

88. Edouard Grenier, *Literary Memories* (*Souvenirs littéraires*), p. 233 and following. See also A. Parmenie and C. Bonnier de La Chapelle, *Story of an Editor and His Authors* (*Histoire d'un éditeur et de ses auteurs*): *P.-J. Hetzel* (*Stahl*), Albin Michel, 1953.

89. *Corr.*, *op. cit.*, vol. 10, to Pierre-Jules Hetzel, May 2, 1851.

90. *Corr.*, *op. cit.*, vol. 9, to Pierre-Jules Hetzel, late April 1850.

91. *Corr.*, *op. cit.*, vol. 9, to Pierre Bocage, October 3, 1850.

92. Ibid.

93. *Corr.*, *op. cit.*, vol. 9, to Pierre-Jules Hetzel, late April 1850. Italics mine.

94. Archives de Paris, civil birth certificate, no. 99728 (former city hall of 12th arrondissement).

95. Archives de Paris, civil marriage certificate, November 28, 1829.

96. Archives de Paris, birth certificates of November 19, 1833, and February 24, 1837 (former city hall of 12th arrondissement).

97. Archives de Paris, marriage certificate of November 3, 1857 (former city hall of 10th arrondissement).

98. Archives de Paris, census document, D1R1 186.

99. Archives de Paris, property registry, 1862.

100. Archives de Paris, civil records.

101. BHVP, Sand fund, G 4174.

102. Archives de Paris, civil records.

103. Archives départmentales de Charente-Maritime, île d'Aix, communal collection, Deaths 1861–1876.

104. Archives de Paris, civil marriage certificate.

105. Archives de Paris, death certificate. George Sand died on June 8, 1876, in Nohant.

106. Archives de Paris, death certificate.

107. Letter from Laure Manceau to George Sand, June 13, 1871, BHVP, Sand fund, G 841.

108. *Corr.*, *op. cit.*, vol. 9, to Pierre-Jules Hetzel, November 9, 1850.

109. *Corr., op. cit.*, vol. 9, to Maurice Dudevant-Sand, May 1849.
110. *Corr., op. cit.*, vol. 9, to Maurice Dudevant-Sand, June 10, 1849.
111. *Corr., op. cit.*, vol. 9, to Pierre-Jules Hetzel, November 5, 1849.
112. *Corr., op. cit.*, vol. 9, to Pierre Bocage, October 3, 1850.
113. *Corr., op. cit.*, vol. 9, to Maurice Dudevant-Sand, December 17, 1850.
114. Ibid.
115. Ibid.
116. After Manceau's death in 1867, George Sand would decide to move into his old room, which can be visited today.
117. *Corr., op. cit.*, vol. 9, November 14, 1850.
118. *Corr., op. cit.*, vol. 3, May 15, 1836.
119. *Corr., op. cit.*, vol. 9, to Maurice Dudevant-Sand, December 24, 1850.
120. BHVP Sand fund, G 4582.
121. *Corr., op. cit.*, vol. 9, to Emmanuel Arago, December 11, 1850.
122. Lovenjoul Collection, Sand fund, letters from Alexandre Manceau to Emile Aucante, Ms, Lov. E 965.
123. *Corr., op. cit.*, vol. 9, to Maurice Dudevant-Sand, April 20, 1852.
124. *Corr., op. cit.*, vol. 9, to Maurice Dudevant-Sand, April 28, 1852.
125. Edmond and Jules de Goncourt, *Journal, op. cit.,* September 14, 1863.
126. *Corr., op. cit.*, vol. 9, to Maurice Dudevant-Sand, January 2, 1851.
127. Letter from Frédéric Chopin to his family, June 8, 1847.
128. *Corr., op. cit.*, vol. 8, to Frédéric Chopin, July 28, 1847.
129. Casimir Dudevant would have a daughter out of wedlock after separating from George Sand. On a related note, although she was legitimized by her parents, Solange also has her place on the long list of the family's "natural" children.
130. *Story of My Life, op. cit.,* pt. 4, chap. 11, p. 875.
131. *Corr., op. cit.*, vol. 2, to Charles Duvernet, May 21, 1832.
132. Ibid.
133. *Corr., op. cit.*, vol. 2, to Alfred de Musset, May 12, 1834.
134. Divorce had been prohibited under the Restoration laws in 1816 and would not be reestablished until 1884.
135. Augustine Brault would eventually marry Charles de Bertholdi, a Polish-born tax inspector.
136. Solange's letter of May 25, 1843, cited in Bernadette Chovelon, *Mother and Daughter, George Sand and Solange (George Sand et Solange mère et fille)*, Christian Pirot Editions, 1994.
137. Marie d'Agoult, *Journal*, June 9, 1837, in *Memoirs, Memories, and Journals of the Countess d'Agoult (Mémoires, souvenirs et journaux de la comtesse d'Agoult)*, notes by Charles F. Dupechez, Mercure de France, coll. Le Temps retrouvé, 2007, pp. 516–517.
138. Wladimir Karénine, *George Sand, Her Life, and Her Works (George Sand, sa vie et ses œuvres)*, Plon, 1899, vol. 3, p. 453.
139. *Corr., op. cit.*, vol. 10, to Caroline Cazamajou, June 27, 1851.
140. *Corr., op. cit.*, vol. 10, to Solange Clésinger, May 24, 1851.
141. *Corr., op. cit.*, vol. 10, p. 269.
142. *Corr., op. cit.*, vol. 10, to Emmanuel Arago, April 8, 1851.

143. *Corr., op. cit.*, vol. 10, to Augustine de Bertholdi, July 19, 1851.
144. *Corr., op. cit.*, vol. 10, p. 372, n. 1.
145. *Corr., op. cit.*, vol. 10, to Solange Clésinger, July 23, 1851.
146. See also Marielle Caors, "*Le Diable aux champs* or the 'monstrous play,'" in *George Sand and the Arts* (*George Sand et les arts*), international colloquium at the Château d'Ars (September 2004), organized by Marielle Caors, Presses universitaires Blaise Pascal, coll. Révolutions et romantismes, 2007.
147. *Corr., op. cit.*, vol. 10, to Solange Clésinger, August 29, 1851.
148. Bousset was a well-known bishop, and court priest to Louis XIV, and renowned orator of the day. [AMC]
149. *Corr., op. cit.*, vol. 10, to Solange Clésinger, November 14, 1851.
150. *Corr., op. cit.*, vol. 10, to Pierre Bocage, January 25, 1851.
151. *Corr., op. cit.*, vol. 10, to Eugène Delanoix, July 19, 1851.
152. *Corr., op. cit.*, vol. 10, to Pierre-Jules Hetzel, October 29, 1851.
153. *Corr., op. cit.*, vol. 10, to Solange Clésinger, September 20, 1851.
154. *Corr., op. cit.*, vol. 10, to Solange Clésinger, August 29, 1851.
155. In 1906, one of the famous Chartier stock restaurants for workers would open at 3, rue Racine. To learn more about the changes, see Leonard Pitt, *Paris: A Journey Through Time* (*Paris. Un voyage dans le temps*), Parigramme, 2008.
156. *Corr., op. cit.*, vol. 10, to Maurice Dudevant-Sand, November 24, 1851.
157. This quotation, as well as the majority in this chapter, comes from *Journal from November-December 1851* (*Journal de novembre-décembre 1851*), in *Autobiographical Works*, vol. 2, Gaillmard, coll. Bibliothèque de la Pléiade, 1971.
158. *Corr., op. cit.*, vol. 10, to General Richepanse, May 27, 1851.
159. *Journal, op. cit.*, p. 1216.
160. *Corr., op. cit.*, vol. 10, to René Vallet de Villeneuve, October 24, 1851.
161. *Corr., op. cit.*, vol. 10, to Louis-Napoléon Bonaparte, January 20, 1852.
162. *Corr., op. cit.*, vol. 10, to Pierre-Jules Hetzel, January 30, 1852.
163. Ibid.
164. Ibid.
165. *Corr., op. cit.*, vol. 10, to Pierre-Jules Hetzel, February 22, 1852.
166. *Corr., op. cit.*, vol. 10, to Pierre-Jules Hetzel, February 18, 1852.
167. *Corr., op. cit.*, vol. 10, to Pierre-Jules Hetzel, July 9, 1852.
168. *Diaries* (*Diaries*), vol. 1, 1852–1856, Sunday March 28, 1852. Transcribed and edited by Anne Chevereau, Jean Touzot Libraire-Editeur, 1990.
169. See the list in *Corr., op. cit.*, vol. 10, p 236.
170. *Diaries*, vol. 1, *op. cit.*, Tuesday, February 3, 1852.
171. *Diaries*, vol. 1, *op. cit.*, Saturday, February 16, 1852.
172. *Corr., op. cit.*, vol. 10, to Alphonse Fleury, April 5, 1852.
173. *Corr., op. cit.*, vol. 10, May 27, 1852.
174. *Corr., op. cit.*, vol. 10, to Maurice Dudevant-Sand, April 3, 1852.

175. Michele Hecquet, "Femininity and Public Space for George Sand" ("Féminité et espace public chez George Sand"), in *Women in the City* (*Femmes dans la cité*), Creaphis, 1992.

176. *Corr., op. cit.*, vol. 8, p. 400.

177. *Bulletin de la République*, no. 6, April 6, 1848.

178. Elizabeth Barrett Browning to Miss Mitford, February 15, 1852, *op. cit.*, p. 50.

179. Elizabeth Barrett Browning to John Kenyon, February 15, 1852, *op. cit.*, p. 56.

180. Elizabeth Barrett Browning to Mrs. Jameson, February 26, 1852, *op. cit.*, p. 59-60.

181. Elizabeth Barrett Browning to John Kenyon, February 15, 1852, *op. cit.*, p. 56.

182. Elizabeth Barrett Browning to Miss Mitford, April 7, 1852, *op. cit.*, p. 63.

183. *Story of My Life, op. cit.,* pt. V, chap. 13, p. 1114.

184. Ibid.

185. *Corr., op. cit.*, vol. 12, to Augustine de Bertholdi, May 26, 1854.

186. *Annual Manual of Health, or Medicine and household pharmacy, containing all necessary theoretical and practical instructions to prepare and use medications at home, prevent illness or heal yourself, quickly and for little cost, from most curable diseases, and relieve enough pain to feel close to healthy in cases of incurable or chronic diseases* (*Manuel annuaire de la santé ou Médecine et pharmacie domestiques, contenant tous les renseignements théoriques et pratiques nécessaires pour savoir préparer et employer soi-même les médicaments, se préserver ou se guérir ainsi, promptement et à peu de frais, de la plupart des maladies curables, et se procurer un soulagement presque équivalent à la santé, dans les maladies incurables ou chroniques*), Bruxelles, 1845.

187. Another note: Raspail especially recommended hammocks for the simplest and most restful sleep. George Sand used them for years (even before the book was published, for lack of space).

188. *Sketches and Hints, op. cit.*, p. 627.

189. *Diaries, op. cit.*, vol. 1, May 10, 1852.

190. *Diaries, op. cit.*, vol. 1, February 14, 1853.

191. *Diaries, op. cit.*, vol. 1, March 28, 1853.

192. *Diaries, op. cit.*, vol. 1, Wednesday, October 19, 1853.

193. *Diaries, op. cit.*, vol. 1, Wednesday, February 2, 1853.

194. *Diaries, op. cit.*, vol. 1, May 10, 1853. Trianon was the garden that George Sand and Alexandre planted for Nini.

195. *Corr., op. cit.*, vol. 11, to Pierre-Jules Hetzel, May 7, 1852.

196. *Sketches and Hints, op. cit.*, p. 628.

197. *Corr., op. cit.*, vol. 10, to Apolline Vallet de Villeneuve, February 2, 1851.

198. *Corr., op. cit.*, vol. 11, to Maurice Dudevant-Sand, April 20, 1852.

199. *Corr., op. cit.*, vol. 11, to Maurice Dudevant-Sand, April 18, 1853. This studio can be visited today in Nohant.

200. *Diaries, op. cit.*, vol. 1, February 12, 1855.
201. *Diaries, op. cit.*, vol. 1, February 13, 1855.
202. She had tied her son's umbilical cord with green silk at his birth, according to Georges Lubin. *Corr., op. cit.*, vol. 12, to Maurice Dudevant-Sand, June 29–30, 1854.
203. George Sand, preface to *Œuvres illustrées* (ill.) by Tony Johannot, P.-J. Hetzel, 1852.
204. *Corr., op. cit.*, vol. 11, to Maurice Dudevant-Sand, October 8, 1852.
205. Vincent Gourdon, *Story of Grandparents* (*Histoire des grands-parents*), Perrin, 2001.
206. *Corr., op. cit.*, vol. 11, August 30, 1852.
207. *Diaries, op. cit.*, vol. 1, November 22, 1852.
208. *Corr., op. cit.*, vol. 11, to Emile Aucante, October 10, 1852.
209. *Corr., op. cit.*, vol. 11, to Maurice Dudevant-Sand, January 24, 1853.
210. *Corr., op. cit.*, vol. 11, to Captain Stanislas d'Arpentigny, September 21, 1852.
211. *Diaries, op. cit.*, vol. 1, April 10, 1854.
212. *Corr., op. cit.*, vol. 11, to Pierre-Jules Hetzel, January 16, 1853.
213. *Diaries, op. cit.*, vol. 1, December 8, 1854.
214. Cited by Pierre de Boisdeffre, *George Sand at Nohant* (*George Sand à Nohant*), edited by Christian Pior, 2000, pp. 50–51.
215. *Diaries, op. cit.*, vol. 1, October 16, 1854. Two Masonic temples existed in Indre: the Etoile du Centre (in Châteauroux) and the Gauloise (in Issoudun). Wherever Manceau was initiated, he was undoubtedly sponsored by Charles Duvernet.
216. For more on this, see Simone Vierne, *George Sand and the Freemasons* (*George Sand et la franc-maçonnerie*), Editions maçonniques de France, 2002.
217. *Corr., op. cit.*, vol. 12, to Rene Vallet de Villeneuve, December 15 1853.
218. *Corr., op. cit.*, vol. 12, to Pierre-Jules Hetzel, January 12, 1853.
219. Ibid.
220. Ibid.
221. Ibid.
222. Ibid.
223. Ibid.
224. *Corr., op. cit.*, vol. 11, to Eugenie Duvernet, December 14, 1852.
225. *Story of My Life, op. cit.,* pt. 5, chap. ii, p. 944.
226. *Corr., op. cit.*, vol. 11, to Pierre-Jules Hetzel, January 16, 1853.
227. *Corr., op. cit.*, vol. 12, to Augustine de Bertholdi, October 28, 1853.
228. *Corr., op. cit.*, vol. 11, to Maurice Dudevant-Sand, May 6, 1853.
229. *Story of My Life, op. cit.,* pt. 1, chap. 1, p. 76.
230. *Diaries, op. cit.*, vol. 1, May 21, 1853.
231. *Diaries, op. cit.*, vol. 1, May 25, 1853.
232. *Corr., op. cit.*, vol. 11, to Pierre-Jules Hetzel, February 19, 1853.
233. *Corr., op. cit.*, vol. 11, to Eliza Tourangin, late March 1853.
234. *Corr., op. cit.*, vol. 12, to René Vallet de Villeneuve, late July 1854.

235. *Story of My Life, op. cit.,* pt. 4, chap. 9, p. 840.
236. *Corr., op. cit.,* vol. 12, to Alexandre Manceau, September 14, 1854. Italics by George Sand, regarding a review of *Consuelo.*
237. In her emotional state, she made a Freudian slip, writing "Maurice is in Paris with his dying mother," instead of Manceau (*Corr., op. cit.,* vol. 12, to Solange Clésinger, December 17, 1854).
238. *Corr., op. cit.,* vol. 13, to Lise Perdiguier, January 15, 1855.
239. *Corr., op. cit.,* vol. 13, to Lise Perdiguier, January 18, 1855.
240. *Diaries, op. cit.,* vol. 2, April 27, 1855.
241. Mona Ozouf, "Aurore ou la génerosité," in *Women's Writing: Essay on the French Uniqueness (Les Mots de femmes. Essai sur la singularité française),* Fayard, 1995.
242. An unexpected similarity between George Sand and Jean-Paul Sartre, who used the same phrase to describe his own community of friends, which was so essential to him (the latter borrowed the phrase from adolescent slang).
243. Alexandre Manceau's letter to Emile Aucante, May 26, 1855, Bibliothéque de l'Institut, Lovenjoul collection, Sand fund, Ms Lov. E 965, *fol.* 73.
244. *Corr., op. cit.,* vol. 13, to Charles Poncy, November 26, 1855.
245. Ibid.
246. Ibid.
247. *Corr., op. cit.,* vol. 13, to Sylvanie Arnould-Plessy, May 1, 1856.
248. *Corr., op. cit.,* vol. 13, to Solange Clésinger, January 9, 1856.
249. *Corr., op. cit.,* vol. 13, to Emile Aucante, January 18, 1856.
250. *Corr., op. cit.,* vol. 13, to Emile Aucante, January 18, 1856.
251. *After the Death of Jeanne Clésinger (Après la mort de Jeanne Clésinger),* 1855, in *Autobiographical Works, op. cit.,* vol. 2, unfinished text. Italics mine.
252. *Corr., op. cit.,* vol. 13, to Pierre-Jules Hetzel, May 24, 1856.
253. *Corr., op. cit.,* vol. 13, p. 606, n. 4.
254. *Corr., op. cit.,* vol. 13, to Solange Dudevant, May 14, 1856. Georges Lubin notes that "checked" means "starting" in the Berrichon dialect.
255. "Please, please fix things with Hetzel and Cie, don't leave things hanging. Our future depends upon it." (*Corr., op. cit.,* vol. 13, to Emile Aucante, May 11, 1856). Her handwriting changed starting with the word "leave."
256. *Corr., op. cit.,* vol. 15, to Pauline Viardot, May 21, 1859.
257. *Corr., op. cit.,* vol. 23, p. 639, November 28, 1871.
258. *Corr., op. cit.,* vol. 13, p. 673. See also Julien Dunilac (alias Frédéric Dubois), *A Close Look at George Sand (George Sand sous la loupe),* Genève, Slatkine, 1978.
259. *Corr., op. cit.,* vol. 14, to Charles Poncy, July 23, 1856.
260. George Sand, *Promenades Around a Village (Promenades autour d'un village),* p. 21, preface by Georges Lubin, edited by Christian Pinot, 1987.
261. Ibid., p. 17.

262. Ibid., p. 57.
263. She was very interested in the idea of realism in art, as her correspond-ence with Champfleury, the movement's philosopher, showed. For more on this, see *Champfleury-Sand, Realism Correspondence* (*Champfleury-Sand, Du Réalisme, Correpondance*), presented by Luce Abélès, Editions des Cendres, 1991.
264. Ibid., p. 80.
265. *Corr., op. cit.*, vol. 14, to Emile Aucante, July 16, 1857.
266. *Corr., op. cit.*, vol. 14, to Maurice Dudevant-Sand, July 30, 1857.
267. *Diaries, op. cit.*, vol. 2, July 27, 1857.
268. *Diaries, op. cit.*, vol. 2, June 26, 1857.
269. *Gargilesse Travel Notebooks* (*Carnets de voyages à Gargilesse*), Christian Pirot Editions, 1999, p. 44.
270. *Diaries, op. cit.*, vol. 2, August 19, 1857.
271. *Corr., op. cit.*, vol. 14, to Solange Clésinger, June 16, 1858.
272. *Diaries, op. cit.*, vol. 2, May 29, 1858.
273. *Corr., op. cit.*, to Solange Clésinger, June 16, 1858
274. *Corr., op. cit.*, vol. 14, to Solange Clésinger, June 16, 1858
275. August 23, 1834, in Sand and Musset, *The Venice Novel* (*Le Roman de Venise*), preface by Jose-Luis Diaz, Actes Sud, coll. Babel, 1999, p. 329.
276. *Corr., op. cit.*, vol. 2, to Marie d'Agoult, May 25, 1836.
277. *Corr., op. cit.*, vol. 2, to Sainte-Beuve, August 25, 1833.
278. *Corr., op. cit.*, vol. 2, to Alfred de Musset, May 12, 1834.
279. *Corr., op. cit.*, vol. 16, to Sainte-Beuve, January 20, 1861.
280. *Corr., op. cit.*, vol. 16, to Charles Poncy, August 15, 1857.
281. Ibid.
282. *Corr.*, vol. 14, to Maria-Laetitia de Solms, late November 1857. Georges Luvin, whose lifelong work provided me with the complete correspond-ence of George Sand, added a note: "Here, the editor of so many intimate letters must respectfully ask a private pardon from G. S."
283. *Corr., op. cit.*, vol. 15, p. 387, n. 1.
284. *Corr., op. cit.*, vol. 15, p. 368, n. 1.
285. *Corr., op. cit.*, vol. 16, to Sainte-Beuve, January 20, 1861.
286. See *Corr., op. cit.*, vol. 2, where Georges Lubin gives a detailed analysis of these corrections.
287. *Corr., op. cit.*, vol. 15, to Emile Aucante, October 15, 1859.
288. *Corr., op. cit.*, vol. 16, to Emile Aucante, February 10, 1861.
289. *Corr., op. cit.*, vol. 16, to Sainte-Beuve, January 20, 1861.
290. *Corr., op. cit.*, vol. 15, to Victor Hugo, August 28, 1859.
291. For more on this wonderful woman, see Patrick Barbier, *Pauline Viardot*, Grasset, 2009.
292. *Diaries, op. cit.*, vol. 2, May 1, 1859.
293. *Diaries, op. cit.*, vol. 2, April 28, 1859.
294. To Ernest Feydeau, August 21, 1859. In *Flaubert-Sand, op. cit.*, p. 4.
295. Maxime Du Camp, *Literary Memories* (*Souvenirs littéraires*), Balland, 1984, p. 244.

296. Ibid., p. 242.
297. Edmond and Jules de Goncourt, *Journal, op. cit.*, March 30, 1862.
298. *Corr., op. cit.*, vol. 16, to Emile Aucante, May 11, 1858.
299. Roughly 13,500 Euros, 9,000 of which were paid in advance (assuming 1 franc in 1860 = 3 Euros today).
300. *Diaries, op. cit.*, vol. 1, January 3, 1855.
301. *Corr., op. cit.*, vol. 14, to Victor Borie, April 16, 1857.
302. *Corr., op. cit.*, vol. 14, to Pierre-Jules Hetzel, October 20, 1856.
303. The Lévy brothers agreed to continue publishing her novels after the first two years of exclusivity. If she didn't renew her contract with them after five years, the editors could release any previously unpublished texts, in exchange for 10 percent of author's rights, in a minimum print run of 3,000 copies at three francs each. Political content was excluded. In that case, they would have to pay 10 percent of the price of any works published elsewhere to the author. George Sand reserved all rights of translation. Also, the same conditions applied to any future plays.
304. *Corr., op. cit.*, vol. 17, to Edouard Rodrigues, April 4 and 17, 1863.
305. See *Corr., op. cit.*, vol. 17, her letter to Sainte-Beuve on June 16, 1863, explaining her position regarding the Commune.
306. *Corr., op. cit.*, vol. 17, to Edouard Rodrigues, January 12, 1863.
307. *Corr., op. cit.*, vol. 18, to Edouard Rodrigues, October 2, 1863.
308. *Corr., op. cit.*, vol. 17, to Edouard Rodrigues, August 29, 1862.
309. "Syllabus of Errors" in the *Quanta Cura*.
310. See *Corr., op. cit.*, vol. 15, p. 610, n. 1.
311. *Corr., op. cit.*, vol. 15, to Pierre-Jules Hetzel, December 23, 1859.
312. *Corr., op. cit.*, vol. 15, to Octave Feuillet, February 27, 1859.
313. *Diaries, op. cit.*, vol. 2, November 20, 1859.
314. Anne Chevereau, *Alexandre Manceau, op. cit.*
315. Lovenjoul Collection, Sand fund, Alexandre Manceau's letter to Emile Aucante, Ms Lov. E 965, *fol.* 48.
316. Ibid., *fol.* 168. He dreamed of taking George Sand on another vacation.
317. Ibid., *fol.* 97.
318. Ibid., *fol.* 76.
319. This wasn't Aucante's companion, also called Marie Caillaud. There were many Caillauds and Maries in Nohant!
320. *Diaries, op. cit.*, vol. 2, October 23, 1859.
321. *Corr., op. cit.*, vol. 14, to Rose Cheri, January 31, 1858.
322. *Corr., op. cit.*, vol. 14, to Ida Dumas, December 18, 1856.
323. *Corr., op. cit.*, vol. 15, to Pierre-Jules Hetzel, December 15, 1859.
324. *Corr., op. cit.*, vol. 15, to Maurice Dudevant-Sand, May 19, 1860.
325. *Corr., op. cit.*, vol. 16, to Victor Borie, August 5, 1860.
326. *Corr., op. cit.*, vol. 16, to François Buloz, November 27, 1860.
327. *Diaries, op. cit.*, vol. , December 31, 1860.
328. *Corr., op. cit.*, vol. 16, to Ludre Gabillaud, April 28, 1861. She was referencing her excursions into Tamaris backcountry.

329. *The Journal of Two Worlds* (*La Revue des Deux-Mondes*), November 15, 1863.
330. *Diaries, op. cit.*, vol. 2, June 9, 1861.
331. *Diaries, op. cit.*, vol. 2, October 10, 1861.
332. *Corr., op. cit.*, vol. 16, to Alexandre Dumas fils, November 7, 1861.
333. Cited in Michele Tricot, *Solange, George Sand's Daughter* (*Solange, fille de George Sand*), L'Harmattant, 2004, p. 142.
334. Recall that the Baroness Dudevant had once forbidden her daughter-in-law, the young Aurore, from writing under her married name. Solange was forbidden from "signing Sand" (see Martine Reid, *Signing Sand, op. cit.*) in the same way.
335. This drawing can be found at the Musée de la Vie romantique.
336. *Corr., op. cit.*, vol. 15, to Solange Clésinger, May 14, 1859.
337. *Corr., op. cit.*, vol. 15, to Solange Clésinger, August 18, 1858.
338. Ibid.
339. Ibid.
340. *Corr., op. cit.*, vol. 19, to Charles Poncy, October 14, 1865.
341. Ibid.
342. This lover of art would order Gustave Courbet's painting *The Origin of the World* (*L'Origine du monde*) in 1866 but went bankrupt two years later and had to return it. See also Thierry Savatier, *The Origin of the World: The Story of a Gustave Courbet Painting* (*L'Origin du monde: histoire d'un tableau de Gustave Courbet*), Bartillat, 2006.
343. *Corr., op. cit.*, vol. 14, to Emile Aucante, December 13, 1856.
344. *Corr., op. cit.*, vol. 16, to Emile Aucante, November 6, 1861.
345. *Corr., op. cit.*, vol. 16, to Emile Aucante, after January 16, 1862.
346. Ibid.
347. *Corr., op. cit.*, vol. 16, to Alexandre Dumas fils, January 25, 1862.
348. *Corr., op. cit.*, vol. 16, to Alexandre Dumas fils, January 4, 1862.
349. In September 1873, Solange would have her friend Madame Brétillot buy the chateau at Montgivray, which had belonged to her uncle, Hippolyte Chatiron. She would live there with her friend and Marie Caillaud (who had crossed enemy lines!). She would live the rest of her life there.
350. *Corr., op. cit.*, vol. 16, to Alexandre Dumas fils, September 9, 1861.
351. *Corr., op. cit.*, vol. 16, to Alexandre Dumas fils, August 26, 1861.
352. *Corr., op. cit.*, vol. 16, to Alexandre Dumas fils, March 10, 1862.
353. *Corr., op. cit.*, vol. 16, to Prince Napoleon, February 26, 1862.
354. Wladimir Karenine, *George Sand, Her Life, and Her Works, op. cit.*, vol. 4, p. 408.
355. Ibid.
356. *Corr., op. cit.*, vol. 17, to Oscar Cazamajou, May 11, 1862.
357. *Corr., op. cit.*, vol. 17, to Alexandre Dumas fils, April 30, 1862.
358. *Diaries, op. cit.*, vol. 3, May 17, 1862.
359. *Corr., op. cit.*, vol. 17, to Alexandre Dumas fils, July 14, 1863.
360. Anne Chevereau, *Alexandre Manceau, op. cit.*, p. 136.
361. *Diaries, op. cit.*, vol. 3, July 21, 1863.

362. *Diaries, op. cit.*, vol. 3, August 1, 1863.
363. Edmond and Jules de Goncourt, *Journal, op. cit.*, March 26, 1860.
364. It's not certain whether these two mixed children were the product of Maillard's liaison with a servant or Madame Maillard's father's liaison with a slave on his plantation. In any case, the Maillards raised Jacques and Joséphine as their own children.
365. *Diaries, op. cit.*, vol. 3, December 31, 1862.
366. Sylvie Delaigue-Moins, *Chopin with George Sand* (*Chopin chez George Sand*), Christian Pirot Editions, 2005.
367. *Corr., op. cit.*, vol. 15, to Aucante, late March 1859, p. 376. "This Manceau pays me (in spite of my wishes, of course) an allowance of 1200 francs each month since last January. He cannot be deterred."
368. *Diaries, op. cit.*, vol. 3, January 23, 1862.
369. *Diaries, op. cit.*, vol. 3, May 11, 1863.
370. Edmond and Jules de Goncourt, *Journal, op. cit.*, September 14, 1863.
371. Lovenjoul Collection, C 475, *fol.* 55. Cited in *Corr., op. cit.*, vol. 18, p. 56.
372. Michele Tricot, *Solange, George Sand's Daughter, op. cit.*, p. 142.
373. This is André Maurois' thesis in *Lélia, or the Life of George Sand* (*Lélia ou la vie de George Sand*), Hachette, 1952.
374. *Diaries, op. cit.*, vol. 3, November 23, 1863.
375. Some also suspect this to be the cause of all correspondence between his mother and Manceau disappearing.
376. A note in Maurice's hand: "Reread the father in *Tartuffe*, my foolish mother, Maurice" (boxed in: *Diaries, op. cit.*, vol. 3, November 24, 1863).
377. *Diaries, op. cit.*, vol. 3, December 6, 1863.
378. *Corr., op. cit.*, vol. 18, to Maurice and Lina Dudevant-Sand, January 26, 1864. Nadar had just suffered a serious ballooning accident.
379. Recall that this is Maurice's wife's first name.
380. *Corr., op. cit.*, vol. 18, to Maurice and Lina Dudevant-Sand, March 5, 1864.
381. *Diaries, op. cit.*, vol. 3, April 25, 1864. George Sand also highlighted the mention *in absentia* of that feast day's saint, in the diary.
382. *Diaries, op. cit.*, vol. 3, June 11, 1864. Maurice's commentary: "How conceited! How asinine!"
383. A note in Maurice's hand: "(my mother is completely stuck)." (*Diaries, op. cit.*, Vol. III, June 12 1864, p. 195.)
384. *Corr., op. cit.*, vol. 18, to Maurice Dudevant-Sand, June 12, 1864.
385. *Corr., op. cit.*, vol. 18, to Charles Duvernet, October 3, 1864.
386. *Diaries, op. cit.*, vol. III, June 23, 1864. A note in Maurice's hand: "He died a year later."
387. *Corr., op. cit.*, vol. 18, to Lina Dudevant-Sand, June 25, 1864.
388. *Diaries, op. cit.*, vol. 3, July 13, 1864.
389. Marc Dudevant-Sand's body would be transferred to Nohant in 1868.
390. *Diaries, op. cit.*, vol. 3, August 2, 1864.

391. *Corr., op. cit.*, vol. 18, to Augustine de Bertholdi, August 1, 1864.
392. About 78,000 Euros.
393. Manceau had added two connecting bedrooms during the renovations.
394. *Diaries, op. cit.*, vol. 3, November 11, 1865.
395. *Corr., op. cit.*, vol. 19, to Sainte-Beuve, January 29 and 30, 1865.
396. *Corr., op. cit.*, vol. 19, to François Buloz, October 23, 1865.
397. *Corr., op. cit.*, vol. 19, to Edouard Rodrigues, February 11, 1865.
398. This is how the play's title would be written.
399. *Corr., op. cit.*, vol. 19, to Alexandre Dumas fils, March 27, 1865.
400. *Diaries, op. cit.*, vol. 3, March 9, 1865.
401. *Diaries, op. cit.*, vol. 3, March 24, 1865.
402. *Diaries, op. cit.*, vol. 3, March 28, 1865.
403. *Diaries, op. cit.*, vol. 3, April 1, 1865.
404. *Corr., op. cit.*, vol. 19, to Doctor Pierre-Paul Darchy, April 26, 1865.
405. *Diaries, op. cit.*, vol. 3, May 20, 1865.
406. *Diaries, op. cit.*, vol. 3, May 28, 1865.
407. *Diaries, op. cit.*, vol. 3, May 26, 1865.
408. *Diaries, op. cit.*, vol. 3, July 7, 1865.
409. *Diaries, op. cit.*, vol. 3, June 25, 1865.
410. *Corr., op. cit.*, vol. 19, to Alexandre Dumas fils, May 13, 1865.
411. *Diaries, op. cit.*, vol. 3, July 6, 1865.
412. *Corr., op. cit.*, vol. 19, to Maurice Dudevant-Sand, August 22, 1865.
413. *Diaries, op. cit.*, August 22, 1865.
414. *Diaries, op. cit.*, August 23, 1865.
415. BHVP, Sand fund, K 240 to 242.
416. *Diaries, op. cit.*, vol. 3, September 4, 1865.
417. The Palaiseau house was undoubtedly placed in Manceau's name to prevent Solange from claiming it. This asset would have still been included in George Sand's inheritance, though. In return, Manceau's parents received an allowance of 125 francs each trimester and weren't bothered by the transaction. George also returned the engraver's watch and old tools to them, keeping the best tools for her own son.
418. Aurore was born on January 10, 1866, and Gabrielle on March 11, 1868.
419. *Flaubert-Sand, op. cit.*, p. 384, January 12, 1876.

SELECTED BIBLIOGRAPHY

For a complete list of George Sand's works, see the bibliography of the Bibliothèque nationale, at www.bnf.fr.

English Translations

Fadette, George Sand, translated by Jane Minot Sedgwick, George H. Richmond & Co., 1893.

Flaubert-Sand, the Correspondence, translated by Francis Steegmuller and Barbara Bray, Knopf, 1993.

The Letters of Elizabeth Barrett Browning, edited by Frederic G. Kenyon, Macmillan, 1898.

Story of My Life, George Sand, a group translation, edited by Thelma Jurgrau, State University Press of New York, 1991.

Other Correspondence and Autobiographical Texts

Correspondance complète, edited by Georges Lubin, Garnier, 26 volumes, 1964–1991.

Lettres d'une vie, introduced by Thierry Bodin, Gaillimard, coll. Folio classique, 2004.

Lettres retrouvées, edited by Thierry Bodin, Gallimard, 2004.

Agendas, transcribed and annotated by Anne Chevereau, preface by Georges Lubin, Jean Touzot Librarie-Editeur, 6 volumes, 1990–1993.

Œuvres autobiographiques, introduced by Georges Lubin, Gallimard, coll. Bibliothèque de la Pléaide, 2 volumes, 1970–1971.

Histoire de ma vie, edited by Martine Reid, Gallimard, coll. Quarto, 2004.

Carnets de voyages à Gargilesse, Christian Pirot Editions, new edition 2007.

Promenades autour d'un village, preface by Georges Lubin, Christian Pirot Editions, 1987.

La Vallée noire, Christian Pirot Editions, 1998.

Selected Works by George Sand, written or published during the years 1849–1865

Antonia, Actes Sud, coll. Babel, 2002.

Autour de la table, Clermont-Ferrand, Paléo, 2007.

François le Champi, Le Livre de poche, 1997.

Les Beaux Messieurs de Bois-Doré, Grenoble, Editions de l'Aurore, coll. Œuvres de George Sand, 1985.

Claudie, followed by *Molière*, Indigo et Côté-Femmes, 1998.

Le Compagnon du Tour de France, Presses universitaires de Grenoble, 1998.

La Confession d'une jeune fille, Clermont-Ferrand, Paléo, 2007.

Les Dames vertes, Magnard, 2004.

La Daniella, Grenoble, Editions de l'Aurore, coll. Œuvres de George Sand, 1992.

Le Dernier Amour, Clermont-Ferrand, Paléo, 2008.

Le Diable aux champs, edited by Jeanne Goldin, Honoré Champion, 2008.

Elle et Lui, Points-Seuil, 2004.

Histoire du véritable Gribouille, Gallimard, coll. Folio junior, 1978.

L'Homme de neige, Actes Sud, coll. Babel, 2005.

Jean de la Roche, Borée Editions, 2001.

Légendes rustiques, illustrated by Maurice Sand, preface by Evelyne Bloch-Dano, Christian Pirot Editions, 2000.

Mademoiselle La Quintinie, followed by *A props des Charmettes*, Presses universitaires de Grenoble, 2004.

Mademoiselle Merquem, Actes Sud, coll. Babel, 1996.

Les Maîtres sonneurs, preface by Marie-Claire Banquart, Gallimard, coll. Folio classique, 1979.

Le Marquis de Villemer, Borée Editions, 2008.

Mont-Revêche, preface by Jean Chalon, Editions du Rocher, 1989.

La Petite Fadette, illustrations by Tony Johannot, Christian Pirot Editions, 2010.

La Ville noire, Borée Editions, 2007.

Tamaris, Clermont-Ferrand, Paléo, 2009.

A photo gallery can be viewed on the website of Evelyne Bloch-Dano, at www.ebloch-dano.com.